RUSSELL ON ETHICS

Russell on Ethics presents a coherent and comprehensive selection of Bertrand Russell's writings on ethics, many of which have been previously unavailable to students and general readers. Charles Pigden provides an accessible introduction, situating the papers within the field of ethics as a whole, together with a detailed set of annotations, analysing Russell's arguments and exploring their relevance to current concerns. *Russell on Ethics* provides a valuable insight into Bertrand Russell as an ethicist that will be useful to both specialist and non-specialist alike.

Charles R. Pigden is a Senior Lecturer in the Department of Philosophy, University of Otago, New Zealand. He is the author of a number of papers on Bertrand Russell and on meta-ethics generally, including the chapter 'Naturalism' in Peter Singer's prize-winning *A Companion to Ethics* (Oxford 1991).

RUSSELL ON...
General editor's introduction
A. C. Grayling

Russell achieved public fame – often enough, notoriety – because of his engagement in social and political debates, becoming known to a wide audience as a philosopher in the popular sense of the term. But his chief contributions, the ones that have made a permanent difference to the history of thought, lie in logic and philosophy; and they are such that his influence both on the matter and style of twentieth-century philosophy, principally in its Anglophone form, is pervasive. Elsewhere I have described his contribution as constituting the 'wall-paper' of analytic philosophy, in the sense that his successors 'use techniques and ideas developed from his work without feeling the need – sometimes without recognizing the need – to mention his name; which is influence indeed'.

Russell devoted much attention to central technical questions in philosophical logic, epistemology and metaphysics. He also wrote extensively and forcefully about moral, religious and political questions in ways not merely journalistic. Much of his work in all these areas took the form of essays. Some have of course been famously collected, constituting a fundamental part of the canon of twentieth-century analytic philosophy. But there are many more riches in his copious output, their value to some degree lost because they have not hitherto been collected and edited in such a way as to do justice to the development and weight of his thinking about these subjects. This series, in bringing together Russell's chief writings on major subject areas in an editorial frame that locates and interprets them fully, aims to remedy that lack and thereby to make a major contribution both to Russell scholarship and to contemporary analytic philosophy.

RUSSELL ON ETHICS

Selections from the writings of
Bertrand Russell

Edited by Charles R. Pigden

London and New York

First published 1999
by Routledge
11 New Fetter Lane, London EC4P 4EE

Simultaneously published in the USA and Canada
by Routledge
29 West 35th Street, New York, NY 10001

Reprinted 2000

Routledge is an imprint of the Taylor & Francis Group

Typeset in Garamond by Routledge
Printed and bound in Great Britain by TJ International, Padstow,
Cornwall

British Library Cataloguing in Publication Data
A catalogue record for this book is available from the British Library

Library of Congress Cataloging in Publication Data
Russell, Bertrand, 1872–1970
Russell on ethics: selections from the writings of Bertrand Russell
Russell / edited by Charles R. Pigden
Includes bibliographical references and index
1. Ethics, Modern – 20th century.
I. Pigden, Charles R. 1956– II. Title
B1649.R91P547 1998 97–42586
170'.92–dc21 CIP

ISBN 0–415–15659–9 (hbk)
ISBN 0–415–15660–2 (pbk)

THIS BOOK IS DEDICATED TO
MY MOTHER AND FATHER,
JEAN AND CHARLES PIGDEN

CONTENTS

CONTENTS

PREFACE AND
ACKNOWLEDGEMENTS

Though Bertrand Russell was famous above all as a practical moralist, he is largely unknown as an ethical theorist. The object of this book is to remedy this state of affairs. It is directed at three classes of readers: (1) professional philosophers, (2) general readers with an interest in Russell, especially those with a tincture of philosophy, and (3) students of philosophy, especially undergraduates. For my fellow professionals, I have written a long introduction explaining Russell's role in the evolution of twentieth-century ethics and noting that he was one of the first in the field with two of the theories (emotivism and the error theory) that have dominated the twentieth-century debate. I hope this introduction will also be of use to the student and the general reader. But I have written for their especial benefit a series of preliminary notes to Russell's writings, summarizing his arguments, emphasizing his insights, noting problems and suggesting further reading.

The distinction between practical or applied ethics and ethical theory is rough and ready, but useful nonetheless. Practical ethics is – well, *practical*; it is concerned with the rights and wrongs of particular issues, of war and peace, marriage and sexuality, eugenics and population policy. Russell wrote an immense amount on such topics, even descending to such trivial questions as 'Should Socialists Smoke Good Cigars?' (the answer is *yes*), but he did not think these writings rose to the dignity of philosophy. Ethical theory is, as the name suggests, more theoretical. It divides into two branches: normative ethics and meta-ethics. Normative ethics supplies (and criticizes) the premises for practical ethics. It is concerned with such questions as the nature of the good life, the nature of virtue, the kinds of acts that are right or wrong, whether we should take consequences into account and what kinds of consequences we should promote. Meta-ethics is a more rarefied study still. It deals with such questions as the following. What do moral judgements mean? How can they be justified? Are they true or false at all or just expressions of emotion? Why should I be moral? And what is the function of morality? Although it is a rarefied study, meta-ethics is not without practical import. At one time Russell believed that if 'the subjectivity of value' were widely recognized, there would be 'less cruelty, persecution, punishment, and moral reprobation' than exists at present (Paper 16). Later, he came to think that if another meta-ethical doctrine – Thrasymachus' thesis that 'justice is the advantage of the stronger' – became widely accepted, this could lead to a disastrous slide into chaos and tyranny (Paper 27).

Russell's writings on practical ethics are readily available and widely read. Not so his writings on ethical theory (with one or two notable exceptions). Accordingly, the emphasis in this collection is on ethical theory, especially meta-ethics. The main questions of ethical theory are of interest to every intelligent person, but they are undeniably difficult and they are not made any easier by the stodgy style of many leading philosophers. Russell's writings afford an introduction to the issues which is *serious* – in the sense that Russell really was concerned to get it right – without being *solemn*. Russell's zest for intellectual activity is evident even in those passages where he is driven to a conclusion that he does not like. His style and wit were such that after he had been expelled from academia for his anti-war activities he was able to make a good living from his pen. He strove for clarity and though he did not always succeed, this makes him vastly more readable than those modern – or post-modern – writers who do not make the effort. My hope then is that this book will provide an entertaining introduction to the chief problems of ethical theory and, specifically, meta-ethics. Indeed, I think it would do duty as a second-year teaching text. At the very least it should amuse my fellow professionals and provide them with a source of quotable quotes.

Most of the books that Russell himself published are still in print, often in cheap paperback editions. There are extracts from these works in the present volume since I could not display Russell's development as an ethical thinker without making use of them. But I have preferred to concentrate on the treasure trove of relatively unknown writings revealed in the successive volumes of *The Collected Papers of Bertrand Russell* (henceforward *CPBR*). My chief debt is to the editors of this splendid (but expensive) series. I have shamelessly exploited their magnificent scholarly achievement and if I sometimes manage to sound like an expert, my expertise is largely derived from them.

My second debt is to the subscribers to the Russell-l email list, particularly Ray Monk, Ken Blackwell, Alan Ryan, Jan Dejnožka (who sent me a very useful set of criticisms in the closing stages), Paul Hagar, John Lenz, Stewart Candlish, Ed Mares and Louis Greenspan, Ray Perkins, Nick Griffin, Ivor Grattan-Guinness and Anthony Grayling. Ken Blackwell, who, until recently, ran the list from the McMaster Russell Archive, managed to create a lively and enjoyable electronic forum which combines the pleasures of serious philosophy with biographical chit-chat. Russell's biographer, Ray Monk, has been an especially inspiring person to correspond with, and I thank him for inviting me to give a paper to the Russell conference at Southampton which helped me to clarify some of my ideas. And thanks too to Anthony Grayling for asking me to edit this collection.

My colleagues in the Department of Philosophy at the University of Otago have tolerated my obsession with Russell and have provided me with friendship and institutional support. Richard Briscoe and Mike Baty have both been prompt and efficient research assistants. Editing this book would have been a much more arduous business without them. Our departmental secretary Marg Newall has been enormously helpful and a real pleasure to work with. My editor at Routledge, Richard Stoneman, and his two assistants, Ruth Schafer and Coco Stevenson, have also been a great help.

Thanks to my family, Zena, Guy, Jemima and Abigail, for putting up with the project especially in the last two rather frantic months.

The Introduction contains material from two articles of mine, 'Bertrand Russell: A Neglected Ethicist' from Ray Monk and Anthony Palmer (eds) *Bertrand Russell and the Origins of Analytic Philosophy*, and 'Bertrand Russell: Meta-Ethical Pioneer' from *Philosophy of the Social Sciences*, vol. 26, no 2. I would like to thank the editors and the publishers (Thoemmes Press and Sage Publications, respectively) for permission to use this material.

I would like to thank the following for permission to reprint material by Bertrand Russell:

Paper 19, 'Science and Ethics', is reprinted from *Religion and Science*, by Bertrand Russell (1935) by permission of Oxford University Press.

Paper 20, an extract from 'Reply to Criticisms' (pp. 720–725) by

Bertrand Russell is reprinted from Paul Arthur Schilpp (ed.) *The Philosophy of Bertrand Russell*, (Library of Living Philosophers Series), by permission of Open Court Publishing Company, La Salle, Illinois, © The Library of Living Philosophers.

I would also like to thank Cambridge University Press for permission to use the translation of Leopardi's poem 'The Infinite' by Russell's friend R. C. Trevelyan, quoted in Paper 29. This first appeared in R. C. Trevelyan, *Translations from Leopardi*, 1941, Cambridge, Cambridge University Press.

In the main, I have retained Russell's original spelling and punctuation, including the rather erratic punctuation and capitalization of his early unpublished writings. However, some of these early essays are disfigured by the promiscuous use of the long dash, which was employed in the nineteenth century as a sort of all-purpose punctuation mark. I have found this a positive barrier to enjoyment and ease of reading, both in Russell's writings and in those of other authors. (For example, it quite spoils Lord Byron's otherwise excellent letters.) I have therefore ventured to remove this barrier, replacing many of the dashes with whatever seemed appropriate. Those who value Russell's prose right down to the last dash should consult *CPBR* vol. 1 where it is preserved in its pristine form.

INTRODUCTION

LIFE, WORK AND ADVENTURES

To understand Russell's ethical writings it helps to know something of his life and times.

Bertrand Arthur William Russell (1872–1970) was born into the Whig aristocracy. His grandfather, Lord John Russell (1792–1878), was twice Prime Minister and introduced the first Reform Bill, which, as Russell boasted, 'started England on the road to democracy'. Russell's parents, Lord and Lady Amberly, were radicals and free-thinkers, disciples of John Stuart Mill whom they asked to stand as a sort of secular godfather to the young Bertie. But they both died young and Russell was brought up by his grandmother, Lady Russell (1815–98), in an atmosphere of puritan piety. 'Only virtue was prized, virtue at the expense of intellect, health, happiness and every mundane good' (Russell 1956a: 3). He rebelled against this atmosphere, but at first his rebellion took the secret form of a series of philosophical meditations in which he abandoned belief in God and adopted utilitarianism (Paper 1). In 1890 he went up to Cambridge to study mathematics. Russell loved Cambridge and the friends he made there (especially the members of the very select discussion club known to outsiders as the Apostles), but he found the mathematics he was taught to be something of a chore ('a set of clever tricks by which to pile up marks in the Tripos'), and gave it up for philosophy in his fourth year. He carried his youthful rebellion further by deciding for philosophy rather than a political career, and by marrying Alys Pearsall Smith (1867–1951), an American Quaker who was regarded by his family as a designing adventuress. His grandmother spoke of his philosophical activities as 'the life you have been leading' and tried to put him off marriage by talk of madness in the family. (She revealed that he had an uncle who was

1

insane.) Russell continued to lead a life of philosophical depravity and solved the madness problem, in true utilitarian style, by using contraceptives. If there was an hereditary taint of madness, then he had better ensure that he had no heirs.

The next twenty years were largely devoted to philosophy, especially the philosophy of mathematics. At first, Russell followed the then fashionable trend and tried to develop a Hegelian system. But under the influence of G. E. Moore (1874–1958), he revolted against Hegelianism, and together they became the founding fathers of what is now known as analytic philosophy. They rejected the monism of Hegelianism (according to which there is really only one thing, the Absolute) and adopted a pluralist view according to which 'there really were such things as tables and chairs' (Russell 1967: 135). Russell's chief project, however, was to reduce mathematics to logic. But to do this he had to invent a logic which could do duty as the basis for mathematics. To begin with, Russell took pleasure in his work, but his discovery of the Russell paradox, which threatened to destroy his entire enterprise, was a dreadful blow. Though he managed, in the end, to arrive at a solution, the completion of *Principia Mathematica*, the *magnum opus* that he co-authored with A. N. Whitehead (1861–1947), was a great and arduous labour which often left him suicidally depressed. To compound his problems he fell out of love with his wife, though they continued to share the same house for many years in a state of aching misery. Nevertheless he acquired an international reputation and became an FRS.

In 1910 Russell took up a lectureship in logic at Trinity College, Cambridge and shortly thereafter began an affair with Lady Ottoline Morrell, like himself a *déclassé* aristocrat. This led to his separation from Alys but it was not an altogether happy relationship. Russell was much more in love with Ottoline than she with him, and, after years of abstinence, he was much keener on sex than she was. But despite the storms and stresses this was a period of intellectual creativity for Russell. He also achieved great success as a teacher. The poet T. S. Eliot (1888–1965), the philosophers C. D. Broad (1887–1971) and Ludwig Wittgenstein (1889–1951) and the mathematician Norbert Wiener (1894–1964) were all his students during this period. It was brought to an end by the Great War. Russell was passionately opposed to British participation in World War I. 'When the War came I felt as if I heard the voice of God. I knew it was my business to protest, however futile protest might be' (Russell 1968: 18). In fact, his protest was far from futile. He became one of the leading anti-war activists, but in the process he lost his job, his respectability and ultimately his freedom. He spent a large part of 1918 in prison because of an article that was allegedly 'likely to prejudice his Majesty's relations with . . . America'.

The War transformed him. The don, the prig and the puritan were gone (he was known in the Peace Movement as 'Mephisto') and in their place was the activist, the popular writer, the socialist – and the philanderer. He continued to do philosophical work, but since he had lost his academic job and given away his inherited fortune he had to earn his living as a freelance writer. The income was especially necessary since he had started a family. He had become convinced that there was no hereditary basis for insanity so he felt free to beget. In 1921 he married Dora Black (1894–1986). One of the great tragedies of his life is that his eldest son, to whom he was devoted, did, eventually, become mentally ill.

Despite his generally left-wing stance, Russell conceived a profound aversion for the Bolsheviks after a brief visit to Russia in 1919. 'The country seemed to me one vast prison in which the jailers were cruel bigots' (Russell 1956a: 8). China, by contrast, pleased him greatly even though he nearly died during his visit in 1921. During the 1920s he and Dora started up a school but it did not prove a financial success. Indeed, it had to be supported by books and lecture tours by both Russell and Dora. Their marriage broke up in the early 1930s, shortly after the publication of *Marriage and Morals*, in which Russell advocated trial marriages and a tolerant line on infidelity. Russell married Patricia Spence in 1936 and they had one son, Conrad. By this time Russell had inherited the Russell earldom from his brother.

In 1938 he left England for America and a succession of academic posts. His reputation as an iconoclast caught up with him when he was deprived of a position teaching logic in New York on the grounds that he was 'erotomaniac, aphrodisiac, irreverent, narrow-minded, untruthful and bereft of moral fibre'. He was the victim of a witch-hunt and experienced some financial stringency. However, he also wrote his *History of Western Philosophy* which thereafter ensured him steady sales and a steady income.

He returned to England in 1944 to a blaze of respectability. He became a Fellow of Trinity, gave the prestigious Reith Lectures and was awarded the OM and a Nobel Prize. However, he had ceased to be philosophically fashionable, having been supplanted by his former pupil Wittgenstein. And he gradually lost his new-won respectability because of his increasingly strident opposition to nuclear weapons and, later on, to the Vietnam War. He was a founder-member of CND and became something of an icon to the 1960s' protest movement. His marriage to Patricia Spence ended in divorce but in 1952 he married Edith Finch (1901–78) and they lived happily ever after (in so far as this was compatible with his geriatric activism).

Such a bald narrative cannot begin to do justice to the drama of Russell's life or the range of his activities, literary, philosophical and political.[1] He wrote sixty books and 2,000 articles. He was one of the co-inventors of modern symbolic logic. He created, or helped to create, a new style in philosophy. For though his various *doctrines* are disputed or denied, his *approach* to philosophy has dominated, and continues to dominate, in the English-speaking world. As Russell's early biographer Alan Wood put it, the *post*-Russellians are all *propter*-Russellians. But his popular writings were also widely influential in helping to create the kind of liberal, left-leaning political culture that has been the source of much that has been most humane in the twentieth century (though this, of course, is a more controversial judgement than the first).

RUSSELL'S MORAL OUTLOOK

This brief biography suggests a certain consistency in Russell's moral outlook. Though his *meta-ethical* opinions – his views on the nature, justification and status of moral judgements – underwent various changes, his *normative* opinions remained fairly constant. He was, with reservations, backslidings and occasional hankerings after something more romantic, a utilitarian of sorts. He thought that the right thing to do was that action which seems most likely to have the best consequences. Usually there is not time to work out *which* action will have the best consequences, so it is sensible to be guided by rules. But Russell was not a rigid rule-utilitarian. The

---

1 For more on Russell's life, see his three-volume *Autobiography* (Russell 1967, 1968 and 1969) now available in a one-volume edition from Routledge, and the biographies by Ryan (1988), Moorehead (1992) and Monk (1996). Russell (1967) is a gem of the autobiographer's art, Russell (1968) is good and Russell (1969) is probably not all his own work. Of the biographies, Ryan is good on the politics but not the personal, Moorehead is lively but sloppy, whilst Monk's book is a masterpiece, though sometimes a little harsh on Russell. Good introductions to Russell's work are his own *My Philosophical Development* (1959), and the books by Grayling (1996) and Slater (1994).

rules are guidelines or rules of thumb, not absolutes, and from time to time they need to be reassessed. Times change, and rules which tend to produce good outcomes under one set of circumstances may produce bad ones under another. Indeed, they may have been based on a mistaken estimate of the consequences to begin with. Thus in his writings on practical ethics Russell is an enlightened rule-utilitarian. It is because the sexual *mores* prevailing in his society did not make for human happiness that he wanted to see them changed. It is because World War I was (visibly) such a disaster for human civilization that he stood out against it.

Mention of human happiness leads to the question of Russell's conception of the good. In totting up consequences, which results are good, which better and which best? It is clear that Russell was not an out-and-out hedonist. There was more to happiness, or at least more to the good life, than pleasure or the satisfaction of preferences. The best life was one that combined creative endeavour and contemplation with loving relations to family, friends and the world at large. The most interesting part of this is the emphasis on contemplation which is partly derived from Spinoza. What Russell valued was enlargement of the self through the contemplation of the Other – other selves but also a universe which is grandly indifferent to human concerns. It was for this reason that he disliked anti-realist doctrines such as idealism and pragmatism. If the world as revealed by science is, in some sense, an emanation of the self or a tool for the prediction and control of phenomena, then the self will not be enlarged by the contemplation of it. If one of the glories of the human mind is to be a mirror of nature, then it must be a nature worth reflecting – and that means a nature which transcends the merely human. Another unusual feature of Russell's conception of the good was his emphasis on what he called 'impulse'. Although his moral psychology was largely derived from Spinoza and Hume (reason being the slave of the passions), he gave it an original twist. Much of what we do – in civilized societies, at least – is done not because we want to do it but because it serves some long-term purpose such as making a living. Indeed, we spend a good deal of time suppressing immediate wants and forgoing particular pleasures. Russell thought that a life in which too many immediate impulses are sacrificed to long-term purposes is liable to be frustrating and boring (Paper 8). Yet we are social beings and cannot give in to every selfish or anti-social impulse. Russell's solution was that we should cultivate 'creative' impulses and desires that are 'compossible' with what other people want. My acquisitive impulses may not be compatible with yours if we both want the same thing, but if we both desire knowledge we can both be satisfied. Russell, therefore, was an ideal utilitarian in that what he wanted to see maximized was not simply pleasure or preference satisfaction but the states that comprise a certain kind of life. I have expressed this ideal in rather high-falutin' terms, but it is rather more rugged than the cultivated aestheticism of G. E. Moore, whose writings might be taken to suggest that the best kind of life can only be lived by a member of the Bloomsbury Group. An affectionate grandfather who cultivated his allotment, took an interest in public affairs and the bird-life he encountered on country walks and enjoyed the occasional glass of whisky would be leading the kind of life that Russell approved of.

RUSSELL UNDERRATED

Russell is underrated as a moral philosopher. This is odd since he was perhaps best known to the general public as a practical moralist. His writings on sex, love, war and politics brought both fame and notoriety. But philosophers have tended to ignore them. This is partly Russell's fault. He adhered to (and argued for) a rather strict interpretation of 'philosophy' which disqualified many of his own ethical writings. Subsequent philosophers have taken him at his word without realizing that their own conceptions of what counts as philosophy were rather more relaxed.

But Russell has suffered a double injustice. It is not just that he is neglected as a practical ethicist. He is ignored as an ethical theorist as well. Again, he may have brought this injustice on himself. 'I do not myself think very well of what I have said on ethics' he wrote in 1963 (Feinberg and Kasrils 1969: 132). And most ethical theorists have agreed with him. Either they do not think very much of what he said or they do not think of it at all. Of course, I do not want to claim for Russell the same status as an ethical theorist that he enjoys as a logician and philosopher of mathematics. But his achievement is not to be sneezed at. To begin with, he was a pioneer of both emotivism and the error theory, the two anti-realist theories that have dominated the twentieth-century debate. His writings reveal the anguish of a philosopher with a yearning for moral truth who cannot reconcile the objectivity of ethics with his philosophical conscience (Papers 20 and 22). Earlier on Russell was an expositor and critic of the ethical doctrines of

G. E. Moore (Paper 13) and played a major part in the Apostolic debates in which those doctrines were developed (Papers 10 and 12). He was also a pupil of the great Victorian moral philosopher, Henry Sidgwick, whose writings continue to loom large in twentieth-century ethics. Russell's reactions to Sidgwick's teachings are well worth preserving, dealing as they do with such hot topics as virtue ethics, the Is/Ought question, and the ethical implications (if any) of Darwinism (Papers 2–8). Even his revolt against Hegelianism had an ethical dimension to it and (as we shall see) his essay, 'Seems Madam? Nay, it is', can be deployed against any attempt to reconcile the claims of morality and self-interest by positing a metaphysical unity of selves (Paper 11). He had some sharp things to say about morality considered as a social institution (Paper 25), and was at one time inclined to wonder whether we would be better off without it, though he later came to favour a less drastic solution. Russell's conception of the human good (and hence the end of moral action) seems to me far more intelligible and at least as interesting as the rival conceptions of Marx and Aristotle to which so many weighty tomes have been devoted. In short, Russell had something to say about most of the questions that have exercised twentieth-century ethical theory. And quite often he was one of the first to say it.

If I am right, there is more to Russell as an ethical theorist than has met many a philosophic eye. But this is partly because those philosophic eyes have not had the chance to meet his writings as an ethical theorist. Many were not published in his lifetime, others were buried in obscure publications (or at least the kind of publication that is not read by philosophers) and sometimes ethical and meta-ethical reflections were incorporated into pieces largely devoted to other topics. My task has been to put together this material (or rather, some of it, since I have had to be viciously selective) to tell a coherent philosophical story.

RUSSELL AND MOORE

Just as the Dark Side of the Force dominated the destiny of Darth Vader, so Russell's destiny as an ethical theorist was dominated by G. E. Moore's *Principia Ethica*. There was a Before, a During and an After *Principia* period (this last being rather protracted) and each phase needs to be understood in those terms. Until 1903, Russell argued with Moore and tried to develop a satisfactory basis for ethics on his own. In 1903, he became an enthusiastic (though not uncritical) convert to the doctrines of *Principia Ethica*. (See Paper 13 for Russell's review and summary.) But in 1913, he lost his faith in the Moorean good and remained a moral sceptic thereafter, vacillating between various forms of moral anti-realism. Even so, he was very much a post-Moorean moral sceptic.

G. E. MOORE AND THE ORIGINS OF ANALYTIC ETHICS

The analytic tradition in ethics begins with Moore's *Principia Ethica*. Yet in many ways it does not seem to be a particularly original book. Moore's central thesis, that moral concepts cannot be reduced to concepts of any other kind, was anticipated by Sidgwick and before him by Richard Price. So what is novel about it? First, its *emphasis*. As Baldwin points out in his introduction to the new edition, 'Moore is primarily concerned to articulate a metaphysical [and I would add *semantic*] thesis about the status of ethical values which he takes to have absolutely fundamental significance' (in Moore 1993: xv). Moore argues (or can be reconstructed as arguing) that if moral concepts cannot be reduced to the non-moral, then a peculiarly moral property of goodness is required to make moral judgements true. And this property cannot be neatly fitted into a naturalistic ontology (i.e. a metaphysic which only recognizes the entities and properties posited by science and common sense). To my mind the chief merit of the book consists in putting the matter so starkly. Second, *Principia* is notable for its rejection of hedonism and its pluralism about the good. In Moore's opinion there are other good things besides pleasure; indeed, pleasure can even contribute to the badness of a whole when accompanied by something vile like lasciviousness. (He proves this by asking us to imagine a Paradise of Ecstatic Bestiality.) Moore even thinks that worlds without minds can be the bearers of value although 'by far the most valuable things which we know or can imagine, are certain states of consciousness, which can be roughly described as the pleasures of human intercourse and the enjoyment of beautiful objects' (Moore 1993: 237).

THE PREHISTORY OF *PRINCIPIA ETHICA*: RUSSELL'S ROLE

During the 1890s Russell thought more about ethical theory than he ever did thereafter. About a third of the papers in *CPBR* vol. 1 are devoted to ethics. This is partly because he did a course with Sidgwick and partly because he seems to have been carrying on a sort of running debate with G. E. Moore at meetings of the Apostles. At least some of Russell's opinions seem to have played a part in the evolution of Moore's ideas.

Two papers, in particular, are worthy of remark: 'Is ethics a branch of empirical psychology?' (Paper 10), and 'Was the world good before the sixth day?' (Paper 12).

In 'Is ethics a branch of empirical psychology?' Russell argues that the good is what we (I, the speaker?) desire to desire. (Hence ethics *is* a branch of empirical psychology.) But the essay ends with a challenge or perhaps a request: 'If our brother Moore will give me an unexceptionable premiss for his definition of the good, or even a hint of where to find one, I will retract.' Could it be that at this meeting, or shortly thereafter, Moore responded with his famous no-definition definition of 'good'? And did Russell consider himself answered? I am inclined to think so given the annotation in Moore's hand ('Good = good') on the back of the paper, and the content of Paper 12, 'Was the world good before the sixth day?'.

Paper 12 (*pace* Levy 1981: 206) is clearly a response to Moore's lecture series *The Elements of Ethics* delivered in 1898. This is an early version of what became *Principia Ethica*. Moore defends his famous no-definition definition of 'good' and disputes Sidgwick's thesis that only states of consciousness are good. Moore argues that a lifeless but beautiful world would be better (i.e. more *good*) than a similarly lifeless world which was 'one heap of filth containing everything that is most disgusting to us'. Hence things other than states of consciousness can be good. Russell attacks a different argument for the same conclusion. Beauty cannot be good only as a means, since the man who derives aesthetic pleasure from the ugly is somehow worse than the man of refined taste who only derives aesthetic pleasure from the beautiful. If beauty were valuable merely as a means, then the state of the clod savouring Tammy Wynette's 'Stand By Your Man' would be as valuable as the state of the aesthete savouring Mozart. Since this is not so, beauty is not valuable merely as a means. (See Moore 1991: 90–1.) Russell concedes that beauty is an objective property, but opposes Moore's view that a world devoid of conscious beings could be good in virtue of its beauty. He denies that the man of low tastes who derives pleasure from the ugly is really experiencing the *same emotion* as the refined gent who appreciates the beautiful. Since the states of the Mozart fancier and the Tammy Wynette fan are distinct, we cannot argue that the difference in the value of their states must be due to the difference in the value of their objects (the productions of Mozart and Tammy Wynette, respectively).

But if Paper 12 represents a partial conversion to Moore's views, Paper 10 is even more interesting, since it represents a position that Moore reacted against. In *Principia Ethica*, Moore denounces a great many naturalistic definitions of 'good'. But he is particularly severe with philosophers who attempt to define goodness in terms of desire. Who are these unnamed miscreants? One, I suggest, is Russell. Moreover, the view that Russell explicitly defends in 'Is ethics a branch of empirical psychology?', namely that ethics is a branch of empirical psychology, is explicitly denounced by Moore in *Principia* (Moore 1993: 92). Finally, in section 13 of *Principia*, in which Moore develops his famous Open Question Argument, the definition he selects for dissection ('one of the more plausible, because one of the more complicated of such proposed definitions') is Russell's 'good' means what we desire to desire (*ibid.* 1993: 67).

ANALYSIS, PARADOX AND THE OPEN QUESTION ARGUMENT

But Paper 10 is now of more than historical interest. For what did away with Russell's Apostolic theory was the Open Question Argument. And this argument proved to be incompatible with Moore's philosophic practice. For the Open Question Argument relies on a publicity condition – that for B to constitute an analysis of A (or for A to be synonymous with B), the equivalence must be obvious to every competent speaker. Moore assumes that if goodness were identical with some other property such as what we desire to desire, 'good' and 'what we desire to desire' would be synonymous. So all he has to do to prove that goodness is not identical with what we desire to desire (or indeed with anything else) is to prove that 'good' and 'what we desire to desire' are not synonyms. How does he do this? He argues that if 'good' were synonymous with 'what we desire to desire', the question 'Is what we desire to desire, good?' would be a silly one, since the answer would be very obvious – yes. Nobody *who understood the words of which it was composed* would bother to ask it, and there could be no two opinions among compet-ent speakers as to what the answer was. Moore takes it to be obvious that 'Is what we desire to desire, good?' is *not* like this; that the question is open; that it makes sense to ask it; and that competent speakers can, and do, disagree about what the answer is. Hence 'good' and 'what we desire to desire' are not synonymous. And the same trick can be used to dispose of alleged synonymies between 'good' and other naturalistic predicates. But note the publicity condition. Moore assumes that *if* 'good' were synonymous with 'what we desire to desire', this would be obvious to all.

This publicity condition came back to haunt Moore in later life. His stock in trade was *analysis*, the breaking down of complex concepts into their components. C. H. Langford proposed a paradox (Langford 1942: 323). Analysis, as Moore conceives it, is either useless or productive of falsehoods. For suppose the *analysans*, or analysing phrase, means the same thing as the *analysandum*, or thing to be analysed. Then, by the publicity condition, everyone would know this, and the analysis would teach us nothing new. Suppose, on the other hand, that the analysis is informative. Then (again by the publicity condition) the *analysans* and the *analysandum* are *not* really synonymous and the analysis is *false*. Indeed, the naturalistic fallacy can be seen as an instance of the Paradox of Analysis. Moore argues, in effect, that any naturalistic analysis of 'good' must either be redundant, because widely known, or false, because not evident to all. It is just that he denies the naturalist the redundant horn of the dilemma.

It seems we must either accept the Paradox of Analysis or reject the Open Question Argument. Either the Paradox is veridical and informative philosophical analyses are impossible, or there is something wrong with the assumptions that generate the Paradox and the Open Question Argument is called into question.

Now it does not seem plausible that Moore's method of analysis (or Russell's for that matter) is *entirely* worthless. Analysis, in something like Moore's sense, is surely capable of turning up results that are both true and interesting. And the reason is that our concepts are not transparent to us. Speakers can *use* concepts without being able to *explicate* them or even being able to recognize an explication when they see one. The purpose of analysis – *one* of the purposes at any rate – is to disinter the buried rules, presuppositions or primitive concepts that govern the use of a word and to express them in English in a perspicuous definition. Such an analysis need not be obvious to every competent speaker. The *analysandum* (in a sense) *means the same* as the *analysans* but this is not something that everyone will be aware of. Thus the Paradox of Analysis can be dissolved if the publicity condition is rejected, but only by reducing the Open Question Argument to rational impotence. Russell's analysis of good as what we desire to desire may be correct after all, and ethics a branch of empirical psychology!

RUSSELL, LEWIS AND THE ARGUMENT
FROM ADVOCACY

Whether or not it is correct, it is at least, a going concern. For a variant of Russell's theory has recently found a distinguished champion in David Lewis. Lewis argues that values can be defined as what we are ideally disposed to desire to desire (Lewis 1989: 113). Although I do not agree with this theory, it is perhaps worth noting that Lewis's account, like Russell's, is immune from another argument of Moore's (sometimes supposed to be *the* argument for the Naturalistic Fallacy) which I shall call the Argument from Advocacy. Suppose that 'good' *is* synonymous with some natural predicate X. Then the assertion that X things are good provides us with no extra reason for promoting them. We are to produce states of affairs of such and such a character, and for no better reason than that 'goodness' is a synonym for the characteristic in question. By defining goodness in terms of X-ness, the naturalist deprives the proposition that X things are good of its motivating power. It becomes a barren tautology. Since the claim that X things are good *does* have an influence on the will (at least when it is believed) and is propounded by the naturalist with the object of *exerting* such an influence, this indicates that the definition is false.

This argument presupposes that 'good' is being defined in terms of some good-making property, as when Bentham, for instance, defines goodness in terms of pleasure. Many naturalistic definitions are in fact like this. The naturalist defines goodness as the property or disjunction of properties he wants to promote. But not all naturalists confuse analysis with advocacy. Hume, for example, does not. Although, like Bentham, he is a utilitarian (though of a rather refined and gentlemanly sort), he does not define goodness in terms of pleasure or happiness. In effect (and I am slurring over some complications here) he defines goodness as what an informed and dispassionate observer would approve of, or would approve of promoting. This means that when *Hume* gets around to saying that pleasure is good, he is saying something more than that pleasure is pleasure. (See the notes to Paper 21 for details.) He is saying that pleasure is what we would approve of at our informed and dispassionate best. This may not be a terribly good reason for promoting pleasure, but at least it is better than a tautology. By distinguishing between analysis and advocacy, Hume makes his advocacy of utilitarianism more rationally persuasive. In much the same way, Russell and Lewis are immune to this version of Moore's argument. When they define goodness or value as what we are (or are disposed to) desire to desire, they are not trying to promote what we desire to desire. They are trying to explain why predicating goodness of something else gives us some sort of reason to promote it. As Lewis puts it, the aim is to secure 'a conceptual connection between value and motivation'. And, like Russell, he wants the connection to be 'multifariously iffy'. After all, we do not always choose the good.

MORE PREHISTORY: THE YOUNG HEGELIANS AND HENRY SIDGWICK

Analytic philosophy began when Moore and Russell revolted against Hegel (or to be more accurate, the brand of neo-Hegelianism that was then fashionable). In Russell's case, as well as Moore's, this revolt had an ethical dimension. During the 1890s Russell hoped that Hegelian metaphysics would provide a solution to a problem posed by Sidgwick, that of the 'Dualism of Practical Reason'. Once Russell realized that Hegelian metaphysics could not be used to reconcile the claims of duty and self-interest, the Absolute began to lose its appeal.

Sidgwick, notoriously, believed in 'the Dualism of Practical Reason'. He thought that 'ought'-judgements express dictates of reason but that reason sometimes speaks with a divided voice. It is rational to promote the public interest and rational to promote one's private interest. And where they come into conflict, you cannot say that the one is more reasonable than the other. Sidgwick considered this 'the profoundest problem in Ethics' and did not profess to have a solution (Sidgwick 1907: 34, 105, xviii–xxiii, 162–75, 506–9).

In Paper 2, 'On the foundations of ethics' (September 1893) Russell suggested a solution based on the Hegelian metaphysics of McTaggart (McTaggart 1931: 210–72). Russell's view on the topic was, he thought, 'that of most of the younger men at Cambridge' and was a rather peculiar variant of utilitarianism (*CPBR* vol. 1: 206). What distinguishes Russell and his young Cambridge contemporaries from standard-order utilitarians is an assumption, derived from McTaggart, that there is a 'most perfect form into which it is metaphysically possible for the universe to develop' and that this consists of an absolute – and, one gathers, blissful – harmony among spirits. It is important that the harmony in which Russell believed in 1893 was a *future* harmony rather than a current harmony (if that is the right way to put it) existing in a timeless Reality. For a future harmony can, perhaps, be promoted or retarded, and hence can be an end for rational action. Not so a harmony that already exists in some timeless supersensible realm. Moreover (since at this time Russell accepted McTaggart's arguments for personal immortality), this future harmony is one in which I can hope to participate. Hence I have a selfish motive for the pursuit of this collective end. Ultimately, as 'sympathy [becomes] more developed . . . selfishness and unselfishness will become indistinguishable and the end of each will become the end of all'. Thus Sidgwick's problem is neatly solved – though at the cost of some metaphysical implausibilities. But McTaggart's solution did not satisfy Russell for long since it relied on personal immortality and a *future* state of absolute harmony, and he soon ceased to believe in either. Reality – the Absolute – may be harmonious, but there is no reason to expect such harmony in the world of Appearance.

The problem is addressed again in Paper 8, 'Cleopatra or Maggie Tulliver?' (November 1894). This represents Russell's first foray into moral psychology. Here Russell develops certain characteristic theses about reason and the passions which remained with him for the rest of his life. He claims (1) that 'as Spinoza says' a passion can only be overcome by a stronger passion; (2) that the 'greatest passions, those which most influence our actions', are not necessarily those of the greatest intensity; and (3) that the greater a passion is the more it ought to be followed. There seems to be a problem here. For if, as a matter of psychological fact, we *do* (and must) follow the strongest or greatest passions, what is the point of suggesting that we *ought* to do so? However, the context suggests that Russell is equivocating here. Though in (2) the greater or greatest passion is simply the one which predominates, in (3) a passion is great if it is permanent and comprehends a larger 'universe'. Thus the greatest passion in sense (2) might not be one of the greater passions in sense (3). In the end, the take-home message seems to be this: (A) We should not stifle our passions lightly, since this leads to frustration, lassitude or maybe even madness (!). Rather, we should cultivate those passions which admit of a harmonious realization and only do away with those which are inimical to the others. (B) That as moral beings, concerned for the welfare of creatures besides ourselves, we should cultivate those passions which harmonize with the desires of other people. In other words, we should cultivate compossible desires, which is pretty much the ethic of *Human Society in Ethics and Politics* (Russell 1954) and most of the books and essays written in between. But this does not solve Sidgwick's problem. After dismissing McTaggart's solution, Russell flirts with the idea (derived from another Hegelian philosopher, F. H. Bradley) that individual selves can be somehow seen as aspects of the one, so that the prudential arguments for cultivating harmonious desires will rule out harmonious but anti-social passions such as those of Napoleon and Iago. The idea is that *really* different selves are not distinct, so that if I have a reason to cultivate desires which are harmonious *inter se*, I have a similar reason to cultivate desires which harmonize with everyone else's. But though Russell professes himself 'vastly tempted' to adopt this hypothesis, he does not do so in the paper.

Why shouldn't he have given in to temptation? An answer is suggested by Paper 11, 'Seems Madam? Nay, it is' (December 1897), the paper which marks Russell's exit from Hegelianism. Its theme is concisely summed up in a letter to Moore: 'that for all purposes which are not *purely* intellectual, the world of Appearance is the real world'. Its basic thesis is this: that if the world of Appearance is bad, it is no consolation to be told that the world of Reality is good, since what we experience is the world of Appearance. (Russell rejects McTaggart's thesis that the timeless harmony which is Reality will one day be manifest in time.) Although Russell does not discuss the matter explicitly, the application of all this to the tempting Bradleian hypothesis of Paper 18 is plain. What does it matter if really you and I are one, if our experience is confined to the world of Appearance rather than Reality? Since I do not experience the pains I inflict on you when pursuing my harmonious but evil desires, why should I worry about the fact that in reality I am inflicting them on myself (or a greater whole of which we are both parts)? After all, it is the phenomenal self that feels, or for that matter desires, and phenomenal selves are distinct. Thus we cannot reconcile self-interest with the public interest by positing a metaphysical unity of selves.

Sidgwick's problem remains unsolved and the Dualism of Practical Reason reasserts itself. Why then should we be moral? Russell has no answer besides the hope that the right sort of upbringing will instil the right motivations. And like a more enlightened version of James Mill, he tried to supply his children with just such an upbringing. The right motivations were not always forthcoming, however. Like most children, Russell's daughter Kate was sometimes inclined to use the classic line 'I don't want to! Why should I?' (Tait 1975: 185). Russell replied, as a good utilitarian, 'Because more people will be happier if you do than if you don't.' Unfortunately that was not the end of the matter.

> 'So what? I don't care about other people.'
> 'You should.'
> 'But why?'
> 'Because more people will be happier if you do than if you don't.'

Little did Kate know that in this dialogue she was displaying the Dualism of Practical Reason. Russell's answer is, of course, a dusty one, but given the Dualism of Practical Reason there is probably no better answer to be had.

BERTRAND RUSSELL, PROTO-EMOTIVIST OR 'NO IS FROM OUGHT'

In 1913 Russell lost his faith in the Moorean good and never regained it again. In later life he put this down to George Santayana's *Winds of Doctrine*, in which his views and Moore's are delicately mocked (Paper 14). As a result, he became a convert to the 'subjectivity of value'. What exactly he meant by this is not entirely clear. In 'The Place of Science in a Liberal Education' (written at about the time he was reading Santayana), Russell states that the 'kernel of the scientific outlook' (something he wants to see more widely inculcated) is 'the refusal to see our own desires, tastes and interests as affording the key to the understanding of the world'. And in the next paragraph he censures Aristotle for allowing 'himself to decide a question of fact by an appeal to aesthetico-moral considerations'. The implication would appear to be that aesthetico-moral considerations are expressions of our 'desires, tastes and interests'. And there are remarks in *Mysticism and Logic* (written in early 1914) to much the same effect (Russell 1917: 57 and 46–8). This suggests emotivism, the view that moral judgements and evaluations generally are neither true nor false (at least with respect to their evaluative meaning) but serve to express attitudes or emotions, rather in the manner of curses or huzzahs. This, in turn, is a variant of non-cognitivism, the view that moral and evaluative judgements cannot be known since they cannot be true or false.

However, the clearest statement of this general idea is in Paper 14, 'On scientific method in philosophy'. I take the argument to be this. As a mere point of logic, it is obviously fallacious to infer facts from values, Is from Ought. It may be that the world *ought* to be thus-and-so or that it would be *better* if it were, but it does not follow that that is the way it *is*. At least it does not follow *unless* we can add an extra premise to the effect that the world, or the relevant bits of it, are as they ought to be. Now many, perhaps most, of Russell's contemporaries thought it possible to establish just such an extra premise. Non-cognitivism affords a reason for supposing them to be wrong. If 'all ethics, however refined, remains more or less subjective', then to use ethical notions in metaphysics is 'to legislate for the universe on the basis of the present desires of men'. And there is no reason to believe that the universe corresponds to our desires.

WHY BE AN EMOTIVIST?

In the above writings, emotivism is alluded to and exploited rather than stated and argued for. It may be that the 'subjectivity of value' forces us to extrude the notions of good and evil from scientific philosophy, but what precisely does this thesis amount to, and why should we believe it in the first place? The answers emerge in dribs and drabs in the course of Russell's anti-war polemics. The first philosopher to challenge Russell's emotivism in print was Perry of Harvard, who took Russell to task for saying that the 'fundamental facts [on the ethics of war], as in all ethical questions are feelings'. ('The Ethics of War', *CPBR* vol. 13: 63). Russell's reply is not very satisfactory (Paper 15). The first decent defence of emotivism occurs as an aside in a magazine article defending pacifism against the aspersions of 'North Staffs' (the pseudonym of T. E. Hulme) (Paper 16). Russell's arguments resolve themselves into two, while a third is hinted at. (1) The moral phenomena (whatever they may be) can be explained without positing moral properties. This suggests that they are ripe for Occam's razor. (2) Disagreements about good and evil – or more generally about basic value judgements – give us reason to doubt whether there is anything corresponding to our alleged perceptions.

The first argument is a little obscure until we know what Russell's theory is and what the relevant phenomena are supposed to be. Given the semantic cast to Russell's thought, I suspect the following. He thinks he can explain how words like 'good' can be meaningful without supposing that there is some thing – some property – that they mean. This can be done *either* on the assumption that they are there to express emotions *or* on the assumption that they are empty predicates. In other words, it might be used to support emotivism, or it might be used to support the 'error theory', the view that moral judgements *are* the kinds of things that can be true or false but that since they refer to non-existent properties of good and evil, they are all of them *false*.

If Russell were simply arguing that the diversity of moral opinion indicates that there is not really a fact of the matter to disagree about, he would be refuted by the second paragraph of his own essay 'War and non-resistance' (Paper 15). There he admits that we cannot agree about what are undoubtedly matters of fact, such as the causes of the Great War and what can be done to bring it to a happy conclusion. But the fact that it is difficult to agree on such topics does not prove that there are no truths to disagree about. Why then should we make this inference when it comes to morals? Moreover, this argument (the 'Argument from Relativity') has been around a long time, and, by now, there is a standard response on the part of moral realists (people who believe that moral judgements have a truth-value and that some of them are true). Our practical moral judgements – that this or that should be done, that this trait is a vice and that is a virtue – are derived from what might be called our ultimate or basic evaluations with the aid of factual premises. This is most obvious if we assume, for the moment, some kind of consequentialism. Why is smoking a vice? Because it undermines one's health and tends to bring on an early death which in themselves are bad things. Why is breast-feeding a good thing to do? Because it promotes the present and future health of the infant which is a good thing in itself and the precondition for other good things. If it turned out that smoking was healthy and breast-feeding harmful we would reverse our value judgements. Now if the bulk of our moral judgements are derived from our basic evaluations with the aid of factual premises, the diversity of moral opinion could be due to differences as to the facts. But Russell's argument is immune to this response. For his point is that people disagree when it comes to their *basic* evaluations, about what kinds of things are intrinsically good or bad. Russell, for instance, approves of the peaceful exercise of man's higher powers whilst 'North Staffs' (so Russell insinuates) despises such a namby-pamby ideal and thinks that strife and combat are good in themselves.

Why should this be a problem? Because it is a disagreement at the level of what are supposed to be *perceptions*. *Theoretical* differences give no cause for concern. The fact that Aristotle thinks the sun goes round the earth and that Copernicus thinks otherwise does not indicate that there is no fact of the matter waiting to be discovered. Once we transcend the observable, truths about the cosmos are hard to come by. It is not at all surprising that rational people come to different conclusions. But suppose there is some alleged realm of fact – the spirit world, say – to be accessed by a special perceptual faculty. The mediums who claim access to this realm do not just disagree in theory. They disagree about what they claim to *perceive*, bringing back completely contradictory accounts of what they have encountered. Under the circumstances we might come to doubt whether the alleged perceptions were perceptions at all and whether the supposed realm of fact was not really a myth. Or we might come to wonder whether we had not misconstrued this entire conversational practice. Perhaps the perceptual 'reports' are not reports at all but – say – fancy ways of expressing one's mood or of influencing other people.

There is a hint – just a hint – of a related argument which falls between the Occamist argument and the Argument from Relativity. It goes like this. People disagree in their basic evaluations. So even if you think your own intuitions are correct, owing to your acquaintance with the good, you must believe in the possibility of *false* intuitions, in which people wrongly perceive goodness to inhere in states which are in fact bad or indifferent. These mistaken intuitions are presumably due to natural causes, to upbringing, indoctrination, temperamental bias and so forth. But if *other people's* basic evaluations can be (and indeed must be) explained away in this manner, why can't the other people return the compliment and explain away your own alleged perceptions in the same way? The diversity of moral opinion – of *basic* opinion, that is – suggests that real properties of goodness and badness are not needed to underwrite the phenomenology of value or to account for people's beliefs – something that even Moorean moral realists must admit when they come to the beliefs of their opponents. And if they are not needed to account for people's beliefs, they are not needed at all, since they can only influence events through the medium of human action. Hence they are ripe for the razor.

EMOTIVISM VERSUS THE ERROR THEORY

Now these arguments are not arguments *for* emotivism or non-cognitivism. Rather, they are arguments *against* the intuitionism of G. E. Moore. And there are more ways than one of not being a Moorean. Perhaps because he realized this, Russell abandoned emotivism in the early 1920s and briefly adopted what has come to be called the error theory. The theory is expressed with admirable conciseness in 'Is there an absolute good?' (Paper 17), which remained unpublished in Russell's lifetime. There are no such properties as goodness and badness. Since ultimate evaluations ascribe these properties to things, they are all false. And falsehood propagates throughout morality since rightness (for example) involves being productive of goodness and no act can be productive of a non-existent property. Morality, therefore, is compounded of falsehoods and rests on a metaphysical mistake. Thus Russell anticipates Mackie, who propounded a similar theory in his famous paper 'The refutation of morals' (Mackie 1946), by over twenty years. Where Russell differs from Mackie is that Russell, unlike Mackie, provides an explanation of how words like 'good' and 'bad' can be meaningful, even though there is no property that they mean. 'Good' and 'bad' are like empty denoting phrases such as 'the present King of France', and are to be analysed in accordance with Russell's theory of definite descriptions. (See the notes to Paper 17 for the technical details.)

The question is not why Russell believed this theory (we have seen reason enough already) but *why he gave it up*. In the absence of hard evidence we can only guess.

Perhaps because it was just too much to bear. Emotivism portrays moral debate as a rather sordid and manipulative business but at least it is not dishonest. The error theory converts the moralist into a purveyor of falsehoods. If the moralist does not believe his or her moral pronouncements, he or she is a hypocrite, and if the moralist does believe (or make believe) them, he or she is a subscriber to a set of comforting falsehoods, just the sort of person that Russell despised. Russell was much addicted to moralizing (no amount of logic, even if it were his own, he said, would make him give it up (Paper 20)) and he would not have liked the thought that he belonged in either category. Of course, it is possible to argue that moral beliefs are necessary fictions, and hence pragmatically true, since, in some sense, it pays to believe them. But, as Russell himself was at pains to emphasize, pragmatic truth is not true truth, since falsehoods do not metamorphose into truths when they turn out to be paying propositions.

But there are more technical objections to Russell's version of the error theory. Despite Russell's claims to the contrary, I think that

Moore's arguments (if they are effective at all) *do* tell against Russell's version of the error theory, given that that theory presupposes his semantics. I define 'predicate' as a word or phrase like 'good' or 'is good', and 'property' as the universal for which a referring predicate stands. Now Moore argues that goodness is a simple or unanalysable property because 'good' is a simple or unanalysable predicate. But *according to Russell's semantics*, if 'good' really were an unanalysable predicate it could not be meaningful and empty. According to Russell, a predicate (or any other non-logical word) can only be meaningful but non-referring if it can be analysed as something like a definite description. That way it can play a part in a sentence, and thus be meaningful, without having a meaning in the sense of some thing or property for which it stands. But according to Moore, 'good' cannot be analysed at all. Hence it cannot be analysed as some sort of definite description. In which case, it cannot be meaningful but non-referring.

Nor is this all. When Russell analyses the predicate 'good' (or better, the contexts in which 'good' occurs), the analysis he propounds is a *naturalistic* one, i.e. just the kind that Moore had professed to prove impossible. What 'M is good' means (in my mouth) is that M possesses the predicate [property] which is common to A, B, C, . . . , where 'A, B, C, . . . ' is a list of the things that I approve of (Paper 17). It is fairly clear that what Russell has in mind is a list of naturalistic items. And this is no mere slip, something that might have been put right in a better formulation of the theory. For *any* analysis that Russell might propound would have to be naturalistic. In Russell's view, many words and phrases are 'incomplete symbols', expressions which can function meaningfully in the context of a larger sentence, but which do not need meanings or referents of their own in order to make sense. But to the end of his days Russell believed that there had to be words of which this was *not* true – words which had to have referents if they were to have any meaning at all. He also believed in a principle of acquaintance, that every proposition that we can understand must (when fully analysed) contain only constituents with which we are acquainted. (The ultimate constituents of a proposition are of course the words which require a referent in order to be meaningful.) Finally, Russell believed that we are acquainted only with items in our direct and private experience. As Grover Maxwell points out, this amounts to a form of concept empiricism (Maxwell 1974). For if you put these doctrines together, you arrive at the claim that all understandable propositions are definable in terms drawn from our private experience. This means that any non-referring but meaningful word must be definable, in context, in terms of items with which we are acquainted – which is to say it must be susceptible to a naturalistic definition.

Finally, Russell's theory falls foul of an argument of Moore's that was neatly reformulated by Russell himself.

> If in asserting that A is good, X meant merely to assert that A had a certain relation to himself, say of pleasing his taste in some way; and if Y in saying that A is not good, meant merely to deny that A had a like relation to himself, there would be no subject of debate between them.
>
> (Russell 1966: 20)

Thus far, the Russell of 1910. But according to the Russell of 1922, 'M is good' in my mouth means that M possesses the property common to A, B, C, . . . , where 'A, B, C, . . . ' is a list of the things that *I* approve of while 'M is bad', in your mouth, means that M possesses the property common to F, G, H, . . . , where 'F, G, H, . . . ' is the list of the things you *dis*approve of. Now, suppose I say M is good and you say that M is bad. Then what I am saying is that M possesses the property common to A, B, C, . . . , whilst what you are saying is that M possesses the property common to F, G, H, ... It is plain that these assertions might be quite compatible even if, as Russell alleges, they are both false. For a thing might possess *both* the property common to A, B, C, . . . , *and* the property common to F, G, H, . . . (if there were such properties). Hence there need be 'no subject of debate' between us since we may not be contradicting each other. But, 'M is good' said by me and 'M is bad' said by you plainly *do* contradict each other, whatever we respectively approve and disapprove of. Hence the analysis is false.

Thus if the naturalistic fallacy really is fallacious, and Russell's semantic theory is correct, Russell's version of the error theory is false. Since both the naturalistic fallacy and Russell's semantics are highly questionable, this might not matter. But it turns out that the Moore/Russell arguments against what is now called 'simple subjectivism' ('X is good' means 'I approve of X') dispose of the theory anyway.

AN UNCERTAIN EMOTIVIST

At all events, Russell reverted to something like emotivism in the middle 1920s (Paper 18), though he did not formulate the theory clearly until 1935 (Paper 19). Russell's version of emotivism is in some ways a cut above that of his successors, Ayer and Stevenson, and it had the additional advantage of allowing Russell to moralize with a clear intellectual conscience. If the purpose of the moral vocabulary is to express certain desires and he *had* the relevant desires, why shouldn't he use this vocabulary to express them (Paper 20)? However, he was never entirely satisfied with emotivism, since he could not help feeling that he was *right* to express certain emotions (e.g. a distaste for the introduction of bull-fighting into America). Accordingly in *Human Society in Ethics and Politics* (1954) he tried to inject a little objectivity into ethics whilst retaining the belief that ethics is based upon feelings and emotions (Paper 21). But he seems to have regarded this attempt as a failure, and, in his last writings, reverted to the perplexed emotivism of the 1930s.

IS MORALITY PERNICIOUS?

At the beginning of World War I, Russell wrote that 'the universal outburst of righteousness in all nations since the war began' had 'given [him] a disgust of all ethical notions, which evidently are chiefly useful as an excuse for murder' (see the notes to Paper 14). Despite his own moralistic propaganda, he continued to take a dim view of morality as an institution and rather hoped that if 'the subjectivity of values' were widely recognized, there would be 'less cruelty, persecution, punishment, and moral reprobation' than currently existed (Paper 16). He even toyed with the idea that we might all be better off if morality were abolished (Paper 25). He later relented, suggesting that although *positive* morality often has a sinister side, protecting predatory elites and encouraging cruelty, it might be reformed and redeemed by the right kind of *personal* morality (Paper 27). I suspect that excesses of the Bolsheviks may have led to this change of heart. They were certainly subjectivists of some kind, and some of their writings suggest the error theory, if not out-and-out amoralism. Yet they were at least as brutal as their moralistic contemporaries. (See Interlude 1, Paper 26 and the attached notes.) At all events, Russell adopted a more balanced view of the function of morality in his book *Power* of 1938 (Paper 27). Despite its sinister side, even positive morality has its uses.

CONCLUSION

I hope I have said enough to stimulate the reader's interest in Russell as an ethical theorist. Reading Russell is not a mere exercise in what is known in the Antipodes as *text-fondling*, the shameful vice of history-for-history's-sake scholarship. Russell is far too stimulating and far too inventive for that. At the very least he is often interestingly wrong. And not many of us can hope to do better than that.

Part I

A MORALIST IN THE MAKING
The pre-*Principia* writings

1

GREEK EXERCISES
Extracts 1888

Reprinted from *CPBR* vol. 1: 8–11. During his teenage years, Russell came to doubt the religious and moral opinions in which he had been brought up by his grandmother, Lady Russell. His first exercise in philosophy was an attempt to come to terms with these doubts. He kept a secret journal, entitled 'Greek Exercises', in which his philosophical reflections, though written in English, were transliterated into Greek letters according to a phonetic system of his own devising. The purpose of this subterfuge was to conceal his thoughts from prying eyes, particularly those of his grandmother. The following extracts deal with his conversion to utilitarianism and his resolution to adopt an ethic based on 'reason' rather than the customs that had helped to preserve that section of the human species to which he belonged. The Miss Buhler to whom Russell could open his heart had been his Swiss governess. For the full text see *CPBR* vol. 1: 3–21.

8

April 18th. Accepting then the theory that man is mortal, and destitute of free will (which is as much as ever a mere theory, as of course all these kinds of things are mere speculations), what idea can we form of right and wrong? Many say, if you make any mention of such an absurd doctrine as predestination (which comes to much the same thing, though parsons don't think so), why what becomes of conscience, etc. (which they think has been directly implanted in man by God)? Now my idea is that our conscience is in the first place due to evolution, which would of course form instincts of self-preservation, and in the second place, to civilization and education, which introduces great refinements of the idea of self-preservation. Let us take for example the ten commandments as illustrative of primitive morality. Many of them are conducive to the quiet living of the community, which is best for the preservation of the species. Thus what is always considered the worst possible crime, and the one for which most remorse is felt, is murder, which is direct anni-hilation of the species. Again, as we know, among the Hebrews it was thought a mark of God's favour to have many children, while the childless were considered as cursed of God. Among the Romans also widows were hated, and I believe forbidden to remain unmar-ried in Rome more than a year. Now why these peculiar ideas? Were they not simply because these objects of pity or dislike did not bring forth fresh human beings? We can well understand how such ideas might grow up when men became rather sensible, for if murder and suicide were common in a tribe, that tribe would die out, and hence one which held such acts in abhorrence would have a great advantage. Of course among more educated societies these ideas are rather modified; my own I mean to give next time.

9

April 20th. Thus I think that primitive morality always originates in the idea of the preservation of the species. But is this a rule which a civilized community ought to follow? I think not. My rule of life, which I guide my conduct by and a departure from which I consider as a sin, is to act in the manner which I believe to be most likely to produce the greatest happiness, considering both the intensity of the happiness and the number of people made happy. I know that Granny considers this an impractical rule of life and says that since you can never know the thing which will produce greatest happi-ness, you do much better in following the inner voice. The conscience however can easily be seen to depend mostly upon educa-tion (as for example common Irishmen do not consider lying wrong), which fact alone seems to me quite sufficient to disprove the divine nature of conscience. And since, as I believe, conscience is merely the combined product of evolution and education, then obviously it is an absurdity to follow that rather than reason. And my reason tells me that it is better to act so as to produce maximum of happiness than in any other way. For I have tried to see what other object I could set before me, and I have failed. Not my own individual happiness in particular, but everybody's equally, making no distinction between myself, relations, friends or perfect strangers.

In real life it makes very little difference to me as long as others are not of my opinion, for obviously where there is any chance of being found out, it is better to do what one's people consider right. My reason is, for this view, first that I can find no other, having been forced, as everybody must who seriously thinks about evolution, to give up the old idea of asking one's conscience, next that it seems to me that happiness is the great thing to seek after, and which practically all honest public men do seek after. As an application of the theory to practical life, I will say that in a case where nobody but myself was concerned (if indeed such a case exist), I should of course act entirely selfishly, to please myself. Suppose for another instance that I had the chance of saving a man whom I knew to be a bad man who would be better out of the world. Obviously, I should consult my own happiness better by plunging in after him. For if I lost my life, that would be a very neat way of managing it, and if I saved him I should have the pleasure of no end of praise. But if I let him drown, I should have lost an opportunity of death, and should have the misery of much blame, but the world would be the better for his loss, and, as I have some slight hope, for my life.

11

April 29th. In all things I have made the vow to follow reason, not the instincts inherited partly from my ancestors and gained gradually by them owing to a process of natural selection, and partly due to my education. How absurd it would be to follow these in the questions of right and wrong. For as I observed before, the inherited part can only be principles leading to the preservation of the species, or of that particular section of the species to which I belong. The part due to education is good or bad according to the individual education. Yet this inner voice, this God-given conscience which made Bloody Mary burn the Protestants, this is what we reasonable beings are to follow. I think this idea mad and I endeavour to go by reason as far as possible. What I take as my ideal is that which ultimately produces greatest happiness of greatest number. Then I can apply reason to find out the course most conducive to this end. In my individual case, however, I can also go more or less by conscience, owing to the excellence of my education. But it is curious how people dislike the abandonment of brutish impulses for reason. I remember poor Ewen getting a whole dinner of argument owing to his running down impulse. Today again at tea Miss Buhler and I had a long discussion because I said that I followed reason not conscience in matters of right and wrong. I do hate having such peculiar opinions, because either I must keep them bottled up, or else people are horrified at my scepticism, which is as bad with people one cares for as remaining bottled up. I shall be sorry when Miss Buhler goes, because I can open my heart easier to her than to my own people (strange to say).

2

ON THE FOUNDATIONS
OF ETHICS

1893

Reprinted from *CPBR* vol. 1: 208–11. Though Russell was
studying philosophy at the time, this paper was not
written for any of his courses, but for the edification of his
sweetheart, Alys Pearsall Smith (1867–1951), soon to be
his first wife. It starts out as a systematic criticism of T. H.
Green's *Prolegomena to Ethics* (1883) but ends up as an exposition of Russell's own view which was, he thought, 'that of
most of the younger men at Cambridge' (*CPBR* vol. 1:
206). Russell was probably right in this, since the opinions
he advocates are largely derived from McTaggart.
McTaggart (1866–1925) was a neo-Hegelian philosopher
who had recently published a pamphlet, *The Further
Determination of the Absolute* (1893). Perhaps because of its
arresting title, this work enjoyed a considerable vogue at
Cambridge and Russell was, in some degree, a convert to
its doctrines. These included personal immortality.

> I found that all I had thought about ethics and
> logic and metaphysics was considered to be
> refuted by an abstruse technique that completely
> baffled me; and by this same technique it was to
> be proved that I should live forever . . . for a time
> I more or less believed it.
>
> (Russell 1961: 35)

McTaggart also argued that since 'reality is exclusively
spirit', 'the universe and ourselves are implicitly in
harmony – a harmony which must some day become
explicit' (McTaggart 1931: 210–11). This harmony would
be a *'civitas dei'*, a community – one might say a communion – of individual spirits in a loving state of mutual
awareness. Russell employs this hypothesis to solve a

problem raised by Henry Sidgwick (1838–1900), Knightsbridge Professor of Moral Philosophy at Cambridge, whose course on ethics Russell was attending. In his classic work, *The Methods of Ethics*, Sidgwick comes to the reluctant conclusion that 'Practical Reason' is subject to a certain 'Dualism'. It is reasonable to promote the general happiness and reasonable to promote one's private happiness, but when the two come into conflict it is not more reasonable to prefer the one to the other (Sidgwick 1907: 496–509). Since Sidgwick thought that 'ought'-judgements express the dictates of reason, this meant that 'the Cosmos of Duty is thus really reduced to a Chaos' (Sidgwick 1874: 473, quoted in Mackie 1976: 77). Russell jokes about the problem in a letter to Alys. 'I wish it were my duty to come to luncheon tomorrow but alas this is one of the cases where enlightened self-interest and universalistic hedonism part company: I must therefore stay at home and read . . . to my grandmother' (Griffin 1992: 16). McTaggart's version of the Hegelian Absolute enabled Russell to restore order to Sidgwick's Chaos. Since we are immortal, we will live to see the future harmony, and since it will be supremely pleasurable for all its participants, it is something we have an egoistic reason to promote. But the future harmony is one of mutual awareness. Hence *my* future happiness is dependent on that of everyone else. I cannot promote the one without promoting the other. Thus in the long run, at any rate, duty and self-interest coincide.

However, this solution rests on two whopping metaphysical posits: personal immortality and a *future* harmony. Russell soon came to disbelieve in them both.

NB. T. H. Green (1836–82) was the first major figure of the British neo-Hegelian movement. Russell says he is 'involved' in a circle in Bk III, chap. II of his *Prolegomena*. It is not clear to me which of several possible circles Russell has in mind.

The Art of Living, with which Ethics is concerned, includes, in its widest sense, every other art. <Art is here used, in its technical sense, as a series of rules, for the guidance of practice, based upon the laws of the corresponding Science: as e.g. the Art of Engineering on the Science of Mechanics.> It must therefore be based upon a Science which shall include every other Science, or at least be logically prior to every other Science; that is, it must be based on

Metaphysics. Before we can determine what ought to be done, we must, if our proceeding is to be logical (which of course is not an obvious requirement), first determine what end we should consider desirable if attainable. If it be said that our moral sense is prior to Science and that this gives us direction as to particular duties, without any consideration of ends, I should admit the first proposition, but should maintain that our moral sense is in itself an empty form, merely telling us that we have a duty; that the filling of this form must be (and is) derived from experience and knowledge. [This process would be similar to that by which the Categories (which are supplied a priori) derive their content from experience, so that all knowledge is subsequent to experience although some elements of it are logically prior to experience.] Such an a priori element there must be in morality: since the idea of duty is obviously not derived from phenomena. But the filling of the idea of duty must be got from considerations not purely ethical and the true procedure would seem to be

1 To determine the most perfect form into which it is metaphysically possible for the universe to develop
2 To discover (if we can) the best means to the attainment of this end.

[It is clear how we require the moral sense at this stage to make us pursue our idea of perfection however the pursuit may conflict with irrational desires.] The second of the above steps is a matter of detail in any particular branch of conduct, depending upon particular sciences: it does not concern us as philosophers, but only as actors. Let us consider further the first of these steps to a philosophic Ethic.

Green throughout considers the ultimate ideal to be a universe of perfect virtue; and supposes the true end of action to be the attainment of a virtuous character by ourselves and those whom we can influence. There is undoubtedly in this view, something which commends itself to the virtuous mind: but in philosophy we must rid ourselves of the bias of virtue as of every other. And when we have effected this, we shall I think be bound to confess that Virtue can be only a means to an end, not itself an ultimate end. For what is Virtue? A disposition to obey the dictates of Ethics. These dictates must themselves then derive their sanction from some consideration which is not ethical. Or again: the perfect state must be timeless: for any change would *ex hypothesi* mar the perfection which had been attained. There will therefore be no action in the perfect state, for action is a process in time; virtue being then that which prompts to right action must also disappear. Or again, if the last argument appears too mystical, virtue depends upon the necessity of acting, and the necessity of acting depends upon the possibility of ameliorating something; and in the perfect state this possibility will cease to exist. Or I might appeal to McTaggart's pamphlet for the proof that emotion alone would remain possible: desirable emotion for all spirits must therefore be the end of action. [The proof of this in the pamphlet depends in no way so far as I can see upon Hegelian metaphysics.] This doctrine is really Utilitarian; but by the assumption of the perfectibility of the universe it has been made to assume quite a different aspect from that of the Utilitarianism which regards every separate pleasure as of intrinsic value. This view would estimate the goodness of an act by its tendency to promote absolute harmony among spirits; since this harmony when established would involve the eternal happiness of all spirits, the passing pleasures and pains of our present existence in time would be of no account to it; and its precepts would often lead to acts which might increase human misery for a time, though it would reckon on an ultimate recompense.

As an example of the great difference between this doctrine (which yet considers happiness the one thing desirable *per se*) and ordinary Utilitarianism I may perhaps parenthetically quote another theorem of McTaggart's, of which I do not know the proof but which we can all verify approximately from our own consciousness. He says that if y be our actual attainment at any given time and x our greatest possible attainment in the time, our unhappiness may be represented by the product $y(x - y)$. This is largest when we have attained half as much as we might; and is zero when we have attained nothing or everything. With those whose development is less than half what it might be it becomes our duty then to make them unhappy, as the only means to greater happiness.

To return from our digression: we can by an ethic of the above kind get out of the circle in which Green is involved in Bk. III, Chap. II; at least so far as the determination of our duty is concerned: though of course if we ask why we should do our duty, the circle reappears and must reappear if the moral sense is part of the 'a priori furniture' of our minds, as I have supposed. But Green's ethic gives no method by which two conscientious people who hold different views about a particular duty can argue the question on which they differ: unless we assume, as he is inclined to do, that self-sacrifice is a good in itself. The fact that his theory suggests this result ought almost to be enough to condemn it; self-sacrifice I suppose means the performance of an action from which we expect more pain than pleasure to ourselves: and although so long as evil exists such actions will be necessary, it is difficult to see how in itself self-sacrifice can be anything but an evil. The view that I have advocated is suggested as an ameliorated Utilitarianism in §360 and objected to in §361 apparently solely on the ground of indefiniteness: this objection is largely removed by such considerations as McTaggart brings forward in his pamphlet, and it seems to me that all the ordinary duties are easily deducible from it, while it draws the limit better than Green's view between valuable self-denial and that which is purely waste, of which there is unfortunately so much just now.

But it must not be supposed that this view in any way minimises the importance of virtue: it is clearly only by action that our condition can be ameliorated, and this must always require virtue: but the more perfection is approached, the less often will self-sacrifice be necessary. When sympathy is more developed no person will be able to feel happiness in the pursuit of his own selfish pleasures if he knows he might be improving the condition of another, and thus gradually selfishness and unselfishness will become indistinguishable, the end of each will be the end of all. Previous virtue is no doubt a condition of the attainment of this state; and of course entire absence of irrational action is necessary. But in the perfect state we shall be neither virtuous nor vicious, any more than the soul is either round or square: the words will have lost their meaning.

Green is to my mind very conclusive against psychological Hedonism (the doctrine that we always do act for pleasure); but this, so far from being logically involved in ethical Hedonism, is strictly speaking (as Sidgwick points out) inconsistent with it. If we always do act for our own greatest pleasure there is no point in saying we ought to do so, and no use in saying we ought not. But as this doctrine had already been rejected by Sidgwick, who kept to Ethical Hedonism, it seems almost superfluous to object to a form of the doctrine which had already been rejected by the champion of Hedonism. I do not entirely understand his objection that a sum of pleasures cannot be enjoyed all at once, but am inclined to agree with it. This objection does not apply to the form of Hedonism I have advocated.

On Free Will Green appears to me not to prove his contention at all. Of course there is in action a non-natural element (using natural as Green does) but so there is in every phenomenon, unless we arbitrarily abstract the mechanical element from the element of consciousness, which latter is just as essential to the intelligibility of the phenomenon (as indeed Green himself sees). But this does not prevent the mechanical explanation of the motion of matter; nor need it interfere with a scientific account of the determining of the will. What Green does prove is that Spirit is the ultimate reality, and that Spirit as a whole is therefore free (i.e. undetermined by anything else, there being in fact nothing else to determine it); but that in no way interferes with the reciprocal determination of individual spirits so far as I can see. I think however that the doctrine has scarcely any ethical importance. But this is too big and too difficult a subject to discuss at the end of this little essay.

3

THE RELATION OF WHAT OUGHT TO BE TO WHAT IS, HAS BEEN OR WILL BE

1893

Reprinted from *CPBR* vol 1: 213–14. This paper, together with Papers 4, 5, 6 and 7, was written for Sidgwick's course on ethics. Russell, like G. E. Moore, was lucky enough to be taught by the great Victorian moral philosopher, Henry Sidgwick (1838–1900), author of the classic *The Methods of Ethics*, a sophisticated and critical defence of utilitarianism. Neither Russell nor Moore seems to have been sensible of their good fortune. 'We called him "old Sidg"', recalled Russell, 'and regarded him merely as out of date' (Russell 1959: 38). Nevertheless, both Moore and Russell were more influenced by Sidgwick than they seemed to realize at the time. It is generally acknowledged that Moore's *Principia Ethica* is a very Sidgwickian work and Sidgwickian themes continue to crop up in Russell's ethical writings right down to his *Human Society in Ethics and Politics* of 1954 (see Paper 21). Russell makes four main points: (1) that 'I ought to do *A*' is a factual claim which involves an 'objective element'; (2) that this 'objective element' is not the fact that the speaker is *of the opinion* that he ought to do *A* (which is implied but not asserted); (3) that ought-claims are not synonymous with any non-moral claims (and hence that morality is *semantically* autonomous); and (4) that as a matter of logical fact, conclusions containing 'ought' cannot be derived from premises in which 'ought' does not appear (and hence that morality is *logically* autonomous). However, Russell's argument only supports the conclusion that there are no *logical* relations between what ought to be and what is, has been or will be, not that there are no relations between them whatsoever. Moreover, there are two problems with

Russell's argument. (1) Russell concedes that 'ought' implies 'can'. Thus if I cannot do A, it would appear to follow that it is not the case that I ought to do it – perhaps a logical relation. (2) It is true that in the syllogistic logic Russell was taught you cannot derive a conclusion containing 'ought' from premises in which 'ought' does not appear. But this does not hold in the vastly more powerful logic that he went on to invent. (See Prior 1960.) However, a modified version of (4) – that 'ought' cannot appear *non-vacuously* in the conclusion of a valid inference unless it appears in the premises – can be demonstrated. (See Pigden 1989: 127–51 and Pigden 1991: 423–5.)

The question is: When we say 'A ought to be done' or 'I ought to do A', do we *mean*, if we are logical, to make any assertion about the real world? It is obvious that such an assertion is *implied* in either proposition, namely the assertion of our opinion; but it is equally obvious that this is not what we mean; an opinion, of whatever kind, is not the same as the assertion that we hold the opinion; such an assertion narrates a fact, which fact is true whether we choose to narrate it or not, and indeed could not otherwise be narrated as a fact. The assertion then that A ought to be done is not a statement of a psychological state; it involves (whether justifiably or not) an objective element; it is supposed true for all minds. But we do not mean to state that the opinion is universally held any more than we mean to state that we hold it; it may be held only by ourselves, but whoever does not hold it is regarded as in error, and it is regarded as just as much a statement of a truth as a proposition of Euclid. But what sort of truth is it? We obviously do not mean to assert that A ever is done or not done; nor that under any imaginable circumstances A would be done. Do we mean that certain consequences will follow if A is done? That the agent or any other person or body of persons will derive any sort of satisfaction from the performance of A? This is plainly not our meaning: it may be that the particular duty in question is held because we believe that the performance of A will lead to some result, but if so we must regard the result attained as desirable. If we call the result attained B, then we have not got rid of our *ought* but merely shifted it onto B, thus: Acts tending to B ought to be done. And if we consider the matter from the point of view of formal logic, it is plain that there are only two alternatives: either (1) we hold the view that 'A ought to be done' unreasoningly as an immediate intuition or (2) it has been obtained as the conclusion of a syllogism in which one premise must have been of the same form as itself, i.e. must have asserted that something ought to be done. Thus it is plain that propositions of the kind considered are *formally* irreducible to propositions about reality: some one or more propositions ethical in form must be regarded as axiomatic, unless such propositions are materially equivalent to some assertion about what is, has been, or will be. Thus we might attempt to found our ethics on psychology: we may say 'because pleasure always is desired therefore pleasure is desirable and ought to be sought'. But even accepting the premise the conclusion cannot by any method be derived from it. It is involved in the notion of 'ought' that there is a power in the agent of choice between two or more courses of action; not necessarily of free choice, since we may suppose the additional motive derived from conscience to determine the will in the direction of the moral precept considered; but a power of choice is involved, that is it must be supposed that a change in the agent's will would produce a change in the resultant action and that such change might be brought about by circumstances; it would be palpably absurd to say e.g. that the earth ought to remedy the obliquity of its axis, however much we may be convinced it would be a good thing if it did so. Therefore to say that we do desire pleasure as a matter of fact lands us in this dilemma: either we must suppose it impossible we should do otherwise and then the word *ought* becomes meaningless; or we must suppose it possible to desire other things than pleasure, and then we find that psychological facts give no indication as to the rightness of following such other desires. And here pleasure of course may be replaced by any other hypothetical object of desire without affecting the argument.

The notion of *ought* implies more than that the prescribed action will realize some end which is considered desirable: for a moral judgment is objective and would not be renounced if we found that the end we considered desirable was not so considered by others. Moreover the fact that some end is desirable or desired may lead to action but cannot lead of itself alone to a precept about action. I may say 'True; I desire pleasure; but I see no reason why I *ought* to pursue pleasure as an end. I pursue pleasure because I desire it, but if any other person chooses to pursue some other end, well and good.' And in reflecting on our self-consciousness it becomes clear that the sense of duty is entirely distinct from the sense of an end to be attained by action (though of course a particular duty may be determined by reference to a desired end); that it enjoins action immediately and not the pursuit of whatever may be desired (though of course we can only act in accordance with desire: but desire may be determined by duty). Thus there seems no relation whatever between what ought to be and what is, has been, or will be.

4

THE RELATION OF RULE
AND END

1893

Reprinted from *CPBR* vol. 1: 216–17. This paper was
written for Sidgwick who, if Russell is to be believed, was
very taken with it. Russell himself considered it 'much the
best Essay I ever wrote' for Sidgwick's course, indeed (as of
October 1894) 'about the best bit of work I ever did in the
way of close reasoning, though there are several fallacies in
it which Sidgwick has spotted' (*CPBR* vol. 1: 215). The
essay is an attempt to refute a claim of Immanuel Kant
(1724–1804) that the only thing that is really good is a
good will, where the good will is the will to do the right
thing (Kant 1959: 10–20). Russell's argument, as I understand it, is this: the good will cannot be the sole good. For
each instance of the good will presupposes an act that is
willed. And the act is willed because it is thought to be
good. Now is this act good or not? If it is, then the good
will is not the sole good. If it is not, then the good will
consists in willing things that are falsely supposed to be
good, which is, to say the least, very odd. Whatever the
merits of this argument, Russell goes too far when he
concludes not only that the good will is *not* the sole good
but that in itself it is only good as a means. Sidgwick's
comments on the paper, recorded by Russell, are, perhaps,
worth repeating.

> I agree, can't will only in order that volition
> subjectively right, but can make this indispens-
> able part of my volition; in fact this state I believe
> normal with man of developed moral conscious-
> ness. Kant allows empirical element in every
> actual volition. Do not admit desire involves
> imagined imperfection. A will to decide by

morality in a case of perplexity is a good will even
in a Kantian sense.

(*CPBR* vol. 1: 215)

Writers on Ethics may be divided into those who consider the Good
to be of the nature of Will and those who consider it to be of the
nature of Feeling. These two views might possibly be harmonized as
far as results are concerned: but in theory they must remain fundamentally distinct. If we adopt the former view, a good Will has
worth in itself and apart from the consequences of the act willed:
the logical procedure then will be first to determine if possible the
nature of a good Will, and the rules by which it must be guided:
and then, if we choose, to try to discover some End or Ends which
will be furthered by the performance of acts dictated by these rules.
The rules are thus logically prior: the ends (if they exist) have only a
relative worth, dependent on the worth of the Will which tends to
their realization. But if we regard the good as of the nature of
feeling, the value of a good Will becomes dependent; the goodness
of the Will is not ultimate, but contingent on its effort to realize
the End, namely the kind of feeling regarded as the Good. In this
case the End is logically prior to the rules, these being determined
as prescribing conduct conducive to the End. [An ethical theory
might be proposed which regarded a good Will as the ultimate
good, and made the production of a virtuous disposition an End:
such a theory would come under the second head, but would differ
radically from the Kantian view, since the excellence of particular
moral acts would have to lie in their tendency to perfect character
and not in the volition itself.]

The question, then, whether Rule or End is the more ultimate
depends upon the following: Is a moral act absolutely good *per se*, or
good only as promoting some other Good? Moral praise or blame
are bestowed on a man considered as an agent, i.e. as having Will.
Moral Good is therefore of the nature of Will: it is the actual volition which is morally good or bad. Thus the question becomes: is
moral good Good *per se*, or Good only as means to an end?
According to Kant the good Will is the ultimate good itself: but
it is impossible to regard it as such in acting, for the will cannot
will itself: it must will some imagined result of the act willed, and
this result must be regarded as good, and must be the cause of the
volition. [This objection might perhaps be made clearer by imagining
a perfect universe constructed on Kantian principles: this would be
a universe in which every individual was willing rationally. But

volition implies desire, desire implies imagined imperfection; thus a perfect universe could only exist if every rational being in the universe believed it to be imperfect.] It may be said, in objection to the above view, that when we will simply for the sake of conformity to the dictates of the moral law we are not willing any result of our volition: but such a volition requires a previous volition in which we will that virtue shall be our sole determining motive in deciding the particular practical question we have in hand: and this volition is determined by an end, namely our conformity to virtue in the immediate future. More clearly thus: suppose a contingency arises in which two courses of action, A and B, are open to us and we have to decide which to follow: in order that our action may be virtuous in the Kantian sense we require first a volition (V say) in which we decide that our choice shall be influenced only by the dictates of the moral law, and then a volition (W say) in which one of the two courses, A or B, is chosen. The first of these two volitions, V, is not made as being good in itself, but as a means to the further good of choosing virtuously between A and B. Thus in willing we must always have some good in view other than the excellence of the volition, and it is impossible for us at the moment of willing to regard our volition as an end in itself. We must therefore have, in willing, some end in view other than momentary conformity to virtue: we must therefore suppose moral action not to be good in itself, but to be good only as tending to some further result. And this result must be sought as a part of the Good or as an indispensable means to a part of the Good; and this Good cannot be regarded as of the nature of Will. The Good will be our end, and the rules of Ethics will be rules for its attainment: we shall obey them, when we act consciously morally, not because they appeal to us immediately, but because we believe duty to consist in the pursuit of the Good and our rules to direct this pursuit.

5

ON THE DEFINITION OF VIRTUE

1893

Reprinted from *CPBR* vol. 1: 219–21. Another essay for Sidgwick. Russell traces Kantian and counter-Kantian intuitions to ambiguities in the common concept of virtue. He prefers to reject Kant and adopts a reformed conception of virtue according to which 'the virtuous disposition is . . . that which is most prone to moral acts'. If this is correct, an ethics of virtue cannot supplant an ethics of duty since the concept of a virtue presupposes the concept of duty, or at least, some conception of the right thing to do.

Russell manages to misquote Wordsworth's 'Ode to Duty' (1807), and to mangle Godwin's Fenelon example. In Godwin's *Enquiry Concerning Political Justice* (1793: Bk II, ch. ii), it is not Fenelon who rescues his housekeeper, but a bystander who must choose between rescuing Fenelon (an author whose works will benefit mankind) and a chambermaid who happens to be the bystander's mother.

In defining a term in such common use as the word Virtue it is important to depart as little as possible from popular usage, for fear of becoming misleading and apparently paradoxical: on the other hand if Ethics is to be at all philosophical, it is important to attach a clear and definite meaning to the word, so far as this may be possible.

That the popular conception of virtue is far from clear, appears at once when we consider the various contradictory propositions about it to which the plain man could with a little ingenuity be got to assent. For example if I say it is more pleasant to me to do wrong than to do right, I shall be supposed to be uttering an immoral sentiment: but again if I say I always do as I like, it will be supposed that I am not in the habit of performing virtuous actions. If I profess that the exercise of kindness is irksome to me, I shall be censured, and should be commended if such exercise sprang from benevolent inclination: on the other hand it will perhaps be said that there is no virtue in merely following inclination. Common sense is also not always clear as to whether subjective or objective rightness is to be made the test: a persecutor, whatever his motive, would usually be censured, while on the other hand it would be easy to make the plain man admit that what the agent honestly believes to be his duty it is virtuous, and alone virtuous, for him to do.

If then we try to get a self-consistent conception of virtue as nearly as may be in accordance with common sense, we shall be forced to make our definition very complicated and full of reservations. There is something tempting about the simplicity of Kant's view of virtue, as consisting solely in the will to do right; and I think we shall have to admit all acts that come under this definition as virtuous. But if we are to avoid paradoxes, it will be necessary to widen our definition considerably. For it is an acknowledged consequence of this view, that for example a kind action done from affection and not from regard for duty is not virtuous; but common sense would probably regard it not only as virtuous but as more virtuous than in the former case. In the family for example it is supposed that mutual forbearance and sacrifice ought not to be the result of a conflict of impulses in which a sense of duty finally conquers, but rather of an emotional desire for the well-being of others which is so strong as to exclude selfish considerations altogether. Yet a man who had reached this state would according to Kant be unable to perform any virtuous acts.

This brings out an important distinction between two different meanings of the word Virtue which common sense seems to allow confusedly to coexist, although they are very apt to come into conflict. According to one view, 'virtuous' is applied to acts considered separately and regarded as separate victories of the sense of duty over inclination. Thus temperance is considered virtuous in one who is strongly tempted to over-indulgence in alcohol, while in another who has no such temptation it is not so considered, though perhaps it might be regarded as praiseworthy in the same way as other non-moral excellences are. This view leads to the paradox (which apparently the plain man shuts his eyes to) that the more irrational desires I have the more virtue I display in living rightly: the man who hates his neighbour and yet acts benevolently is more virtuous than the man who so acts from kindliness. And so we come to the other view, that virtue consists not in particular acts but in the whole disposition and character. On this view it is necessary to have some standard of objective rightness first: it then appears that certain impulses tend to promote acts objectively right, others to discourage them: a character in which the former class of motives is strong is then virtuous, while one in which the latter is strong is at least less virtuous. And common sense would admit probably that a perfect man could have no conflict of impulses but would act rightly without effort; just as in the orthodox view God is not regarded as liable to temptation. And I think it could hardly be maintained that the conflict of impulses would cease because the moral sense had become so overpowering that all other desires were negligible compared to the desire of doing right: rather we should look for such an ordering of the other desires that they should always prompt of themselves to the action which the moral sense would approve. It is for this reason that emotions, such as Benevolence and Sympathy, are commonly reckoned among virtues: because they normally afford a motive tending to facilitate the performance of duty, and if they become strong enough may in most cases be safely allowed to supersede conscious conformance to the moral code. But it is thought dangerous to allow conscience to be altogether in abeyance: as Wordsworth says

> There are who ask not if thine eye
> Be on them: who in simple truth,
> Where no misgiving is, rely
> Upon the genial sense of youth:
> Glad hearts, without reproach or blot,
> Who do thy will and know it not,
> O if through confidence misplaced
> They fail, thy saving arms dread power around them cast.

But some virtuous acts can only be performed impulsively, their performance requiring immediate action, without time for reflection: such acts can hardly arise from conscious virtue, but must spring from an impulse, which would be regarded as virtuous. Indeed sometimes common sense would disapprove of reflection even where it could be performed: for example when Godwin censures Fenelon for his effort to rescue his housekeeper from his burning house, on the ground that his life was more valuable than hers, we feel that although, if Fenelon had stopped a moment to reflect, he might have seen the justice of the argument, it was more virtuous to rush in and be burned. This view may be erroneous, but I think it would certainly be the view of common sense. And generally, even in deliberate action, where the agent incurs considerable pain by his act, this act is usually regarded as virtuous although perhaps mistaken. This may be explained by the consideration that the disposition shewn in such acts is one which would in general lead to conduct such as the moral sense would approve, although the particular act may be Quixotic.

In conclusion then: Virtue will apparently be defined most nearly in accordance with common usage if applied to disposition or character, as manifested in acts: it being supposed that the moral sense is able to decide, or at least that the decision can somehow be made, as to what conduct is moral and what immoral. The virtuous disposition or character is then that which is most prone to moral acts, that in which the desires (including among these the desire to act morally) are so graduated as always to prompt to the best action; and further in which some acts are performed without conscious reference to the moral sense (though it must always be supposed that the moral sense would approve if it judged at all); indeed the perfectly virtuous disposition would I suppose *always* find sufficient motive for moral action without calling in the moral sense, though this must be supposed strong. We should then call a person more or less virtuous according as he approximates more or less to this ideal.

6

THE ETHICAL BEARINGS
OF PSYCHOGONY

1894

Reprinted from *CPBR* vol. 1: 223–5. Psychogony as a
subject is the enquiry into the psychological and evolutionary origins of concepts, emotions and conventions.
Russell seems to conceive of it as a department of human
sociobiology (though 'sociobiology' was not a word that
had been invented at the time). Since he has already argued
(Paper 3) that what is, has been or will be can have no
logical bearing on what ought to be, it is not surprising
that Russell considers psychogony of little relevance to
ethics. An evolutionary account of our moral beliefs or our
moral sentiments cannot tell us whether our beliefs are true
or whether our sentiments are to be trusted. Thus Russell
seems to have abandoned the thesis of 'Greek Exercises'
(Paper 1) that *because* our common-sense moral intuitions
are the products of evolution and education, they ought to
be given up in favour of the dictates of 'reason'.

There are several points to note:

1   Russell's understanding of the evolutionary process is
    rather crude. Like many Victorians he is a 'group-
    selectionist'. That is, he believes that nature selects for
    traits which favour the group – the tribe, the nation or
    the race – rather than the individual and his or her kin.
    This is nowadays regarded as a mistake (see Dawkins
    1989: 7–10 and Wright 1994: 186–8) though it is
    allowed that a trait can spread because it favours the
    group if it *first* favours the individual (Mackie 1978:
    126–9). However, this modern consensus is now
    coming under challenge (Wilson and Sober 1998).
2   Russell argues that just because a trait – such as a
    moral sentiment – has evolved, this does not mean
    that it is 'life-preserving' or confers a selective advant-
    age in the present. It may be a 'morbid bye-product'.

THE ETHICAL BEARINGS OF PSYCHOGONY

Or it may have become maladaptive in the present (in 'the altered conditions of civilized society') even though it paid its way in the past (in the primitive societies in which human beings evolved). Modern sociobiologists have sometimes been slow to see this point. (See Kitcher 1985: 213–40 but also Wright 1994: 37–8.)

3   Could the psychogony of a moral belief undermine its credentials? Perhaps yes. Suppose the belief that p only qualifies as an instance of knowledge if it is partially caused by the fact that p. (This condition has to be considerably qualified if it is to escape refutation, but perhaps a more elaborate version can be defended.) Then, if we can explain why people believe that p without recourse to the (alleged) fact that p, their shared belief may be true, but it no longer qualifies as an instance of knowledge. Moreover, if the only reason to posit the fact that p is that people believe in it, then a successful psychogony may call the truth of the belief into question. If the reason we posit the fact that p is to explain the widespread belief that p, and if we can explain this belief without the aid of the alleged fact, then the fact that p can be dispensed with. It is for these two reasons that a psychogony of morals can be a subversive enterprise. (Some writers on Nietzsche, who was famous for his subversive 'genealogies', come close to appreciating these points but I have not come across one who makes them explicit. See Schacht 1983: 126–30.) If this is right, then the teenage Russell of 'Greek Exercises' is more nearly correct than the Cambridge Russell of the 1890s.

4   Despite the examples which are plainly intended to shock, Russell's conclusions in this essay would have met with Sidgwick's approval. 'Cautious willingness to accept the hypothesis of evolution by natural selection as a valuable scientific theory, coupled with scepticism as to its bearing on philosophy in general and ethics in particular, characterized Sidgwick's attitude throughout his life' (Schneewind 1977: 385).

At first sight we might be tempted to say that Psychogony, being concerned with what is and what has been, cannot possibly have any bearing on what ought to be: and in this opinion we should be at least so far justified, that of itself no mere history of the moral sentiments or science of their development can afford any ground for a belief in their ethical validity or invalidity as they at present exist. But on a closer inspection we may find that Psychogony has considerable indirect bearings on Ethics, that it is important, if not as a constructive, at least as a negative and regulative force. Let us first see briefly what Psychogony can tell us about the moral sentiments.

If we accept an Evolutionary account of the development of this as of every other set of impulses, we can easily point out the importance of many simple virtues both to the primitive tribe and to the still more primitive family. In the struggle for existence it would be an advantage to a family if the father protected the mother until she ceased to bear children and if the parents protected the children until they grew up. In the primitive tribe it would be essential to its existence that some feeling of patriotism, of self surrender for the good of the whole, should exist; and as soon as it did exist in any tribe, this tribe would be able to exterminate its enemies with comparative ease. Even a certain amount of mutual forbearance within the tribe might possibly be advantageous, as an aid to cooperation against common enemies and also as facilitating the propagation of the species and the maintenance of children. And as society became more complex, more and more of such cooperation would be required and this would introduce the need for more and more action of the kind usually known as virtuous. Also with greater stability comes in the possibility of excessive self-indulgence and therefore the necessity of prudence and self-control.

Thus it is easy to see how the existing virtues are on the whole and in the main of use in the Struggle for Existence and may have been produced by Survival of the Fittest. But in the first place it by no means follows that morality has been developed precisely in the way most adapted to its original evolutionary purpose: what are known to the biologist as morbid bye-products may have been produced along with the directly useful virtues, and perhaps the race would prosper better without these bye-products. For example it is difficult to see what use a woman is to society, from an evolutionary point of view, when she has ceased to bear children, or at least to bring them up. The Indian custom of Suttee seems far more suitable than ours: why waste the means of sustenance on one who can serve no longer for the preservation of the species? Again the humanitarian habit of carefully preserving the lives of weak and sickly members of the community, and of even allowing them to propagate their weakness and sickliness, is undoubtedly the result of sentiments which must be put in the category called *moral*: and yet I suppose no one will deny that on the whole it is a disadvantage from the evolutionary point of view, and that the Spartan habit of exposing sickly babies was far preferable. But secondly: even if we were to admit that all our moral sentiments are such as tend to the maximising of Life (in Herbert Spencer's phrase), or if we construct or could construct a morality which should serve this end, what warrant have we for accepting it as ethically valid? Because evolution has brought forth a certain morality tending on the whole to the maximising of Life, why accept this end as ours? Since we have survived, we have of course bodies and minds which are liable to survive: but how does the mere fact of our survival prove us ethically superior to those whom we have succeeded in exterminating? The murderer is not usually considered more virtuous than the man he murders: yet on the principle of survival he ought to be, having proved himself the stronger. For his position is in reality not materially different from that of a tribe which by superior patriotism and courage has succeeded in exterminating another tribe and so in propagating the virtues which led to its success. Nothing compels us to regard life in itself as valuable and alone valuable: this must of course appear the end of nature since those organisms only which best attain this end survive: but why blindly follow nature? why survive? or if we choose to survive, why not endeavour to attain some other end beside mere life? These questions belong to Ethics, and no account of the origin of ethical opinions can answer them.

So far, then, Psychogony would not seem to give us much help in Ethics. But when we have determined the most fundamental questions of Ethics, we may be helped in details by Psychogony. For psychogony can give some light as to the ends which will be served by following the morality of common sense; and therefore in so far as we consider these ends desirable or undesirable we shall accept or reject this morality. If for example we consider happiness the end of moral action, and if we hold further with Mr. Herbert Spencer, that pleasure springs from life-preserving actions, existing morality will no doubt help us in ordinary circumstances. But the more we examine into such indirect bearings of Psychogony on Ethics, the more evanescent they seem to become. Apart from the glaring fallacies involved in the proof of the proposition quoted above from Mr. Herbert Spencer (among which Psychological Hedonism is prominent), we cannot at all trust that moral sentiments will be always life-preserving in their character: for in so far as they have arisen through evolution, they are likely to be adapted, as most of our other impulses are, to a much more primitive state of society: and they are bound always to lag a little behind the needs of the age. It is true that those whose moral sentiments are too grossly out of touch with these needs will be unable to propagate their quixotism (if examples were needed one might instance a curate who leaves the church in consequence of religious scruples and is therefore unable to afford marriage): but these people are genuinely following their moral impulses, and so we can never be sure in acting (as we think) virtuously that we shall not become those very victims of imperfect adaptation who are eliminated in the struggle. Such cases are similar to those of death or loss of health from excessive sensual indulgence: here too a man is following an impulse originally produced by natural selection, but which owing to the altered conditions of civilized society has become more powerful than it need be for evolutionary purposes. These instances shew how dangerous it is in a complex and changing society to trust to impulses which originally had a life-preserving or life-producing tendency: they may be slightly injurious, but not to the extent of loss of life; or again they may be normally so restrained by self-control as to fail of the destructive effects which they cause when not so controlled. On the whole then it would seem that even the indirect bearings of Psychogony are very limited and doubtful.

7

ETHICAL AXIOMS

1894

Reprinted from *CPBR* vol. 1: 227–8. This is the last essay
that Russell wrote for Sidgwick's course. Russell's problem
is this: what are the axioms of ethics and how are they to
be justified? There must be such axioms, Russell thinks,
since no moral conclusion can be derived from premises
that do not contain at least one moral judgement (Paper 3).
Hence there must be 'ethical maxims not themselves based
on any further propositions'. And it is 'sufficiently obvious
that [their justification] cannot be sought in any proposition about what is or has been' (Papers 3 and 6). So where
is it to be sought? The axioms do not seem to be self-
evident since they are not evident to every self. And Kant's
principle – 'I ought never to act in such a way that I could
not also will that my maxim should be a universal law'
(Kant 1959: 18) – is no help since it is 'purely formal' and
does not tell us which maxims to will. At the end of the
essay Russell seems close to theoretical despair though he
appears to be moving towards the doctrines of the Oxford
idealist philosopher F. H. Bradley (1846–1924). Russell's
definition of the Good as that which satisfies desire seems
to be borrowed from Bradley's *Appearance and Reality*
(1893) whilst his talk of self-realization suggests the same
author's *Ethical Studies* (1876). (See Bradley 1930: 356 and
Bradley 1927: 64.) However, Russell does not record
reading either of Bradley's books until some months after
this paper was written (*CPBR* vol. 1: 353). Perhaps he had
a preliminary peek.

Although Russell 'takes it as a datum' that moral
judgements are 'liable to truth and falsehood', the essay
suggests an undercurrent of doubt. He feels it necessary to
argue that we are 'precluded from scepticism' because we
must choose and choice is based on evaluative judgements.

Perhaps it is, but those evaluative judgements (1) need not be ethical and (2) need not be liable to truth and falsehood. Indeed, his own attempt to define the good in terms of desire suggests that they might be construed as expressions of desire. He finds it necessary to argue against subjectivism (the view that 'X is good', means something like 'I desire X', or 'I approve of X') on the grounds that moral judgements are liable to error whereas 'statements of [one's] psychological state' are not.

We may take as our datum here that we do make moral judgments, as a matter of fact; and that we regard these, like judgments as to what is, as liable to truth and falsehood. Hence there must be some criterion, implicit or explicit, to which we refer such moral judgments: if we allow the possibility of error, we must regard propositions as to what ought to be as deducible from some one or more fundamental ethical maxims, not themselves based on any further propositions. Of course in framing any particular moral precept, Do this or Avoid that, our premises are partly matter of fact, or may be; but one premise at any rate, if we have any premises at all, must be ethical, and thus finally we are brought to the necessity for ethical maxims which have no further basis. And however impossible we may find it to compel everyone to accept such maxims, however unfounded the whole structure may appear, we are precluded from scepticism by the mere fact that we will and act: for to choose one action rather than another, where two or more courses are open to us, or even to abstain from acting, involves some ground for preference of our choice, and thus involves the distinction of better or worse: volition must imply a good presented to the imagination as possible but not actual, a contrast, that is, between what is and what ought to be.

Thus some basis must be found for ethical judgments. And it is sufficiently obvious that such a basis cannot be sought in any proposition about what is or has been. No theory of the origin of the moral sentiments, no general consensus of common sense can afford even the shadow of an ultimate ethical axiom, being themselves concerned with what is and not with what ought to be.

But where are we to find the axioms we are seeking? Unfortunately the immediate dictates of conscience are always more or less particular: they may prohibit lying or murder, they may enjoin kindness to my neighbour, but such precepts are not sufficiently general for our purpose. Can we then find axioms as self-evident as those of Arithmetic, on which we can build as on a sure foundation, which could be shaken only by a scepticism which should attack the whole fabric of our knowledge?

It becomes important here to distinguish between formal and material axioms. The Kantian maxim, which Kant himself apparently regarded as sufficient, is purely formal: it gives no indication as to the sort of conduct we ought to will to become universal. I see no reason why an astute pick-pocket in galloping consumption should not will picking pockets to become the universal rule: for he might thus avoid spending his last days in prison and might be so convinced of his superior skill as to be certain of making more by picking the pockets of others than he lost by having his own picked: and though society would rapidly fall into ruin, he might hope to be dead before this result followed. But as a formal rule, Kant's precept really amounts to no more than that moral judgments claim objective validity (since there is no knowing what perverseness a man might shew in willing universal laws of conduct). And this objectivity of moral judgments is involved in their liability to truth and error: if they were merely statements of a psychological state, and claimed to be nothing more than this, they could not err (except by the speaker's mistaking his own feelings). This one formal axiom, then, as soon as its meaning is clear, must I think be admitted as self-evident by all who pass moral judgments.

But when we come to seek a material precept the case seems to me very different. No maxim of this kind has obtained the universal consent of moralists, and therefore we can scarcely hope to find one which shall command our assent by its self-evidence. Let us endeavour to find out the sort of axiom we should require.

As was said above, all action implies an imagined good sought by the agent: where we may define the Good as that which satisfies desire. This good which is sought must be, strictly speaking, the agent's own good: though he may of course find this in any object of desire, as for example in complete self-surrender to the good of others. But from the above definition it follows that the agent must seek his own imagined good by his act, since all action must aim at the satisfaction of desire. There may be error in his view of his own good, for the frequent failure to find satisfaction in the attainment of our desires is a commonplace of moralists. But if in all action I necessarily seek what I imagine to be my good, the difference between moral and immoral action must consist in the difference of the conception I form of my own good. The good for me is obviously dependent on myself and my surroundings, but is not dependent upon my idea of it at any moment, since it is that which *will* satisfy desire, and not that which I merely believe will satisfy desire. Thus the material axiom which we are seeking will have to contain a precept that we are to seek our own good, with a definition of this good, more or less partial of course. Our duty will consist in self-realization, but self-realization may of course be best attained by what is commonly called self-sacrifice: and so long as we live in a society, our own development must be closely connected with that of the society we live in. But in what more particularly self-realization would consist I cannot here discuss: this is a metaphysical rather than an ethical question.

8

CLEOPATRA OR MAGGIE TULLIVER?

1894

Reprinted from *CPBR* vol. 1: 92–8. This paper (like Papers 10, 11 and 12) was delivered to the Cambridge Conversazione Society, otherwise known as the Apostles, a secret and very exclusive Cambridge club that met on Saturday evenings to discuss a paper read by one of the members. According to Russell, 'The Society' (as it was also known) included most of the people of any intellectual eminence who had been at Cambridge since 1820. And though this is something of an exaggeration, it is perhaps a pardonable one, since the list of members includes Russell himself, Sidgwick, Whitehead, Keynes, Lytton Strachey, Leonard Woolf, Wittgenstein and F. P. Ramsey. Its active membership was generally confined to undergraduates and some of the younger dons. 'With rare exceptions, all the members at one time were close personal friends. It was a principle in discussion that there were to be no *taboos*, no limitations, nothing considered shocking, no barriers to the freedom of speculation' (Russell 1967: 68–9). Apart from Russell himself, the two leading philosophers in the Society at this period were McTaggart and the young G. E. Moore (1873–1958), whose work on ethics would culminate in the epoch-making *Principia Ethica* of 1903. Papers 8 and 11 deal with the work of McTaggart whilst Papers 10 and 12 represent Russell's contribution to the Apostolic debates that led up to *Principia Ethica*.

Paper 8 was written during a period of enforced separation from Alys when Russell was working as an honorary *attaché* at the Paris embassy. Appropriately enough, it deals with the passions and whether they should be suppressed. (Shakespeare's voluptuary heroine Cleopatra represents the voice of passion whilst George Eliot's Maggie Tulliver from *The Mill on the Floss* represents duty and self-restraint.)

There are two points to note:

1   Since 'as Spinoza says, a passion can only be overcome by a stronger passion' the dichotomy in the title is a false one. The choice is not between passion and duty but between wayward and dutiful passions, or rather between base and possibly fleeting passions (which may be more intense) and those which comprehend 'a larger universe'. One gathers that these latter passions are rather refined affairs since the practical effect of indulging them is to 'scorn delights and live laborious days'. (A passion for knowledge, art or perhaps the public good is the sort of thing that Russell seems to have in mind.) But given the dire effects of suppressing even our wayward passions, the moral seems to be that we should indulge those passions that can be combined in a harmonious system. Russell retained these views in later life though as time went on he became more friendly towards the wayward passions. He came to think that in civilized societies, too much of what we do is done for the sake of something else. We are dominated by refined passions such as a desire for success, security or respectability. These ruling passions demand the sacrifice of spontaneous impulses, wayward desires for immediate activities or pleasures. This leads to joylessness or, worse, a frustration which finds release in violence or patriotic hysteria. The solution is to cultivate 'creative' impulses, spontaneous desires that can be combined with the pursuit of some larger and (one hopes) beneficent purpose. 'Laborious days' are all very well but they must be leavened with the indulgence of spontaneous impulses. There should indeed be harmony between the passions but this should be the harmony of a jazz improvisation rather than a Gregorian chant. (See for example, Russell 1916: 9–32 and Russell 1949: 11–22.)

2   Now it may be that psychological health requires a harmonious system of passions. But such a system is quite compatible with selfishness or even malice. (Russell cites Napoleon and Iago in this connection.) Is there any reason why we should stifle selfish or anti-social passions if we have a reasonable prospect of indulging them with impunity? This is a variant of Sidgwick's problem. 'This paradox', Russell wrote, 'has been to me for years a worry – a solution would be

a real solid addition to my happiness' (*CPBR* vol. 1: 91). Paper 8 represents Russell's second attempt to solve this problem using the machinery of Hegelian metaphysics. By November 1894 when this paper was read, Russell no longer believed in personal immortality so McTaggart's solution would not do. However, he *did* believe in a more or less Bradleian Absolute. Bradley's Absolute is a timeless reality in which the experiences of every conscious being are dissolved. Since separate selves are illusory, you and I are really one – or rather we are both aspects of the Absolute which alone is truly real (Bradley 1930: chaps X, XIII, XIV and XXV, and Sprigge 1993: 264–88). Thus when I hurt you in the service of my selfish desires, I am really hurting myself – or rather, since the Absolute is not a self, the separation between the pains I cause and the pains I experience is based on a sort of metaphysical mistake. Hence if I have a motive for cultivating a system of harmonious passions I have essentially the same motive for cultivating a set of passions which harmonize with other people's – or, at least, I would have such a motive, if I saw reality as it truly is. The neo-Hegelian solution to Sidgwick's problem is to posit a metaphysical union of selves, either in the future or in some timeless reality. Thus I have as good a motive for promoting other people's welfare as I do for promoting my own. The modern solution, pioneered by Parfit, is to break the self into a set of person-stages linked by a rather loose relation of psychological continuity that progressively weakens over time (Parfit 1984: 245–347). Thus I have no better reason for promoting my own (future) welfare than I do for promoting other people's. However, it should be noted that Bradley's metaphysic allows you to partake of both solutions. Before dissolving separate selves into the Absolute he breaks them up into a series of 'finite centres of experience' unified, in part, by a mistaken conception of the not-self (Sprigge 1993: 264–88 and 511–72).

NB. The Whitmaniacs were the followers of the American poet Walt Whitman (1819–92) whom Russell greatly admired.

What shall we do with our passions? Slay them, say Stoicism and

Mediaevalism: fix our minds on the sovereign contemplation of virtue, or the Deity, and live a calm, unchanging unruffled life. This is Descartes' 'remède souverain contre les passions': its ideal is calm, in which perhaps some joy may be found, but for which the real recommendation is that it avoids pain. Mrs. Grundy's answer is different: to hold our tongues about them and draw down the blinds before we indulge them is her gospel. To her, there is no harm in them if the blinds are thick enough and we don't allow the indulgence to interfere with dinner and Success – but to make any sacrifice to them is improper and shows that one is not 'safe'. Above all it is shocking to admit their existence. As a reaction against both these, the French, and the English aesthetes of the last generation, admit them and glory in them. To indulge them beautifully is morality, to be able to resist them is to be Machiavellian and disgusting; to feel the appropriate passion at the critical moment is the acme of virtue – and passions in this Ethic are judged aesthetically, not by their practical consequences. It is amusing to compare this, the creed of all that Mrs. Grundy abhors, with her own sentimental professions, which agree exactly with this if we substitute the word sentiment for the word passion. Only with her they are merely professions, while with the others they are real beliefs. I ought to mention too the Whitmaniacs, whose views on the subject are none of the above: they have two gods, tolerance and sanity: hence they have a derived worship for all those passions which the sane and healthy man or woman feels – these are great Nature, and to be ashamed of them is to be ashamed of sane and normal humanity. Hence they too, like the French, glorify passion: but unlike the French, they glorify it only when it makes for health, when, in Mr. Carr Bosanquet's words, it is 'sane lusty and adequate'. 'Without shame the woman I love avows the deliciousness of sex' says Walt: but also – spite of his tolerance – 'no diseased person, no venereal taint', is with us ('Song of the Open Road').

Sidgwick would admit then that there is here no 'consensus of common sense'. Let us therefore abandon common sense and define our terms. If I don't use them quite in the ordinary way, that will be only for the sake of precision. I shall then define a *passion* as a body of particular desires coordinated by direction to a single end or to a closely related system of ends. I shall use *emotion* as the State of Mind accompanying the fruition or frustration (final or temporary) of a Passion, with special reference to its aspect of pleasure and pain.

Starting from these definitions I shall maintain (1) That, as Spinoza says, a passion can only be overcome by a stronger passion (2)

That the greatest passions, those which most influence our actions, are not necessarily those of greatest intensity (3) That from an ethical standpoint, the greater a passion is the more it ought to be followed, and that the problem of self-control is to give the victory to the great and permanent passion rather than to the small and temporary one.

Before beginning the regular discussion of these points, I may observe that it follows from my definition that a passion cannot be valuable for its own sake, though an emotion may. For the essence of passion is desire, and desire is consciousness of imperfection, of contrast between the ideal and the actual. Thus a passion is only the *condition of an attempt* to realize the Good, and is not intrinsically good in itself; it is a means, not an end. But as a means it can hardly be valued too highly – the passions for knowledge, for beauty, for love are the very condition of all development, of all that is good. If the Good is that which satisfies, the desire is essential to the struggle after it, and to imagine the Good, to be conscious of it, is to desire it. Hence a passion may be ethically defined as a more or less imperfect conception of the Good, combined with the consciousness of its absence and the consequent desire for its realization.

After this parenthetical remark, I will try to tackle my question. Being ethical in form, I fear it will be necessary to plough through some rather dry ethical theory first, before attempting any more practical conclusions.

I will begin by a classification of desires, which I put forward subject to criticism, though I shall state it dogmatically. Lowest in the scale are immediate desires for physical objects for their own sakes – *on account*, doubtless, of some quality they possess, but without conscious isolation of this quality as that which gives them value. To this class belong animal appetites, for food and drink, etc.; a jackdaw's love of a shilling and a savage's love of beads. Next come desires for particular states of mind in ourselves, desires relative to our own psychical life. These involve self-consciousness and there-fore stand on a distinctly higher plane than the first class. They are in the first place no doubt desires for pleasure. And the wish for pleasure has peculiar importance, because, since *every* satisfied desire is pleasant (even if the thing desired be pain, which may be the case in moods of morbid sentimentality), the desire for pleasure rein-forces every other, though not in equal degrees, for not all satisfactions are equally pleasurable. But this class does not consist exclusively of desires for pleasure – we may equally desire know-ledge or a particular kind of volition for their own sakes. The last indeed cannot be an immediate motive in action, because volition is not the proximate effect of volition. However, defining *virtue* as a *potentiality* of desirable volition, the desire for virtue can be a motive, since every volition affects our power of making future volitions. This however involves self-consciousness in the second degree, and is a complex and presumably rare motive. Third come desires relative to other people's psychical life; these certainly exist pure – e.g. hatred is a desire for another's pain for its own sake. Indeed I am inclined to think that it is normal to desire for others – for our friends, our acquaintances, even perhaps our relations – everything we desire for ourselves. This constitutes sympathy, and it seems to me an ultimate and unanalyzable fact. I do not mean of course that sensible people desire every particular thing for others as for themselves – because as desires grow complex we like things for their uses more often than for their own sakes – but whatever we regard as intrinsically and *per se* good for us we cannot but desire also for our friends, though in most cases less intensely than for ourselves. Then come desires for relations between ourselves and other people, or between ourselves at one time and at another – even, as is shown by the match-making instinct in women, between others, without reference to self. Thus in the development of desire we get further and further from the passing moment, and from wishes which can be gratified immediately. We have to search for means, and when the object of our desire is abstract, e.g. power (which consists in a relation between our volitions and those of others), no particular thing can wholly satisfy the desire, which thus prompts to a long series of actions all directed to one end. This sort of desire is what I have called a Passion and generally speaking, the further a desire is removed from sense, the higher it comes in my scale, the more extended is its universe, and therefore the more commendable it is, ethically considered. The intensity of a passion may be very slight, that is, our desire at any moment for the particular thing to be attained by the act we are deliberating about may be weak, and yet, being reinforced by the thought of all the future occasions where similar desires will recur, and of the lasting loss if we let the passing moment slip by, the passion may acquire great power in deciding us, and may overcome a much more intense desire less bound up with our future. But we must always do as we wish – this is a mere tautology – the stronger desire is that which conquers; and if we are capable of realizing the future, a passion will overcome an isolated desire, and a passion with a larger universe will overcome one with a smaller universe. Self-control, a strong will, a firm character, etc., are all names for the power of vividly bringing to mind the larger and perhaps remoter universe of the less intense desire, and so resisting the more intense but more limited one. I will say nothing for the moment as to 'selfish' and 'unselfish' desires and the like vague terms, because they seem to me to have no ethical importance at any rate at our present level. The thing that *has* ethical importance is the extent of a desire's universe, because the larger its universe, the more permanent is its possible satisfaction, and the more self-consistent can the life be made which is regulated by it. Although in my phraseology this is a plea for indulging the larger passion, it is in common language the plea of morals for what it calls 'resisting one's passions' – it is the command to 'scorn delights and live laborious days', to resist passing allurements and be what the world calls passionless.

So far so good: this is theoretical and I hope sound, but when we try to apply such principles to practice – and the question we started with was a practical one – many things have to be considered which make our problem far more complex than before. I don't know any general principles invariably applicable here – one can only indicate a few broad lines along which to conduct the process of balancing by which practical questions have to be decided. First of all, there are two different conditions which make it possible to resist one's passions: strong will, or weak desires. It is because we are apt to imagine the latter (which is wholly despicable) that we feel a sort of contempt sometimes for people who renounce happiness for what they believe to be their duty – women who sacrifice intelligence to family or to childbearing, children who obey their parents, etc. For nothing can be accomplished without powerful passions. The most efficient men are the men wholly in the grip of some great passion which carries them over difficulties and obstacles and makes them neglect all but what conduces to their end: the Napoleons and Newtons and men of single powerful purpose. And here lies the danger of too rigid repression of passing passions: in time our desires sicken and die: we become purposeless anaemic beings, saints perhaps, but totally incapable of any achievement. Like Mr. Gilfil in George Eliot, we cease to take an interest in anything but our whiskey and soda if we are men, or our tea if we are women: or worse still, a person who has resisted a great passion and prevented it from venting itself in action may come to regard with hatred all those who do not so resist, even where there are no grounds for resisting. Such a person is apt to idolize pain, to regard all enjoyment as wicked, and to become in consequence the most fiendish person imaginable in daily life. The passion remains, and not being allowed to take its natural course, it turns to mute rage against all who are more fortunate, and leads to the most ghastly morbid developments. It is therefore very necessary to gauge one's own strength before denying any really strong craving, and the dangers involved in doing so may make it well worth while to indulge a passion even where it seems to interfere with some wider and nobler one. It is necessary to keep the spring of desires fresh, otherwise the character dries up, the energy and life goes out of it, and it loses perhaps the very passion for which it made the sacrifice. Also the amount of self-control of which a person is capable at any time is limited, and by a too great exercise of it in one direction one loses the power of using it in others.

The effects of too great repression of passions are somewhat curious and interesting. First comes an extraordinary lassitude – a complete absence of will or desire. Then, in this void, arise various instinctive impulses, chiefly trivial, which may have existed before, but were never attended to because of the energy of other thoughts which drove them out. Now however, owing to the mind's emptiness and weariness, it has not the energy to drive them out, and they persist – partly morbid, partly belonging to a more primitive state, a reversion to which is a common symptom of degeneracy. At first they are *mere* ideas – what little vigour remains is spent in keeping them so – but gradually they work like madness in the brain, and it becomes impossible to resist. Where, as in Dostoevsky's *Crime and Punishment*, the impulse is not trivial, it produces pronounced mania; where, as is more usual, there are a number of trivial impulses, they merely turn to eccentricity or ill-temper or nagging or nervousness. A very common result, and one of the earliest, is an unreasoning hatred of almost every body, and a joy in giving and watching pain. Superstitious dread, of one knows not what, or of some trivial thing such as one fly getting to the top of a pane before another, is also common. And unless some strong and healthy passion is found to replace the one resisted, these impulses are apt to grow more frequent and more dominant, until, at worst, they develop into insanity.

A passion may be resisted from laziness just as easily as from strength of will. Most conventional women who have any intelligence are examples of this. But the same morbid effects follow as in the other case, provided the possibility of a fine free indulgence is realized. Princess Casamassima in Henry James is an instance of what I mean. The passion for thought, for intellectual activity for its own sake, when it exists, is particularly liable to be neglected through laziness or the pressure of circumstances, and to take revenge by list-lessness and savage self-analysis and self-contempt – also by a freezing of all other passions: the little thought that is possible easily shows them to be valueless, but is unable to go on to the harder task of proving that they are invaluable. All these effects depend upon the fact that strength of will is not inexhaustible: up to the limits of our self-control, the pure theory seems to me to hold.

From a practical point of view, when once a passion is given, there is not much more to be said. I suppose a moraliser would propound the education of the passions and a close watch over the birth and growth of those that may prove dangerous, but this involves an amount of self-consciousness and an absence of spon-taneity which I shudder to think of. The only solution then would be an education of them by others by which I am sure very much may be done. But if others have neglected this duty, the problem for the individual seems insoluble. No ethical theory is likely to have any permanent effect in the presence of an intense passion, so that the only hope lies in a correct psychology to strangle an inconve-nient one in its infancy. But it is just in infancy that passions are often so alluring, and few people's estimate of themselves can stand out against such seductions. Since I am going away tomorrow, why not make the most of today? When tomorrow comes, today has been made such good use of that it is impossible to go away, and so the last chance is gone. Here we stumble against the ghastly ques-tion of free-will: many acts would be desirable, but they *can't* be done unless the agent desires them. I have hitherto spoken as if only a conflict of passions presented difficulties because only then is deliberate choice possible: but many passions – like Iago's hatred of Othello – may exist perfectly pure and yet be ethically condemned. I am afraid this forces me to revise part of my theory.

This necessity is annoying, the more so as I see no very satisfac-tory way of revising it. McTaggart will say that all my difficulties arise from the attempt to make goodness an ultimate point of view – and so no doubt they do – but in an ethical discussion one is forced to take up this position, and only where a definite dilemma compels one to rise above the level of the Science in question is one justified in using this method of escape. Short of this, the objections to what James calls making capital out of our intellectual defeat are good. I will then briefly recapitulate my former theory: Just as truth is true, ultimately, because we cannot but believe it if we judge at all, so the Good is good because we cannot but desire it if we desire at all. But as there may be error in belief, so there may be error in desire – a desire is erroneous when and in proportion as the attainment of its object will not bring satisfaction, i.e. when the desire conflicts with the general body of desires.

No reason can, at bottom, be given for desires. Desire and Knowledge are separate and independent realms, which may, I suppose, be brought together by a Metaphysic, by proving that what we desire must be real, and that Reality must be what Desire pronounces good – though I confess I have never understood any metaphysic which proves the world ethically as well as logically perfect. Knowledge is concerned with fact. Desire can (and does) damn facts, and construct an utterly different world of its own, a self-subsistent world, for which the ultimate and entire justification is that it is desired, and would satisfy desire if it were actual. As soon as we *talk* about desire, we are no longer in the *realm* of Desire, but in that of Knowledge, which is apt to cause confusion – we are dealing with the desire, which is a fact, not with its object, which is not a fact. That is why knowledge cannot judge desire as a whole, but only postulate that desires should form a harmonious system, otherwise they must, partially at least, defeat their own end of satisfaction, since the satisfaction of one is inconsistent with that of another. If we leave the Self out of account here, and require that Desires should not clash anywhere, whether in the same or in different individuals, we have the whole, it seems to me, that ethics can say on conduct: for since we do as we wish to do, judgments on conduct are reducible to judgments on desires. But how to prove, a priori, that the satisfaction of the individual is necessarily that of the Universe, I do not see, and this is to me *the* fundamental difficulty of Ethics.

So far I had not raised the question: Satisfaction to whom? and with this question a host of difficulties arise. The desires are of the Self, and hence, it seems, the satisfaction should be of the Self too. If, with McTaggart, we bring in personal immortality and a progress towards perfection (waiving the difficulty about Time), this limitation to the Self involves no great difficulties, for with higher sensibility comes acuter sympathy, and so personal satisfaction cannot be perfect until it is shared by all. But with a more Bradleian view of the Subject this theory becomes unsatisfactory – though it is difficult to see how Ethics can be expected to transcend the Self. But how, without such transcendence, are we to condemn an Iago or a Napoleon? They acted in the way most conducive to personal satisfaction, and common sense condemns them only because their gain was others' loss. I am vastly tempted to regard the Subject, as apparently Bradley does, as a mere fluid nucleus of

Feeling, of uncertain and constantly changing boundaries, and so adopt an almost Spinozistic monism, in which our terms become merely Desire on the one hand and Satisfaction on the other. This would obviate all these ethical difficulties, and reduce Hatred and similar passions to my former case of a conflict, for reciprocal hatreds do not form a harmony like reciprocal loves, and cannot both be satisfied. Also all I said in the early part of my paper about desires with large universes would hold – the harmonious passions bring satisfaction to their objects as well as to the agent. An object such as knowledge or beauty, whose attainment is a gain to all, has obviously a wider universe than dinner, which is a gain only to the eater and to those who profit by his subsequent good-humour; and it has a larger universe than (say) power, which is limited to the individual. Thus if I am allowed, in estimating a desire's universe, to consider things outside the agent himself, all becomes easy. And yet Conduct is my Conduct, and therefore Virtue is my Virtue, so that nothing can be plainer than the egotistic nature of the whole question. McTaggart may draw what conclusions he will from this dilemma, and I shall probably accept them – only it is not my business now to draw them.

However we are to get out of this maze fairly, *I* shall do it by climbing over the hedges. I shall simply state dogmatically that though the Desires are of the Self, the Satisfaction required to make them ethically good is *not* necessarily of the Self. The problem of Ethics is to produce a harmony and self-consistency in Conduct, but mere self-consistency within the limits of the individual might be attained in many ways. There must therefore, to make the solution definite, be a universal harmony; my conduct must bring satisfaction not merely to myself, but to all whom it affects, so far as that is possible. In the face of what may be called the disharmonious passions (hatred, malice, etc.) this is not completely possible. And this would make one person's virtue necessarily incomplete so long as others are not completely virtuous. But to this conclusion I see no theoretic objection. The practical modification of the previous results then would be that it is better to sacrifice personal consistency than to obtain it from desires directly opposed to those of the others whom they affect; so that desires themselves can be judged ethically according as they are such as can be satisfied universally or such as must conflict in different individuals. This is really only the old Kantian rule, and is an eminently commonplace conclusion for so long an argumentation. But having got back to common sense, I feel it is quite time I should hold my tongue.

9

ARE ALL DESIRES
EQUALLY MORAL?

c. 1896

Reprinted from *CPBR* vol. 1: 243–4. This paper was not
written for public consumption but to clarify Russell's own
thinking. He is still struggling with the idea that 'good'
must somehow be defined in terms of desire, but he has
abandoned Bradley's view that the good is that which satisfies desire. This leaves him with the uncomfortable
doctrine that 'the Good, for me, at any moment, *is* what I
want' or more precisely that 'X is good' means nothing
more than 'I want X'. Thus moral judgements (or at least
judgements about what is good) are little more than 'statements of a psychological state' (Paper 7). The problem
with this doctrine, as Russell realized in Paper 7, is that
judgements about what is good cannot err '(except by the
speaker's mistaking his own feelings)'. It has the further
unhappy consequence that I cannot desire the bad, since
the very fact that I desire it means that for me, at least, it is
good. But surely I can both be mistaken about the good
and desire the bad – a consideration Russell later came to
think decisive (Russell 1966: 18). Russell's solution is to
suppose that 'the Good [is] the object exclusively of the
primary desires', our desires for ends as opposed to our
secondary desires, which are desires for means. What I
want for its own sake cannot be bad, but what I want as a
means *can* be bad if it does not achieve my ends. This
suggests a distinction between being 'good-as-a-means and
being good-as-an-end'. 'X is good-as-a-means' is presumably equivalent to 'X conduces to something that I want as
an end', but 'X is good' (*simpliciter*) means that I (the
speaker) want X for its own sake. But the problem merely
reduplicates itself at the 'primary' level. We normally
suppose that people can be mistaken about what is good
even if they want it as an end not a means. And people can
desire evil ends as well as mistaken means.

Ethics must have a postulate, which cannot be disputed. This postulate is, that the Good, for me, at any moment, is what I want, and cannot be other: that it is useless, therefore, to say it ought to be other. I always shall act from desire, and it is a counsel of perfection to urge that I had better act otherwise. I desire objects which will satisfy desire, but not, except derivatively, the satisfaction of desire. Therefore the Satisfaction of Desire is *not* the Good, but the things desired *are* the Good. But what then becomes of morals? *All* acts are virtuous, since they pursue the Good. May it be that vice lies in a bad choice of means? That desiring A, I regard B as a means, and commit an act, β, which brings B, but turns out not to bring A with it? This gives the Socratic maxim, that no man sins wittingly. It brings into relief the distinction between *primary* desires, for ends, and *secondary* desires, for means. In this way, the Good, the object exclusively of the primary desires, might acquire some permanence amid the changing secondary desires. And this is essential: if Ethics is to be a definite body of knowledge, the Good must be a fixed standard, by which to test the moral worth of acts.

Is it essential to the goodness of a desired object that its attainment should really bring satisfaction? This satisfaction seems logically involved in the desire, and yet it is a platitude that attainment brings disgust. This platitude is true, I believe, only because most of our desires are secondary, and our choice of means is often bad. If we desire a thing truly for its own sake, and not as a means, its attainment *must* bring satisfaction, by the very meaning of terms.

This seems a theoretically possible ethic: *primary* desires are *not* subject to moral praise or blame, being the data, in morals, for the construction of the Good; but *secondary* desires are immoral, when they are mistaken, i.e. will not attain the ends to which their objects are supposed to be means.

The problem of Ethics then becomes: What things do we desire for their own sakes? The problem of practical morals becomes: How are we to get these things? If we fail to adopt the right means, *we* are immoral: if the world does not provide any possible means, the *world* is immoral.

If Ethics could prove that the only primary desire is the desire for *harmony*, we should have a Good which would be the same for all, which therefore, given adequate knowledge, all would attain. But how prove that this is the only primary desire?

If it were proved that desire for harmony is the only primary desire, further constructions as to the Universal Will would follow of themselves. For the Universal Will would be desire for universal harmony, and submission to it would be the best way of attaining individual harmony. But how prove this?

Desires may be classified as

I Immediate desires for some relation to objects of sense.
II Desires for a state of ourselves as to

    1 Feeling
    2 Knowledge
    3 Volition – the latter, however, a derivative desire.

III Desires for states of mind in other people, known to ourselves,

    1 Having no direct reference to ourselves
    2 Having direct reference to ourselves.

A compound of II and III 2 gives desires for certain relations between ourselves and others. A complication of III gives desires for relations between others.

As regards I, the relation desired must be one which gives pleasure, and must therefore be a harmonious relation. As regards II 1, pleasure results directly from harmony, 2 is already a harmony, 3 depends on a previously established standard of virtue, and is thus irrelevant in discussing what is virtue. III is the crux.

We may say, straight off, desire is always for a harmony between idea and existence, and this seems to settle the question. But what idea?

10

IS ETHICS A BRANCH OF EMPIRICAL PSYCHOLOGY?

1897

Reprinted from *CPBR* vol. 1: 100–4. This paper was delivered to the Apostles on 6 February 1897. Russell was obviously very tempted to define 'good' in terms of desire. Why? Perhaps because Bradley had created a vogue for this sort of definition, and the young Russell wanted to be up-to-date. Or perhaps because Russell wanted to secure some sort of conceptual connection between value and motivation. If goodness has something to do with what I want, then we can begin to see why thinking something good disposes me to promote it. If so, the conceptual connection is bought at a high price. We normally think that judgements about what is good are 'liable to truth and falsehood'. Yet they risk becoming trivially true since they merely describe the speaker's state of mind. Moreover, the good cannot constitute a standard for adjudicating between different desires, since (for the speaker at least) what is desired is automatically good. In Paper 9, Russell tried to solve the problem by distinguishing between primary and secondary desires. But he obviously came to feel that this would not work. Paper 10 represents his second attempt at a solution. After a complex and bewildering argument he defines 'good' as what we (though I think he means 'I, the speaker') desire to desire. Thus something is good (for me) if I desire to desire it. This gives me an *internal* standard for adjudicating between different desires and makes it conceptually possible to desire the bad. It converts ethics into a branch of empirical psychology, since what we (variously) desire to desire is a matter of psychological fact. Thus what (psychologically) is, has been or will be turns out to be crucially relevant to what ought to be. But good-judgements continue to be immune to error (except in

71

those rare cases when we are mistaken about what we desire to desire). And since it is part of our common conception of morality that good-judgements *are* liable to falsehood, this counts against the theory.

This paper is of interest for three reasons:

1   Moore almost certainly had Russell's paper in mind when he penned §13 of *Principia Ethica*, the famous passage in which he expounds the Open Question Argument.

> To take, for instance, one of the more plausible, because one of the more complicated, of such proposed definitions, it may easily be thought, at first sight, that to be good may mean to be that which we desire to desire,

he writes, before going on to dismiss this definition on the grounds that it remains an obstinately open question whether what we desire to desire is good. (See Moore 1993: 67 and Paper 13 below for Russell's exposition of the argument.) And in §26 Moore censures efforts to reduce ethics to some other science such as psychology, which is precisely what Russell professes to do (Moore 1993: 92). Russell's definition at least gets the back-handed accolade of being the best of a fallacious bunch.

2   Inspired, in part by Moore's hostile reference, David Lewis has unwittingly developed a version of Russell's theory (Lewis 1989: 113–37). Russell's theory cannot accommodate the conceptual truth that we can desire to desire the bad and has the further unfortunate consequence that good-judgements are not (as they ought to be) liable to error and falsehood. Lewis solves both problems by weakening the conceptual connection between value and motivation. Value (rather than 'good') is what we (humane and right-thinking persons) are ideally disposed to desire to desire under conditions of full imaginative acquaintance. Thus I can desire to desire the bad if I am not a humane and right-thinking person or if I am not imaginatively acquainted with the bad thing in question. And I can be mistaken about what is valuable for much the same reasons. I may not be a humane and right-thinking person or my imagination may not be sufficiently vivid. The conceptual connection between value and

motivation, as Lewis himself admits, is now 'multifariously iffy' (Lewis 1989: 116). To be moved by value, I must be a humane and right-thinking person with a vivid and sensitive imagination whose desires correspond with what that person desires to desire – rather a tall order! Lewis, however, glories in his multifariously iffy connection, and, like Russell himself, rejoices in the reduction of ethics to psychology.

3   The reading of this paper would appear to mark the beginning of Russell's conversion to the doctrines of *Principia Ethica*. Moore was notorious for his no-definition definition of 'good'. 'If I am asked "How is good to be defined?"', he wrote, 'my answer is that it cannot be defined and that is all I have to say about it' (Moore 1993: 58). The last page of Paper 10 is marked in Russell's hand with the apparent question 'Shall we spell {Good/good} with', to which Moore replies 'Good = good' (*CPBR* vol. 1: 105).

Between the foundations of ethics and the foundations of Epistemology, a certain analogy may be traced. The one is a theory of the good, the other a theory of the true. Both are due, in a sense, to the existence of states of consciousness with an objective reference. In desire, as in knowledge, we have a mental state with a reference to something other than itself. The two differ in the *manner*, but agree in the *fact* of reference. In knowledge, we distinguish the act of knowing from the thing known: in desire, we distinguish the act of desiring from the thing desired. In the theory of knowledge, we isolate the thing known, as the objectively true, from the act of knowing: in ethics – so it is usually held – we can isolate the thing desired, as the objectively good, from the act of desiring.

But let us examine a little more closely the justification, in the theory of knowledge, for this isolation from the fact that we know. The psychological investigation of belief or cognition, as we know, analyses the causes of belief, and assigns, empirically, many causes which cannot, by logic, be regarded as valid grounds. Why does not this undermine our faith, as it undermined Hume's, in the correctness of our logical postulates? The reason is, that the results we obtain by empirical psychology are themselves knowledge, and therefore postulate the correctness of our methods of cognition. To call in question the correctness of these methods, on the ground of results obtained by postulating them, is therefore a vicious circle.

To put the matter otherwise: knowledge, in the concrete, has two aspects, the objective fact asserted, and the psychological fact of assertion. But any study of the psychological fact of assertion can only lead to fresh knowledge, having the same two aspects, with the logically irrelevant difference that now the objective fact asserted is that I previously made an assertion. Hence again the validity of knowledge has to be postulated, before our manner of knowing can be investigated: this investigation cannot, therefore, shake our belief in the validity of knowledge. Thus the theory of knowledge is, in its foundations, independent of empirical psychology, and the objective reference of our judgments can be studied apart from the fact that we know.

In the same way, it is suggested, we can study the objects of desire apart from the fact that we empirically desire them. The primary assertion would thus be: 'This is good', and only psychological reflection would lead to: 'I desire this'. But to this view there is a fundamental objection. The state of mind in which I desire an object does not, abstractly considered, contain an assertion or a cognitive element: to say, 'This is good', is not the same as to desire this. Reflection is involved in the transformation of the desire into the assertion: the assertion is made on the ground of the desire, and is not itself the same mental state as the desire. Thus the two statements: 'This is good', and: 'I desire this', are strictly equivalent to one another: both are made by a reflection on the desire, and both assert one and the same fact. This is not the case with the previous couple: 'This is true', and: 'I believe this'. Here the first assertion actually *is* the state of mind of the person believing, while the second assertion asserts the existence of that state of mind. In the ethical couple, on the contrary, neither assertion is the original state of mind, but both, as the result of reflection, assert that state of mind.

Put briefly, the distinction is this. When we reflect on knowledge, the result is fresh knowledge: when we reflect on desire, the result, so far as ethics is concerned, is not fresh desire, but knowledge. For an ethical proposition, considered as a psychical occurrence, is not a desire, but a cognition. In reflecting psychologically on desires, therefore, we are not bound to postulate beforehand the ethical justification of all desires, since the result of our reflections is not itself desire, but knowledge. The result of psychological reflection on knowledge is to know our manner of knowing: the validity of this result therefore presupposes the validity of knowledge. To obtain a strict parallel in ethics, we should have to consider an attitude towards our desires which led to our desiring our manner of desiring. If this were the result of psychological reflection on desires, the objective reference of desires would remain ultimate and irreducible: in the practical sphere, where desire is ultimate, this is the case: but in the theoretical sphere, where only knowledge is ultimate, we cannot establish any such contention. Now ethics belongs to the theoretical sphere: it is *knowledge* of the practical sphere, and thus not itself practical. Knowledge of desire is as little practical as desire for knowledge is theoretical.

Thus the relation of ethics to desire is quite different from the relation of the psychology of cognition to knowledge. Ethics asserts the desire for an object, whereas the psychology of cognition asserts the assertion of an object. Thus the objection to psychology as a legitimate method in the theory of knowledge does not exist in the ethical sphere. The practical fallacy, parallel to this theoretical fallacy, would be to take desire for virtue as our criterion of the good, where virtue is defined as the possession of those desires which we desire to have. This would be plainly absurd, for if our desires are ever a criterion of the good, they must be so equally whether their objective reference is to other desires or not. Thus for ethics, the primary assertion is the knowledge that something is desired, which is already at the psychological level. The unreflective level does not, as in the theory of knowledge, afford any component of ethics, but self-knowledge is an indispensable condition of ethical judgments.

Thus the only method for ethics, it would seem, is to investigate as best it can the nature and objects of our desires. It cannot investigate the objects of desire, without at the same time and in the same terms investigating desire itself, since the objects referred to by desire are not cognitively referred to, and are therefore only *known* as objects of desire by a distinct reflective act. An a priori system of desires, independent of reference to psychology, would have to be primarily desired, not known, and could be known only empirically, by reflection on the state of mind in which it was desired. Unless, therefore, the good can be defined otherwise than in terms of desire, ethics, properly studied, must always remain, it would seem, purely a branch of empirical psychology, dependent through and through on investigation of the things which people desire or find to satisfy their desires. From this conclusion there seems no escape.

If, then, the good is the desired, it follows that ethics is a wholly empirical study, that ethical judgments have not any objectivity or permanence in ascribing goodness to things, and indeed that goodness is a relation to ourselves which varies with our every whim. We may take this result either as condemning ethics, or, as our brother

Moore will certainly take it, as condemning the identification of the good and the desired. There are several ways, historically, of escaping from this identification. We may regard the good, as the Hedonists mostly intend to regard it, as the pleasant; or we may regard it, with Mr. Bradley, as that which satisfies desire. There is very little to choose between this and the Hedonist definition: as soon as we have amended pleasure into the pleasant, it becomes practically the same as that which satisfies desire; except that Mr. Bradley's definition omits those pleasures which come unsought, and omits them with little apparent justification. It is to be observed that what satisfies desire is very different from what is desired: it excludes all foolish desires, whose attainment is disappointing; it affords an ethical meaning for error, and it makes the good less dependent on the particular degree of knowledge of the person desiring, since what would satisfy desire is more constant than what is actually desired. Moreover, if there be a dialectic of desire, to be gone through in practice, Mr. Bradley's definition places the good in the ultimate goal, and not in the ever-changing will-o'-the-wisp which we pursue on the way. These are solid advantages; but it seems impossible not to challenge the premise. Why should I call good what satisfies desire, rather than what I desire?

The ultimate premiss of any subject should have an evidence which cannot be questioned. The premiss of Logic and Metaphysics is that truth is true of reality, and that some knowledge is true. This depends on the ontological argument, which again depends on the impossibility of total scepticism. But where are we to find corresponding evidence for an ethical premiss? We have it, if we define the good as the desired, but not, so far as I can see, on any other definition. A man needs no argument to convince him that what he desires is good: he can accept no argument to prove anything else good. When Sigmund refuses Valhalla because Sieglinde will not be there, it is useless to argue that he will forget her, that he will have satisfaction of desire, etc., etc.: the fact remains that his present desire is for Sieglinde, not for Valhalla, and to speak of error in his estimate of the good seems absurd. It is to be observed that in Economics, the only science worth the name which deals with human nature, the same definition of goods prevails. Goods are whatever people desire. Brackish water which could be disposed of as fresh, for example, would come under the head of goods, though it would not satisfy desire. We cannot escape by saying people desire things because they believe they will give satisfaction: that would plunge us into the fallacies of psychological hedonism. With any other definition of the good, it is open to us to say Why? People said Why? to pleasure, as soon as it became evident that the desired was not always pleasure. Similarly, one may say Why? to that which satisfies desire. If we do not happen to desire it, there is no way of convincing us that we ought to do so. It may be said, nothing can satisfy desire unless it is desired. True; but the desire presupposed is here a hypothetical one, or else Mr. Bradley's definition becomes mine. There seem to be three ways of defining the Good by reference to desire: (1) The satisfaction of desire (2) That which satisfies desire (3) The desired. (1) The first is open to all the objections to Hedonism: it places the good in a mere frame of mind, not in a state of the universe. But for these objections, it would lead, in a few moves, to a satisfactory and beautiful ethic. For it would lead us to assert that those things only ought to be desired which the Universe will let us have, since only so can our desires be satisfied. This would place virtue in submission to, or harmony with, the universal will – a very pious doctrine, which I should like extremely to believe. It would prove, also, that the Universe is neither good nor bad, since both good and bad exist only in our attitude towards the Universe. But, unfortunately, it affords no argument against the man who stubbornly desires what the Universe will not give, and its definition is wholly arbitrary.

(2) The second definition, as that which satisfies desire, also allows of moral error, not now in our estimate of the world, but in our estimate of ourselves. The first definition placed the good in that which, if we desired it, we could obtain. The second places it in that which, if we obtained it, would satisfy our desires. Error, here, consists in a wrong estimate of the things which would give lasting satisfaction. All the banal objections to the man of pleasure, all the homilies on the vanity of human wishes, fall under this definition. These things, it is said, turn to dust and ashes as soon as they are attained. But if this is used as an argument for a change of life, it presupposes that what people really want is desires for things which can give lasting satisfaction: if they retort, But I desire human things, though I know they will prove a disappointment, the unhappy moralist is left shocked and speechless, but without arguments.

(3) The third definition alone, it would seem, needs no argument to prove it – and this is fortunate, since all argument in proof of a definition of the good is impossible. The good, we say, is simply the desired. Since people always act from desire, this destroys the possibility of moral error. But, oddly enough, it does not destroy the

possibility of bad conduct. For good conduct, on our definition, is desired conduct, and our conduct is only too often not such as we desire. The habitual drunkard normally desires to keep sober, and drunkenness is therefore bad conduct. Since many of our desires, in short, have other desires for their objects, we can distinguish good and bad among all those desires which are themselves objects of desire or aversion. The desires we desire to have are good; those we desire not to have are bad. In general, the desires we wish not to have are those which interfere with our master passions: the drunkard objects to his desire for drink, because it interferes with work or worldly success. Thus good desires will be those which form a harmonious system *inter se*, and bad desires those which clash. Though this will be only approximate and empirical, it is odd to see so old an ethical friend returned from so anarchical a quarter.

To sum up: An ethic which merely says: The good is the desired, leaves the good a prey to changing fancies. An ethic which says: The good is the satisfaction of desire, is open to all the objections to Hedonism: it chooses an aspect of the good, a mere result of desire, as the whole good. On the other hand, since we always do act from desire, an ethic which takes all desires as equally ultimate loses all criterion, all standard of judging action: all acts become alike good or alike bad. Now morality is exhibited only in action, and action springs only from desire. Therefore moral judgments must discriminate between desires. But since all contrast of ideal and actual rests on desire, since all goodness, all morality, rest on the contrast of ideal and actual, desire alone can supply the criterion among desires. The criterion must be supplied, therefore, by the contrast between ideal and actual desires, by the contrast between desires we desire and desires we dislike. Whether we have them or not, for example, most of us desire a wish for the good of humanity, and dislike a craving for drink or morphia. In fact, the desired has as wide a range in conduct as in feeling. The man, then, who desires always and only what he wishes to desire, is perfectly good in his conduct: in all that depends upon himself there is no conflict, but the most perfect harmony possible.

That my conclusion is satisfactory, I do not pretend. If our brother Moore will give me an unexceptionable premiss for his definition of the good, or even a hint of where to find one, I will retract. At present, I see no way of distinguishing between the good and the desired. I regard the good, therefore, as totally devoid of objectivity, and as matter for purely psychological investigation.

11

SEEMS MADAM? NAY, IT IS

1897

Reprinted from *CPBR* vol. 1: 106–11, first published (at Russell's suggestion) in Russell (1957) *Why I am Not a Christian*. This paper was read to the Apostles on 11 December 1897. Russell describes it in a letter to Moore as 'a scratch sort of paper' written at a 'dry time' but it is, in fact, a glittering piece, written in something like Russell's mature style. The awkwardness and affectation of some of his early writings are gone and it displays his characteristic combination of wit and clarity. The title is taken from *Hamlet*, Act I, Scene ii, and expresses Russell's theme that if the universe *seems* bad then (for us, at least) it *is* bad since we have no experience of the timeless Reality that it is alleged to be truly good. As Russell himself put it in his letter to Moore, 'for all purposes that are not *purely* intellectual, the world of Appearance is the real world' (*CPBR* vol. 1: 105) and Hegelian metaphysics with its notion of a timeless and somehow perfect Reality, the 'Absolute', is deprived of its power to console. This paper marks the beginning of Russell's break with Hegelianism, since he soon came to feel that even for purposes that *are* purely intellectual, world of Appearance is indeed the real world.

But there is a corollary to Russell's argument that he does not explicitly draw. In Papers 2 and 8, he tries to solve Sidgwick's problem of the Dualism of Practical Reason with the aid of Hegelian metaphysics. Specifically, in Paper 8, he suggests that if you and I are really one, I have the same motive not to bruise your feelings in the pursuit of my selfish desires as I have for not indulging one of my passions at the expense of all the rest. For if in Reality you and I are one, then I cannot hurt you without hurting myself, or rather without hurting that one great experiencer, the Absolute, of which our separate selves are delusory aspects. But if our experience is confined to the world of Appearance, and if in this world you and I are distinct, then I will not feel the pains that I inflict on you. So why should I care that in Reality I am suffering too (or rather that both of us are components of a greater whole in which suffering has been created) if this is a Reality which I do not experience? In the world of Appearance I do not seem to feel your pains, and when it comes to feelings, what seems to be is what is. Thus there is no selfish or prudential motive for avoiding harms to others if we think we can get away with it. Reality or the Absolute is not only useless as a source of consolation – it cannot provide us with a basis for morality.

Russell's reference to 'the rigid Science of Mr F. W. H. Myers' is not entirely serious. Myers (1843–1901) was chief of the Society for Psychical Research.

Philosophy in the days when it was still fat and prosperous, claimed to perform, for its votaries, a variety of the most important services. It offered them comfort in adversity, explanation in intellectual difficulty, and guidance in moral perplexity. No wonder if the younger Brother, when an instance of its uses was presented to him, exclaimed with the enthusiasm of youth

How charming is divine Philosophy!
Not harsh and crabbed, as dull fools suppose,
But musical as is Apollo's lute.

But those happy days are past. Philosophy, by the slow victories of its own offspring, has been forced to forego, one by one, its high pretensions. Intellectual difficulties, for the most part, have been acquired by Science. Philosophy's anxious claims on the few exceptional questions, which it still endeavours to answer, are regarded by most people as a remnant of the dark ages, and are being transferred, with all speed, to the rigid Science of Mr. F. W. H. Myers. Moral perplexities – which, until recently, were unhesitatingly assigned by philosophers to their own domain – have been abandoned by McTaggart and Mr. Bradley to the whimsies of statistics and common sense. But the power of giving comfort and consolation is still supposed by McTaggart to belong to philosophy. It is this last possession of which, tonight, I wish to rob the decrepit parent of our modern gods.

It might seem, at first sight, that the question could be settled very briefly. 'I know that philosophy can give comfort,' McTaggart might say, 'because it certainly comforts me.' I shall try to prove, however, that those conclusions which give him comfort are conclusions which do not follow from his general position – which, indeed, admittedly do not follow, and are retained, it would seem, only *because* they give him comfort.

As I do not wish to discuss the truth of philosophy, but only its emotional value, I shall assume a metaphysic which rests on the distinction between Appearance and Reality, and regards the latter as timeless and perfect. The principle of any such metaphysic may be put in a nutshell. 'God's in his heaven, all's wrong with the world' – that is its last word. But it seems to be supposed that, since he is in his heaven, and always has been there, we may expect him some day to descend to earth – if not to judge the quick and the dead, at least to reward the faith of the philosophers. His long resignation, however, to a purely heavenly existence, would seem to suggest, as regards the affairs of earth, a stoicism on which it would be rash to found our hopes.

But to speak seriously. The emotional value of a doctrine, as a comfort in adversity, appears to depend upon its prediction of the future. The future, emotionally speaking, is more important than the past, or even than the present. 'All's well that ends well' is the dictum of unanimous common sense. 'Many a dull morning turns out a fine day' is optimism; whereas pessimism says:

> Full many a glorious morning have I seen
> Flatter the mountain tops with sovereign eye
> Kissing with golden face the meadows green
> Gilding pale streams with heavenly alchemy;
> Anon permit the basest clouds to ride
> With ugly rack on his celestial face
> And from the forlorn world his visage hide
> Stealing unseen to west with this disgrace.

And so, emotionally, our view of the universe as good or bad depends on the future, on what it will be; we are concerned always with appearances in time, and unless we are assured that the future is to be better than the present, it is hard to see where we are to find consolation.

So much, indeed, is the future bound up with optimism, that McTaggart himself, while all his optimism depends upon the denial of time, is compelled to represent the Absolute as a future state of things, as 'a harmony which must some day become explicit'. It would be unkind to urge this contradiction, as it is mainly McTaggart himself who has made me aware of it. But what I do wish to urge is, that any comfort, which may be derived from the doctrine that Reality is timeless and eternally good, is derived only and exclusively by means of this contradiction. A timeless Reality can have no more intimate connection with the future than with the past: if its perfection has not appeared hitherto, there is no reason to suppose it ever will – there is, indeed, every likelihood that God will stay in his heaven. We might, with equal propriety, speak of a harmony which must once *have been* explicit; it may be that 'my grief lies onward and my joy behind' – and it is obvious how little comfort this would afford us.

All our experience is bound up with time, nor is it possible to imagine a timeless experience. But even if it were possible, we could not, without contradiction, suppose that we ever *shall* have such an experience. All experience, therefore, for aught that philosophy can show, is likely to resemble the experience we know – if this seems bad to us, no doctrine of a Reality distinguished from Appearances can give us hope of anything better. We fall, indeed, into a hopeless dualism. On the one side we have the world we know, with its events, pleasant and unpleasant, its deaths and failures and disasters – on the other hand an imaginary world, which we christen the world of Reality, atoning, by the largeness of the R, for the absence of every other sign that there really is such a world. Now our only ground for this world of Reality is, that this is what Reality would have to be if we could understand it. But if the result of our purely ideal construction turns out so very different from the world we know – from the real world, in fact – if, moreover, it follows from this very construction that we never shall experience the so-called world of Reality, except in a sense in which already we experience nothing else – then I cannot see what, as concerns comfort for present ills, we have gained by all our metaphysicizing. Take, for example, such a question as immortality. People have desired immortality either as a redress for the injustices of this world, or, which is the more respectable motive, as affording a possibility of meeting again after death those whom they have loved. The latter desire is one which we all feel, and for whose satisfaction, if philosophy could satisfy it, we should be immeasurably grateful. But philosophy, at best, can only assure us that the soul is a timeless reality. At what points of time, if any, it may happen to appear, is thus wholly irrelevant to it, and there is no legitimate inference from such a doctrine to existence after death. Keats may still regret

> That I shall never look upon thee more,
> Never have relish in the fairy power
> Of unreflecting love

and it cannot much console him to be told that 'fair creature of an hour' is not a metaphysically accurate phrase. It is still true that 'Time will come and take my love away', and that 'This thought is as a death which cannot choose But weep to have that which it fears to lose'. And so with every part of the doctrine of a timelessly perfect Reality. Whatever now seems evil – and it is the lamentable prerogative of evil that to seem so is to be so – whatever evil now appears may remain, for aught we know, throughout all time, to torment our latest descendants. And in such a doctrine there is, to my mind, no vestige of comfort or consolation.

It is true that Christianity, and all previous optimisms, have represented the world as eternally ruled by a beneficent Providence, and thus metaphysically good. But this has been, at bottom, only a device by which to prove the future excellence of the world – to prove, for example, that good men would be happy after death. It has always been this deduction – illegitimately made of course – which has given comfort. 'He's a good fellow, and '*twill* all be well.'

It may be said, indeed, that there is comfort in the mere abstract doctrine that Reality is good. I do not myself accept the proof of this doctrine, but even if true, I cannot see why it should be comforting. For the essence of my contention is, that Reality, as constructed by metaphysics, bears no sort of relation to the world of experience. It is an empty abstraction, from which no single inference can be validly made as to the world of appearance, in which world, nevertheless, all our interests lie. Even the pure intellectual interest, from which metaphysics springs, is an interest in explaining the world of appearance. But instead of really explaining this actual palpable sensible world, metaphysics constructs another fundamentally different world, so different, so unconnected with actual experience, that the world of daily life remains wholly unaffected by it, and goes on its way just as if there were no world of Reality at all. If even one were allowed to regard the world of Reality as an 'other world', as a heavenly city existing somewhere in the skies, there might no doubt be comfort in the thought that others have a perfect experience which we lack. But to be told that our experience, as we know it, is that perfect experience, must leave us cold, since it cannot prove our experience to be better than it is. On the other hand, to say that our actual experience is not that perfect experience constructed by philosophy, is to cut off the only sort of existence which philosophical reality can have – since God in his heaven cannot be maintained as a separate person. Either, then, our existing experience is perfect – which is an empty phrase, leaving it no better than before – or there is no perfect experience, and our world of Reality, being experienced by no one, exists only in the metaphysics books. In either case, it seems to me, we cannot find in philosophy the consolations of religion.

There are, of course, several senses in which it would be absurd to deny that philosophy may give us comfort. We may find philosophizing a pleasant way of passing our mornings – in this sense, the comfort derived may even, in extreme cases, be comparable to that of drinking as a way of passing our evenings. We may, again, take philosophy aesthetically, as probably most of us take Spinoza. We may use metaphysics, like poetry and music, as a means of producing a mood, of giving us a certain view of the universe, a certain attitude towards life – the resulting state of mind being valued on account of, and in proportion to, the degree of poetic emotion aroused, not in proportion to the truth of the beliefs entertained. Our satisfaction, indeed, seems to be, in these moods, the exact opposite of the metaphysician's professions. It is the satisfaction of forgetting the real world and its evils, and persuading ourselves, for the moment, of the reality of a world we have ourselves created. This seems to be one of the grounds on which Bradley justifies metaphysics. 'When poetry, art and religion', he says, 'have ceased wholly to interest, or when they show no longer any tendency to struggle with ultimate problems and come to an understanding with them; when the sense of mystery and enchantment no longer draws the mind to wander aimlessly and love it knows not what; when, in short, twilight has no charm – then metaphysics will be worthless.' What metaphysics does for us in this way is essentially what, say, *The Tempest* does for us – but its value on this view, is quite independent of its truth. It is not because Prospero's magic makes us acquainted with the world of spirits that we value the *Tempest*; it is not, aesthetically, because we are informed of a world of spirit that we value metaphysics. And this brings out the essential difference between the aesthetic satisfaction, which I allow, and the religious comfort, which I deny to philosophy. For aesthetic satisfaction, intellectual conviction is unnecessary, and we may therefore choose, when we seek it, the metaphysic which gives us the most of it. For religious comfort, on the other hand, belief is essential, and I am contending that we do not get religious comfort from the metaphysic which we believe.

It is possible, however, to introduce a refinement into the argument, by adopting a more or less mystical theory of the aesthetic emotion. It may be contended that, although we can never wholly experience Reality as it really is, yet some experiences approach it more nearly than others, and such experiences, it may be said, are given by art and philosophy. And under the influence of the experiences which art and philosophy sometimes give us, it seems easy to adopt this view. For those who have the metaphysical passion, there is probably no emotion so rich and beautiful, so wholly desirable, as that mystic sense, which philosophy sometimes gives, of a world transformed by the beatific vision. As Bradley again says: 'Some in one way, some in another, we seem to touch and have communion with what is beyond the visible world. In various manners we find something higher, which both supports and humbles, both chastens and supports us. And, with certain persons, the intellectual effort to understand the Universe is a principal way of thus experiencing the Deity. . . . And this appears', he continues, 'to be another reason for some persons pursuing the study of ultimate truth'.

But is it not equally a reason for hoping that these persons will not find ultimate truth? if indeed ultimate truth bear any resemblance to the doctrines set forth in *Appearance and Reality*. I do not deny the value of the emotion, but I do deny that, strictly speaking it is in any peculiar sense a beatific vision, or an experience of the Deity. In one sense, of course, all experience is experience of the Deity, but in another, since all experience equally is in time, and the Deity is timeless, no experience is experience of the Deity – 'as such' pedantry would bid me add. The gulf fixed between Appearance and Reality is so profound, that we have no grounds, so far as I can see, for regarding some experiences as nearer than others to the perfect experience of Reality. The value of the experiences in question must, therefore, be based wholly on their emotional quality, and not, as Bradley would seem to suggest, on any superior degree of truth which may attach to them. But if so, they are at best the consolations of philosophizing, not of philosophy. They constitute a reason for the pursuit of ultimate truth, since they are flowers to be gathered by the way; but they do not constitute a reward for its attainment, since, by all that appears, the flowers grow only at the beginning of the road, and disappear long before we have reached our journey's end.

The view which I have advocated is, no doubt, not an inspiriting one, nor yet one which, if generally accepted, would be likely to promote the study of philosophy. I might justify my paper, if I wished to do so, on the maxim that, 'where all is rotten, it is a man's work to cry stinking fish'. But I prefer to suggest that metaphysics, when it seeks to supply the place of religion, has really mistaken its function. That it can supply this place, I admit; but it supplies it, I maintain, at the expense of being bad metaphysics. Why not admit that metaphysics, like science, is justified by intellectual curiosity, and ought to be guided by intellectual curiosity alone? The desire to find comfort in metaphysics has, we must all admit, produced a great deal of fallacious reasoning and intellectual dishonesty. From this, at any rate, the abandonment of religion would deliver us. And since intellectual curiosity exists in some people, it is probable that some attempts would still be made to understand the world, and it is possible that they would be freed from certain hitherto persistent fallacies. 'The man', to quote Bradley once more, 'whose nature is such that by one path alone his chief desire will reach consummation, will try to find it on that path, whatever it may be, and whatever the world thinks of it; and if he does not he is contemptible.'

12

WAS THE WORLD GOOD BEFORE THE SIXTH DAY?

1899

Reprinted from *CPBR* vol. 1: 113–16. This paper was read to the Apostles on 11 February 1899 and is distinguished by the grisly excess of Apostolic banter in the first three paragraphs. (The Society was jocularly supposed to be Reality and non-members mere Phenomena.) The paper is a response to an early draft of *Principia Ethica*, a typescript entitled *The Elements of Ethics*, which Moore had delivered as a set of lectures to the London School of Ethics and Social Philosophy (Moore 1991). Russell seems to have accepted Moore's doctrine that 'good' is indefinable and even agrees that beauty is an objective property. But he disputes Moore's opinion that 'a world of matter alone . . . may be good or bad' in itself. Russell prefers the Sidgwickian doctrine that 'among the things we know there is nothing good or bad except psychical states'. The argument is discussed in the Introduction.

Our brother Moore has been engaged, by order of the Society, in a heroic work, involving the very highest degree of danger and difficulty. He has been endeavouring – I believe with success – to corrupt still further (an arduous task) the morals of those phenomena who frequent the shallow abyss known among shadows as 'The London School of Ethics and Social Philosophy'. As the glory of God is enhanced by the damnation of the wicked, by which they are rendered still more wicked than they intended to be, so the glory of the Society is enhanced by increasing the phenomenality of phenomena. And as it is the mark of the Society to be wise and good, so it is the mark of phenomena to be foolish and wicked. Moore has been endeavouring, then, to render these shadows even more foolish and more wicked than they naturally are. That this is difficult, is certainly undeniable; but the difficulty seems to have been successfully overcome. For according to an emissary, sent by the Society to report upon Moore's success, he persuaded the assembled phenomena that their so-called lives were of such value to each other, that, if they saw one of the wise and good drowning, they ought not to risk death in an endeavour to save him. The danger of Moore's mission, however, was even more overwhelming than the difficulty, and has, I greatly fear, been less effectually avoided. It is well-known that whatever is dangerous to a brother is unreal, and that contact with the unreal may entail fatal consequences. What, then, was my horror, when I discovered that these views, designed for the corruption of the non-existent, had – I shudder at the thought – infected our lamented brother himself. To free him from these dreadful toils is my purpose tonight.

Moore contends that God, when he looked upon the world in its early stages, was right in maintaining it to be good – that it was already good in and for itself, and would have continued so even if God had not been looking. A world of matter alone – so says our misguided brother – may be good or bad. For it may certainly be beautiful and ugly, and beauty is better than ugliness. It cannot be said – so the argument proceeds – that beauty is good only as a means to the production of emotion in us. For we judge the man who is moved by beauty to be better than the man who is equally moved by ugliness. This judgment can only be valid, if beauty is good *per se*; for in this case, the man who enjoys ugliness more is to be condemned for liking what is bad. But if beauty were only good as a means, ugliness would be equally good if it produced the same effect; this however, is manifestly false. Hence beauty is good *per se*, and a purely material world, with no one to contemplate it, is better if it is beautiful than if it is ugly.

Such is the argument which, though invented for the further perdition of shadows, has, alas! deceived our brother himself. Let us now endeavour to persuade him that this sophism, like the world of matter, can only be good as a means, and must never be taken as an end.

There are several lines of argument, commonly taken as regards beauty, which I shall avoid. Many would urge that beauty is purely subjective, and exists only in the spectator, or begins when a spectator is seen to be coming. This is rather like the Berkeleian theory, that when a house is tumbling down, it doesn't begin to make a noise till some one comes along the road, and then only if the some one is not deaf. This theory I shall not adopt. I shall admit that beauty is a quality of the object, and that persons of bad taste – if there be any such – are those who are unable to see this quality.

Another course which might be taken, would be, to admit that ugliness is as good as beauty if it produces as much pleasure. This course would be unavoidable for a utilitarian, and is much to be commended as a method of irritating hedonistic but fastidious art critics. The objection to it is, as Moore says, that it makes the person of bad taste as good as the person of good taste, provided only he enjoys bad art as much as the other enjoys good art – a proviso which, one must admit, is fully satisfied by the facts. To maintain that 'Home Sweet Home' gives less pleasure than a Bach fugue, would only be possible for one in bondage to a theory. Nor shall I adopt the really radical puritanical view, that beauty is good neither as means nor as end, but is an invention of the fiend to tempt us to damnation. This is a view I have much sympathy with, and should like, outside the Society, to advocate. But for the present I will adopt another and less thorough-going argument.

That nothing is good or bad in itself except psychical states, is a position which could only be maintained by omniscience. For we do not know of what nature other possible existents than mind or matter may be, and of what we do not know we cannot judge whether it is good or bad. But it is possible to maintain, and I intend to maintain, that among the things we know there is nothing good or bad except psychical states. Of matter I affirm, that it can only be good or bad as a means. When a smut falls on my nose, it is bad as a means; when it falls on the bald head of the Vice-Master, it is similarly good; but in neither case is it an end in itself. But how, then, are we to account for our ethical judgment that the man who sees and enjoys beauty is better than the man who enjoys ugliness? It seems to me that Moore's argument on this point presupposes, what he would be the last to affirm, that psychical states can only derive value from the pleasure they contain. For the pleasure derived from ugliness may certainly be greater than that derived from beauty; but no evidence is offered that there are not other differences between the state in which the fastidious man perceives beauty and that in which the other perceives ugliness. No evidence is possible, since indeed the opposite is the case. The man who knows beauty when he sees it is *ipso facto* different from the man who does not. There is no reason to deny, therefore, that there is a specific aesthetic emotion, only to be had by the man who consciously perceives beauty; just as there is a feeling of red only to be had by the man who looks at something red, and does not, through colour-blindness, take it to be blue. If there be such a specific emotion, there is no ground for denying that beauty is to be valued as a means to this and that this emotion is good *per se* in a degree quite out of proportion to its pleasurableness.

Let us examine this possibility more minutely. We will suppose two people, A and B, the first having perfect taste, the other having the very reverse. We will suppose two objects, α and β, the first perfectly beautiful, the other utterly hideous. Then A gets from α the aesthetic emotion, which is good, and from β he gets its opposite, which is bad. B, on the other hand, being a person of bad taste, judges α to be horrid and β to be quite lovely. Are we bound to hold that B gets the aesthetic emotion from β? I do not see that we are. For there is no reason to suppose the emotion the same merely because the judgment is the same. We may maintain, on the contrary, that only beautiful objects can give the aesthetic emotion, and only people who perceive their beauty can feel this emotion. People of bad taste, before an ugly object, we shall say, falsely judge it to be beautiful, and falsely judge that they feel the aesthetic emotion. In this I see no more difficulty than in the fact that some people mistakenly think themselves in love. Indeed it would be very curious if the emotional effect of beauty on one person were exactly the same as that of ugliness on another, nor do I see the shadow of a reason for such an assumption. It does not follow, because a person thinks he sees beauty, that he will have the same emotions as he would have if he really saw it. Indeed, even though it be admitted that beauty is objective, we may still regard the beautiful as that which can produce the aesthetic emotion, though this is of course no definition of it. And there is no reason to suppose all people capable of this emotion or of the perception of beauty. That many people, when they use the word, have no idea of what it means, seems a plausible way of accounting for the disputes which rage about it. We learn what red means by having red things pointed out to us. But if the vast majority of mankind, when a red thing was pointed out, saw in it only hardness, smoothness, shape, etc., and not colour, great disputes would doubtless rage as to what was red. One man would pitch on hardness, and call all hard things red; another on smoothness, and so on. Thus we may suppose most people use the word beauty in some wholly irrelevant sense, and do not, when they use the word, mean by it at all what should be meant.

But even when they mean the same, it is quite likely that they are subject to a sheer error, and do not obtain the same emotion from many of the things they call beautiful as the more cultivated obtain from things which really are so. You may think so-and-so a very amusing fellow, through mere lack of self-consciousness, when, as a matter of fact, you are bored to death whenever he is in the room. And the same may happen with regard to beauty.

Thus broadly, the people of bad taste are of two kinds. There are first those who don't know what the word means, but are ignorant even of their own ignorance. The judgments of these are quite irrelevant. Secondly there are those who know what the word means, but through defective perception sometimes apply it falsely. There remains the question why these two classes are less good than the faultless critic.

As regards the first class, who do not know even what beauty means, they are to be condemned because, first, they are ignorant, but secondly because they have never felt the aesthetic emotion, which, it is contended, is *sui generis* and good as an end. The second class are less condemnable. They have at some time seen beauty and felt its charms. But they have not seen it clearly enough to recognize it when they saw it again, nor yet felt its charms strongly enough to recognize the feeling when they felt it again. These people may again be of two kinds. They may always feel the appropriate emotion, without recognizing it as such, or recognizing the beauty of the object. Such people are essentially people of good taste: their error is purely intellectual, and is no greater than that of people who can't do sums. But – and this is probably the more common case – they may be very seldom capable of aesthetic emotion, and feel it only slightly when they have it. In this case the slightness of their sensibility is the source both of their bad taste and of their ethical inferiority.

If, then, we admit a specific aesthetic emotion, which can only be produced by beautiful objects, and then only in those who are not aesthetically blind, there is no reason, even though we admit the objectivity of beauty and the inferiority of those who have bad taste to admit so monstrous a paradox as the possible goodness of a purely material world. There is a sense, I admit, in which such a world is *bad*, since it contains nothing good; but this applies equally to all such worlds, and does not distinguish the beautiful from the ugly. That the good is confined, as far as objects of experience are concerned, to what is psychical, is a conclusion, then, if there be an aesthetic emotion, which the objectivity of beauty cannot alone destroy. Whether any other arguments exist against this view I do not know, but I expect to be soon informed.

Part II

META-ETHICS

13

THE MEANING OF GOOD
1904

Reprinted from *CPBR* vol. 4: 571–5. Originally published in *The Independent Review*, March 1904, 2: 328–33. G. E. Moore's *Principia Ethica* was published in October 1903 and on the 10th Russell wrote thanking Moore for a complimentary copy.

> Many thanks for your book, which I have now read. It strikes me as a triumph of lucidity – except unavoidably in regard to Metaphysical Ethics, the whole seems to me intelligible to any attentive and candid reader.
>
> The only matters on which I disagree with you are a few immediate judgements of value, and some of your maxims in Practical Ethics, which seem to me unduly Conservative and anti-reforming. But I should be willing to agree if you merely said that rational opinion on such points is unattainable. Your motto strikes me as admirable; and I think the book all through is a model of exposition. I am to review it in the 'Independent', so I shall be reading it again more carefully.
>
> *(CPBR vol. 4: 567)*

Russell's praise of Moore both public and private was particularly generous since Moore had recently subjected him to a nasty snub. In the spring of 1903 Russell had asked to join an Apostolic reading party that Moore was organizing, and Moore had written to him curtly telling him that he was not wanted. (See Moorehead 1992: 129–30 and Monk 1996: 164–5.) Russell was hurt, but he was not the man to let personal feelings get in the way of philosophy. There is not a trace of bitterness in the above letter nor in the three articles he wrote expounding Moore's doctrines. Of these the longest and most famous is 'The Elements of Ethics' (not to be confused with Moore's type-script of the same title) which was originally intended as part of a projected Moore manifesto and first appeared in its entirety in Russell's *Philosophical Essays* of 1910. (See Russell 1966: 13–59.) It has been much anthologized, but it is rather long and I have preferred to devote the space to papers in which Russell expounds his own opinions rather than those of Moore. Still, *something* on *Principia* was called for, since Russell remained a convert to its doctrines for about nine years. So I have included Russell's second review, 'The Meaning of Good', which is shorter, better written, and less readily available.

There are several points to note:

1   Russell distinguishes (as Moore perhaps does not) between two arguments against the naturalistic fallacy: the Open Question Argument proper and what might be called the Argument from Advocacy. The first contends that 'good' cannot be synonymous with any naturalistic predicate 'X' since 'Are X things good?' is a significant or open question for every 'X'. The second contends that 'good' cannot be synony-mous with any naturalistic 'X', if 'X things are good' is supposed to be a reason for action rather than a 'barren tautology'.

2   Russell writes that the naturalistic fallacy is involved in 'every attempt to infer what ought to be, from what is or will be'. While there is a lot of truth in this, it suggests a confusion that has bedevilled twentieth-century ethics. The idea that Ought cannot be *logically* derived from Is does not depend on the alleged inde-finability of 'good'. It is a simple point of logic that a moral word (or any other word) cannot appear non-vacuously in the conclusion of a valid inference unless it appears in one of the premises. But it is a *trivial* point unless 'good' is indefinable. For if it *is* definable, it should be possible to bridge the gap between the non-moral premises and the moral conclusion with the aid of a definition, i.e. without bringing in any *substantial* or *synthetic* moral premiss. (See Pigden 1989.) Nevertheless the *logical* autonomy of ethics (no moral conclusions from non-moral premises) should be distinguished from *semantic* autonomy (moral words cannot be defined in terms of any others).

3   Russell argues that Moore's attempt to *define* what we ought to do as that action which will produce the best results on the whole commits the naturalistic fallacy. This point was made much of by Ross and was finally accepted by Moore himself (Ross 1930: 8–11 and Moore 1942: 558). But this leaves the substantive issue undecided. Moore thinks that we ought to do what *will* produce the best consequences whereas Russell thinks we ought to do what *we think* will produce the best consequences (so long as our thoughts are based on a due consideration of the evidence). This is still a matter of dispute between utilitarians. Moore's view entails that Stalin's mother did wrong when she failed to strangle him at birth whereas Russell's view entails that she did the right thing though it is a pity (perhaps a bad thing) that she did so. As Russell remarks, paradox is unavoidable, though Russell's view is, perhaps, the less paradoxical of the two.

4   Russell is evidently unfazed by the metaphysical oddity of the Moorean good. This is because at the time he himself was something of a Platonist (though of a rather peculiar sort). Hence he could accept Moore's meta-ethics without metaphysical strain (Hylton 1990: 117–236).

In 1913, Russell began to doubt the Moorean good. His response was anti-realism. If there is no such thing as goodness, then it cannot be true that pleasure (for example) is good. Either moral judgements are not the kinds of things that can be true of false (emotivism) or they *can* (in principle) be true or false although they are largely condemned to falsehood by the non-existence of good and evil (nihilism or the error theory). Russell explored both these options in his later writings. But modern philosophers who share Russell's scepticism about the Moorean good do not suppose that they have to give up on moral truths and moral facts. There are at least three alternatives:

1   Perhaps the Open Question and Advocacy Arguments are not as decisive as Moore and Russell supposed and 'good' is not indefinable after all. If 'good' can be analysed then there is no need to posit a non-natural property of goodness in the first place. We can have moral truths and moral facts without other-worldly

moral properties. (See the Introduction above for a consideration of this option.)

2   Even if 'good' is not synonymous with any natural predicate or combination of predicates, this does not entail that goodness is not identical with some natural property. After all, 'water' (which connotes the drinkable liquid found in lakes and rivers) is not synonymous with 'H$_2$O' (which names a chemical compound) even though both of them stand for the same stuff. Perhaps goodness is identical with some natural property of X-ness even though the words 'good' and 'X' suggest rather different ideas (Durrant 1970: 360–1).

3   Moore's argument presupposes that 'good' is a *predicative* adjective like 'yellow' rather than an *attributive* adjective like 'big'. If a garment is a yellow jacket, it is both yellow and a jacket, but if a creature is a big flea, it does not follow that it is both big and a flea. Geach has argued that 'good' is a purely attributive adjective, that it makes sense to talk of good men, good cats or good can-openers but not of Good Things or things which are good *period* (Geach 1956: 33–42). Moore's argument, therefore, is based on a sort of grammatical mistake. First he misconstrues 'good' as a predicative adjective and then he invents a mysterious non-natural property to correspond to this grammatical illusion. So though there may be no such thing as the Moorean good, there can still be good men and good deeds and hence moral facts and moral truths. This is now the orthodox view, though in my opinion it is mistaken. (See Baldwin 1990: 73, Wong 1984: 101, Blackburn 1993: 160–1 and Pigden 1990: 129–54.)

Principia Ethica. By G.E. Moore. Cambridge: Cambridge University Press, 1903. Pp. xxvii, 232.

Works on Ethics suffer, as a rule, from two opposite defects. From a desire for system and simplicity, reinforced by logical confusions, they flagrantly outrage common sense in their estimate as to what things are good in themselves; and then, from a dread of consequences which are felt to be immoral, they endeavour, by flimsy and inconclusive arguments, to prove that their estimate of goods leads to the usual code of duties and sins. Both these defects are absent from

Mr. Moore's work. There is throughout a frank appeal to what appear as ethical facts, combined with an extraordinary subtlety and care in the analysis of their implications. But, in spite of the subtlety, all the discussions are admirably clear, and are intelligible, except in one chapter, without any previous knowledge of philosophy.

It is a merit rarer, perhaps, than is supposed, to aim solely, in philosophy, at the discovery of truth. Most philosophers are interested, almost exclusively, in establishing some apparently valuable conclusions, for which they seek to find premisses. The premisses, when found, do not interest them on their own account; and any questioning of the premisses is regarded as trivial and carping. Thus attention is concentrated on results, and a hasty, practical tone of mind is generated. In the present author, no trace of this mistake is to be found. 'It may be thought', he says on one occasion,

> that my contention is unimportant, but that is no ground for thinking that I am not in the right. What I am concerned with is knowledge only – that we should think correctly and so far arrive at some truth, however unimportant.

In accordance with this theoretical spirit, Mr. Moore begins by dismissing the notion that ethics is solely concerned with human conduct, or with the goods attainable by human beings: ethics is the general inquiry into what is good, and into what *good* is. The chief contention of the first chapter is that *good* itself is indefinable: an ultimate, simple notion, like yellow. Not that it is impossible to define *the good*, i.e. the things which are good; but that what we mean when we say that a thing is good, cannot be explained in any other terms. This is established by observing that, however we may propose to define *good*, it is always significant to say that that which is suggested as the definition is itself good. If we say: 'pleasure is good', we say something different from: 'pleasure is pleasure'; thus *good* cannot mean the same as pleasure. And the same process may be applied to any other suggested definition. The notion that *good* can be defined, is called by Mr. Moore the *Naturalistic Fallacy* because usually some natural object (*i.e.* something which exists) is taken to be the meaning of good. He shows that, in one form or other, it has been committed by almost all ethical writers; it is involved, for example, in every attempt to infer what ought to be, from what is or will be. The remainder of the chapter is concerned, first, with distinguishing *good as end* from *good as means* – what is called good as means is merely a cause of what is good, while *good as end* is the same as good *simpliciter* – and, next, with the principle of what are called *organic unities*, *i.e.* wholes whose value is not the sum of the values of the parts. These have a very important place in estimating goods, and are frequently discussed in later chapters. An instance is the enjoyment of a beautiful object. A beautiful object which no one sees has little or no value, and a mistaken admiration also is not much prized; but, when the object admired has beauty, we get a whole which is often very good indeed.

Chapter II, on *Naturalistic Ethics*, discusses theories which hold that the only good things are certain natural objects, in so far as these theories are advocated as derivable from the very meaning of *good*. It is shown that such theories always confuse *good*, in its correct and indefinable sense, with the sense which they assign to it by definition. For example, Evolutionist Ethics are apt to argue that *good* means *more evolved*, and on this to base practical recommendations. Yet, if their contention were correct, no practical consequences could follow. We ask: Why should I prefer this to that? And they reply: Because the more evolved is the better. But if they were right in the reason they give for thinking so, they have only said that the more evolved is the more evolved; and this barren tautology can be no basis for action. The meaning of two phrases cannot be the same, if it makes any difference whether we use one of them or the other; and, applying this test, it is easy to see that *more evolved* does not mean the same as *better*.

The doctrine that pleasure is the sole good is next discussed; and its refutation appears as complete as any refutation can be. Sidgwick who, alone among Utilitarians, has recognised clearly that 'good' is indefinable, argues that, though other things than pleasure are valued, they appear not to be valued apart from the pleasure which accompanies them. But this only proves that pleasure is a *constituent* of valuable wholes, which we may admit to be usually true. In virtue of the principle of organic unities, it may happen that a whole would be worthless without a certain constituent, and yet that its value does not lie wholly in that constituent. And this appears to be often the case with pleasure. For example, pleasure is essential to the goodness of enjoyment of works of art; yet such enjoyment is commonly held to be much better than other pleasures which are quite as keen. Thus, though many enjoyments are good, they are not good in proportion to the pleasure they contain; and yet it may be that without the pleasure they would cease to be good.

Metaphysical Ethics, which are discussed in Chapter IV agree with Naturalistic Ethics in thinking that the question: 'What is real?' has a bearing on the question: 'What is good?' They thus come within the scope of the Naturalistic Fallacy. But they are distinguished by the belief, that the reality which is relevant is supersensible and timeless. All the discussions on this subject are excellent, but they are impossible to reproduce within the limits of a review.

Chapter V, on *Ethics in Relation to Conduct*, though it abounds in important distinctions, appears to me the least satisfactory in the book. The question discussed in this chapter is: 'What ought we to do?' It is held that what we ought to do is that action, among all that are possible, which will produce the best results on the whole; and this is regarded as constituting a definition of *ought*. I hold that this is not a definition, but a significant proposition, and in fact a false one. It might be proved, in the course of moral exhortation, that such and such an action would have the best results; and yet the person exhorted might inquire why he should perform the action. The exhorter would have to reply: 'Because you ought to do what will have the best results.' And this reply distinctly adds something. The same arguments by which good was shown to be indefinable can be repeated here, *mutatis mutandis*, to show the indefinability of ought. And, at a later stage, Mr. Moore becomes untrue to his own definition. In regard to moral principles, such as: 'Thou shalt do no murder', which are generally useful and generally obeyed, he holds that there must be instances where better results would follow from breaking them; yet, since we can never know when such an instance is before us, he holds that we ought *always* to obey such rules. This implies that we ought to do what we have reason to think will have the best results, rather than what really will have the best results. It is certain that some people, whom I refrain from naming, might with advantage to the world have been strangled in infancy; but we cannot blame the good women who brought them up for having omitted this precaution. Mr. Moore's objection to this view is, that he thinks it a contradiction in terms to say that it was a pity a man did his duty. It must be admitted that this sounds paradoxical; yet paradox of some kind is apparently unavoidable. Mr. Moore, in consequence of his definition, is led to infer, that we can never be sure what we ought to do, since we cannot calculate all the consequences of our actions; also that no moral law can be self-evident, as the Intuitionist school suppose. If *ought* is indefinable, these consequences do not follow. They may, nevertheless, be true in the main; but there must be at least one self-evident proposition as to what ought to be done. This will be some such rule as, that we ought to do what, so far we can judge, will have the best consequences; though it is doubtful if this particular rule is itself quite true.

A virtue is defined as an habitual disposition to perform acts which usually have the best results; and the notion that virtue is the sole good is discussed and rejected. It is pointed out, that those who have professed this view have yet thought it possible that virtue should be rewarded in heaven by happiness, thereby showing that they regarded happiness as also good; for if virtue were the sole good, it would be logically compelled to be its own reward. But it is admitted that such virtues as are not *mere* habits are good in themselves, as well as being useful as means. Their value as ends is, however, scarcely enough emphasised; and it seems a pity that so little is said about them, and about right actions informed by virtues, in the description of the things which have a high degree of intrinsic goodness.

The last chapter, on *The Ideal*, is the best in the book. It consists chiefly of an enumeration, analysis, and comparison, of those among the things we know which are very good. Although the results differ widely from those usual in works on ethics, they are almost all unhesitatingly affirmed by common sense. It is quite extraordinary and surprising with what certainty the author is able to appeal to our intuitive perception of values, not only in regard to fairly simple matters, but even in very complex and elaborate organic unities. There is a keen pleasure, as we read, in the sure assent with which we follow his estimates, and in the discovery that our power of judging is at once more subtle and more certain than we had supposed.

To judge of the intrinsic value of anything, Mr. Moore says, we must consider what we should think of that thing existing in isolation. We thus avoid two errors: first, the ascription of value to mere means, and, secondly, the supposition that, when one part of a good whole has no value, all the value must lie in the other parts. Applying this test, it appears obvious, that by far the best things we know are the enjoyment of beautiful objects and the pleasures of human intercourse. These two are separately considered.

Aesthetic enjoyments require for their goodness, not merely perception of the object, but also an appropriate emotion. But the emotion apart from the object has little or no value, and, if directed to an ugly object, the whole so formed may be very bad; it is necessary both to see the beautiful qualities of the object, and to see that they are beautiful. We must further distinguish according as there is or is not a belief that the object exists; in the case of imagination and the representative arts, such a belief is absent. The presence of this belief, if true (i.e. if the object does exist), makes the whole much better; if false, it makes the whole worse. Mr. Moore does not decide whether, in this last case, the whole is good or bad; yet this is a question of some practical importance. The love of God, plainly, is in itself a thing of great value; and it is almost always much weakened, if not destroyed, by unbelief. Ought an unbeliever, under these circumstances, to seek to destroy belief in others? Though the effects of belief are here relevant, it is also important to know whether the love of a good object falsely believed to exist is, on the whole, in itself good or bad; and this is one of those rare questions upon which our intuition gives no certain answer.

In regard to personal affection, all the elements present in the previous case exist, together with the fact that, when not misdirected, the affection has an object which is not merely beautiful, but good in a high degree. But, from the point of view of analysis, there is not much to add to the previous discussion of beauty.

A discussion of evils follows. Three evils are recognised as preeminent: namely, the admiration of what is evil or ugly, the hatred of what is good, and consciousness of great pain. Admiration of evil is made worse, both by judging it to be evil and by judging it to be good; but is unaffected by the existence of its object. Hatred of good is better if the good is thought to be evil, and worse if acknowledged to be good. It also becomes worse if the object is perceived to exist. With regard to pain, Mr. Moore is, so far as I know, the first to point out its lack of parallelism to pleasure, though many must have felt this. Pain, he says, is in itself a grave evil, whereas pleasure is not a great good; but, conversely, pleasure often much improves a whole, whereas pain does not make a whole much worse, and may even make it better, as in the case of sympathy for suffering. In this and other such cases, a whole formed of two evils may, *as a whole*, be good; hence, when one evil exists, it is sometimes good to create another. But there seem to be no cases where the whole and the parts together are good on the balance, and where yet one of the parts exists and is evil, and no good part exists. Thus we cannot maintain that the existence of evil is essential to the ideal. But its mere apprehension *is* essential, as may be seen by the excellence of Tragedy.

In conclusion, Mr. Moore points out that the lack of symmetry and system in his results is not an objection to them, since there is no reason to suppose the truth symmetrical. In this we must agree most entirely: philosophy will never advance, until the notion is dispelled, that sweeping general principles can excuse the patient attention to detail which, here as elsewhere, can alone lead to the discovery of truth.

14

ON SCIENTIFIC METHOD
IN PHILOSOPHY

Extract 1914

Reprinted from *Mysticism and Logic* 1917 (1986 edn):
103–7 and *CPBR* vol. 8: 62–4. 'When I was young', writes
Russell, 'I agreed with G. E. Moore in believing in the
objectivity of good and evil. Santayana's criticism in a book
called *Winds of Doctrine*, caused me to abandon this view,
though I have never been able to be as bland and comfortable about it as he was' (Russell 1956a: 87–93). George
Santayana (1863–1952) was a Harvard philosopher and a
close friend of Russell's brother Frank. Russell liked him
but thought him unduly smooth and smug. In his *Winds of
Doctrine* (1913) Santayana ridicules the Moorean good as a
metaphysical illusion bred of intolerance. Ethical abso-
lutism is a 'mental grimace of passion' which 'refutes what
it says by what it is'. Santayana seems to have been something of an emotivist at least as regards basic value
judgements. 'But to speak of the truth of an ultimate good
would be a false collocation of terms; an ultimate good is
chosen, found or aimed at; it is not opined.' Thus ethical
intuitions are not debatable since 'they are not opinions
that we hazard but preferences we feel; and it can neither
be correct nor incorrect to feel them'. Moreover, Santayana
believed this doctrine would conduce to greater tolerance.
'A consciousness of the relativity of values, if it became
prevalent, would tend to render people more truly social.'
Ideological strife would not be at an end but it would be
conducted in a more chivalrous spirit. 'Moral warfare
would continue but not with poisoned arrows' (Santayana
1970: 130–7). Russell came to agree, both about the non-
existence of an objective good and about the beneficial
effects if this doctrine were widely believed. The first hints
of a change of heart are contained in 'The Place of Science
in a Liberal Education' which Russell wrote at about the

time that he was reading Santayana. But the text I have selected to illustrate the change is 'On Scientific Method in Philosophy' which was composed during the autumn of 1914, delivered at Oxford as the Herbert Spencer Lecture on 18 November, and published as a pamphlet in the same year. Russell had long believed that you cannot derive an Ought from an Is (or more precisely, moral conclusions from non-moral premises). In this paper he argues that it is illegitimate to derive an Is from an Ought or a non-moral conclusion from moral premises. Thus the notions of good and evil should be 'extruded from scientific philosophy', that is a philosophy which 'aims only to understand the world'. The argument is discussed in the Introduction. It depends partly on what Russell means when he says that 'all ethics, however refined, remains more or less subjective'. Does he think that 'X is good' means something like 'I (the speaker) approve of X'? (In modern parlance this is usually what is meant by subjectivism in ethics.) But as Russell had realized long before (Paper 7) this theory would reduce ethical judgements to 'statements of a psychological state'. Moreover, it would prevent them contradicting one another.

> If in asserting that A is good, X meant merely to assert that A had a certain relation to himself, say of pleasing his taste in some way; and if Y in saying that A is not good, meant merely to deny that A had a like relation to himself, there would be no subject of debate between them.

But since X and Y *do* contradict each other this cannot be what 'X is good' means (Russell 1966: 20–1). One solution is to deny that basic moral judgements make any sort of a statement at all whether about psychological states or anything else. In later elaborations of the theory Russell suggests that basic evaluations are really in the optative mood and express a certain kind of wish or desire. (This is nowadays known as emotivism.) What 'X is good' means is something like 'Would that everyone desired X!' Since this states nothing at all (not even that the speaker desires that everyone desire X) it is neither true nor false. But there is a sense in which 'X is good' said by one person contradicts 'X is bad' said by somebody else, since the two wishes cannot both be satisfied. But Russell's emotivist theory was not formulated in an unambiguous way until 1935 (Paper

19). Until that time it is not quite clear whether he was a subjectivist or an emotivist or whether he distinguished between the two positions.

But whether moral judgements express or state the speaker's feelings Russell had come to take a dim view of moralizing by 1914.

> My H[erbert] S[pencer] lecture was partly inspired
> by disgust at the universal outburst of righteous-
> ness in all nations since the war began. It seems the
> essence of virtue is persecution, and it has given
> me a disgust of all ethical notions, which evidently
> are chiefly useful as an excuse for murder.
> (Letter to Samuel Alexander,
> 5 February 1915, *CPBR* vol. 8: 56)

The *real* title of the paper, he explained to Perry, was 'Philosophers and Pigs' (letter to Perry, 21 February 1915, *loc. cit.*). It was 'inspired by the bloodthirstiness of the professors both here and in Germany'. However, the Oxford philosophers to whom it was addressed were not persuaded to give up their immoral *penchant* for moralizing. 'J. A. Smith', writes Russell. 'was preparing to pontificate as soon as I was gone. Schiller, bounder and cad though he is, was the only person with whom I felt in any degree of sympathy' (letter to Ottoline Morrell, 18 November 1914, *CPBR* vol. 8 : 55). History does not record why Russell considered Schiller (1864–1937) a bounder and a cad. Perhaps the fact that he was a pragmatist was enough.

(2) The philosophy of evolution, which was to be our second example, illustrates the same tendency to hasty generalization, and also another sort, namely, the undue preoccupation with ethical notions. There are two kinds of evolutionist philosophy, of which both Hegel and Spencer represent the older and less radical kind, while Pragmatism and Bergson represent the more modern and revolutionary variety. But both these sorts of evolutionism have in common the emphasis on *progress*, that is, upon a continual change from the worse to the better, or from the simpler to the more complex. It would be unfair to attribute to Hegel any scientific motive or foundation, but all the other evolutionists, including Hegel's modern disciples, have derived their impetus very largely from the history of biological development. To a philosophy which derives a law of universal progress from this history there are two

objections. First, that this history itself is concerned with a very small selection of facts confined to an infinitesimal fragment of space and time, and even on scientific grounds probably not an average sample of events in the world at large. For we know that decay as well as growth is a normal occurrence in the world. An extra-terrestrial philosopher, who had watched a single youth up to the age of twenty-one and had never come across any other human being, might conclude that it is the nature of human beings to grow continually taller and wiser in an indefinite progress towards perfection; and this generalization would be just as well founded as the generalization which evolutionists base upon the previous history of this planet. Apart, however, from this scientific objection to evolutionism, there is another, derived from the undue admixture of ethical notions in the very idea of progress from which evolutionism derives its charm. Organic life, we are told, has developed gradually from the protozoon to the philosopher, and this development, we are assured, is indubitably an advance. Unfortunately it is the philosopher, not the protozoon, who gives us this assurance, and we can have no security that the impartial outsider would agree with the philosopher's self-complacent assumption. This point has been illustrated by the philosopher Chuang Tzu in the following instructive anecdote:

> The Grand Augur, in his ceremonial robes, approached the shambles and thus addressed the pigs: 'How can you object to die? I shall fatten you for three months. I shall discipline myself for ten days and fast for three. I shall strew fine grass, and place you bodily upon a carved sacrificial dish. Does not this satisfy you?'
>
> Then, speaking from the pigs' point of view, he continued: 'It is better, perhaps, after all, to live on bran and escape the shambles. . . . '
>
> 'But then,' added he, speaking from his own point of view, 'to enjoy honour when alive one would readily die on a war-shield or in the headsman's basket.'
>
> So he rejected the pigs' point of view and adopted his own point of view. In what sense, then, was he different from the pigs?

I much fear that the evolutionists too often resemble the Grand Augur and the pigs.

The ethical element which has been prominent in many of the

most famous systems of philosophy is, in my opinion, one of the most serious obstacles to the victory of scientific method in the investigation of philosophical questions. Human ethical notions, as Chuang Tzu perceived, are essentially anthropocentric, and involve, when used in metaphysics, an attempt, however veiled, to legislate for the universe on the basis of the present desires of men. In this way they interfere with that receptivity to fact which is the essence of the scientific attitude towards the world. To regard ethical notions as a key to the understanding of the world is essentially pre-Copernican. It is to make man, with the hopes and ideals which he happens to have at the present moment, the centre of the universe and the interpreter of its supposed aims and purposes. Ethical meta-physics is fundamentally an attempt, however disguised, to give legislative force to our own wishes. This may, of course, be questioned, but I think that it is confirmed by a consideration of the way in which ethical notions arise. Ethics is essentially a product of the gregarious instinct, that is to say, of the instinct to cooperate with those who are to form our own group against those who belong to other groups. Those who belong to our own group are good; those who belong to hostile groups are wicked. The ends which are pursued by our own group are desirable ends, the ends pursued by hostile groups are nefarious. The subjectivity of this situation is not apparent to the gregarious animal, which feels that the general principles of justice are on the side of its own herd. When the animal has arrived at the dignity of the metaphysician, it invents ethics as the embodiment of its belief in the justice of its own herd. So the Grand Augur invokes ethics as the justification of Augurs in their conflicts with pigs. But, it may be said, this view of ethics takes no account of such truly ethical notions as that of self-sacrifice. This, however, would be a mistake. The success of gregarious animals in the struggle for existence depends upon cooperation within the herd, and cooperation requires sacrifice, to some extent, of what would otherwise be the interest of the individual. Hence arises a conflict of desires and instincts, since both self-preservation and the preservation of the herd are biological ends to the individual. Ethics is in origin the art of recommending to others the sacrifices required for cooperation with oneself. Hence, by reflexion, it comes, through the operation of social justice, to recommend sacrifices by oneself, but all ethics, however refined, remains more or less subjective. Even vegetarians do not hesitate, for example, to save the life of a man in a fever, although in doing so they destroy the lives of many millions of microbes. The view of the world taken by the philosophy derived from ethical notions is thus never impartial and therefore never fully scientific. As compared with science, it fails to achieve the imaginative liberation from self which is necessary to such understanding of the world as man can hope to achieve, and the philosophy which it inspires is always more or less parochial, more or less infected with the prejudices of a time and a place. I do not deny the importance or value, within its own sphere, of the kind of philosophy which is inspired by ethical notions. The ethical work of Spinoza, for example, appears to me of the very highest significance, but what is valuable in such work is not any metaphysical theory as to the nature of the world to which it may give rise, nor indeed anything which can be proved or disproved by argument. What is valuable is the indication of some new way of feeling towards life and the world, some way of feeling by which our own existence can acquire more of the characteristics which we must deeply desire. The value of such work, however immeasurable it is, belongs with practice and not with theory. Such theoretic importance as it may possess is only in relation to human nature, not in relation to the world at large. The scientific philosophy, therefore, which aims only at understanding the world and not directly at any other improvement of human life, cannot take account of ethical notions without being turned aside from that submission to fact which is the essence of the scientific temper.

If the notion of the universe and the notion of good and evil are extruded from scientific philosophy, it may be asked what specific problems remain for the philosopher as opposed to the man of science? It would be difficult to give a precise answer to this question, but certain characteristics may be noted as distinguishing the province of philosophy from that of the special sciences.

15

WAR AND
NON-RESISTANCE:
A REJOINDER TO
PROFESSOR PERRY

Extract 1915

Reprinted from *CPBR* vol. 13: 186–7 and originally published in *The International Journal of Ethics*, 26 (1915): 23–30. This article is a reply to Ralph Barton Perry's article 'Non-Resistance and the Present War' in the April issue of *The International Journal of Ethics*, which is, in turn, a reply to Russell's 'The Ethics of War' (*CPBR* vol. 13: 63–73). 'The Ethics of War', as its title suggests, is largely devoted to the ethics of war. But before getting down to business, Russell espouses what looks like emotivism:

> Opinions on such a subject as war are the outcome of feeling rather than thought. . . . The fundamental facts in this, as in all ethical questions are feelings; all that thought can do is to clarify and harmonize the expression of those feelings, and it is such clarifying and harmonizing of my own feelings that I wish to attempt in the present article.

Perry took him to task for this, and the following extract is an attempt to justify these rather throw-away remarks. Russell's argument leaves much to be desired. Judgements about what ought to exist are matters of taste. Why? Because we cannot arrive at a rational consensus. But we cannot arrive at a rational consensus on the causes and consequences of the Great War. Yet it does not follow that history and politics are matters of taste, however biased our judgements may be. As Russell himself had argued in 'The Elements of Ethics', 'the difficulty of discovering the truth does not prove there is no truth to be discovered' (Russell 1966: 20).

Perry (1876–1957) was a professor at Harvard and a leader of the 'New Realists', a set of young philosophers who largely agreed with Moore and Russell.

Professor Perry is surprised that I should speak of my opinions as merely an expression of 'feeling'. It is true that I formulated judgments and supported them by what was meant to be as like reason as I could make it. But all that can be *proved* in this way is that the opinion one is combating is by no means certainly true, and that the opinion one is advocating has as much in its favour as that of one's opponents. If our views as to what ought to be done were to be truly rational, we ought to have a rational way of ascertaining what things are such as ought to exist on their own account, and by what means such things are to be brought into existence. On the first point, no argument is possible. There can be nothing beyond an appeal to individual tastes. If, for example, one man thinks vindictive punishment desirable in itself, apart from any reformatory or deterrent effects, while another man thinks it undesirable in itself, it is impossible to bring any arguments in support of either side. In regard to means, the difficulty is just the opposite: so many arguments can be brought on both sides of the question that no rational decision is possible. Take again the question of punishment. Is punishment reformatory? Obviously sometimes it is, and sometimes it is not. Will it be reformatory on the present occasion? The answer, however supported by a wealth of argument, will turn on whether we feel a vindictive impulse or not. Those who feel such an impulse will persuade themselves that the punishment will be wholesome; those who do not will persuade themselves that it will only produce exasperation.

The subjectivity of men's opinions on political questions is much greater than is generally supposed. Whether a certain course of action will have a certain effect cannot, as a rule, be ascertained, and yet all argument for or against depends upon the effect which is expected. Unavowed and often unconscious desires lead men to feel convinced that a certain effect will result, when they ought to be full of doubt. Many men, before the war had an unconscious impulse toward war, which led them to advocate, in the name of peace, various measures which seemed to genuine lovers of peace, ideally calculated to produce war. The few who frankly avowed a desire for war, like Bernhardi, maintained that war leads to moral regeneration. The *Morning Post* maintains this view still, although it is easy to see that war has provoked hatred, brutality, and vice. It is not hypocrisy that promotes positive opinions of this kind, it is merely failure to allow for the influence of passion on thought. In the case of private quarrels, we all know how anger alters men's judgment. And on the other hand pacifism before the war made many of its advocates blind to facts which took them by surprise last August, and led them sometimes to repudiate the convictions of a lifetime. It was the attempt to do justice to such sceptical considerations which led me to speak of my own views as an expression of feeling.

16

CONTROVERSY WITH 'NORTH STAFFS'

1916

Reprinted from *CPBR* vol 13: 324–6, originally published in *The Cambridge Magazine*, 5, 12 February 1916 and 11 March 1916. 'North Staffs' was the *nom de guerre* of T. E. Hulme (1883–1917), an amateur philosopher, whose posthumously published *Speculations* won him a certain fame. He published a series of articles on the War in *The Cambridge Magazine* which was at the time under the editorship of C. K. Ogden (1889–1957). They were not of a pacifist tendency. In one of these, which Ogden (who obviously enjoyed stoking the flames of controversy) had mischievously entitled 'The Kind of Rubbish We Oppose', Hulme accused Russell of a 'faded Rousseauism' and of setting up a false distinction between the warmongers, motivated by 'impulses of aggression', and pacifists motivated by 'disinterested intelligence' (*The Cambridge Magazine*, 5, 12 February 1916). Russell replied with 'Mr Russell's Reply' and Hulme returned to the attack with two articles, 'North Staffs Resents Mr Russell's Rejoinder' and 'North Staffs Continues Where He Left Off' (published on 26 February and 4 March, respectively). Hulme was perceptive enough to notice that the apparent subjectivism of Russell's lectures (subsequently published as *The Principles of Social Reconstruction*) was at odds with the objectivism of 'The Elements of Ethics'. In 'North Staffs' Praise of War', Russell owns up to his change of heart. It is still not clear exactly what he means by the 'subjectivity of ethics' (emotivism, subjectivism or the error theory?) but the arguments have begun to solidify. These are discussed at length in the Introduction, so I shall not go into them here. However, it is worth noting that Russell had a *moral* (as opposed to an intellectual) reason for advocating the subjectivity of ethics. He thought it would lead to 'less

cruelty, persecution, punishment and moral reprehension'
if it were widely believed. This echoes the view of
Santayana, who hoped for 'moral warfare' but without
'poisoned arrows'. The Bolsheviks, who were certainly
subjectivists of some sort (see Paper 26), were soon to prove
them wrong.

Hulme (who had already been wounded) rejoined his
regiment in March 1916. He was killed a year later.

Mr Russell's Reply

SIR,

Your correspondent 'North Staffs' has contributed to the
Magazine a criticism of a recent lecture by me, with the courteous
title 'The Kind of Rubbish We Oppose'. This criticism shows such
profound misunderstanding of the lecture that I suspect 'North
Staffs' of being the gentleman who ostentatiously read the Daily
Express during the greater part of the hour.

He begins by suggesting that I regard the bellicose as moved by
impulse and the pacifists as moved by reason. My whole lecture, on
the contrary, was concerned to represent *both* sides as moved by
impulse, and to show that impulse is essential to *all* vigorous
action, whether good or bad: 'Blind impulses' – so I contended –
'sometimes lead to destruction and death, but at other times they
lead to the best things the world contains. Blind impulse is the
source of war but it is also the source of science and art and love. It
is not the weakening of impulse that is to be desired, but the direction of impulse towards life and growth rather than towards death
and decay.' And again: 'It is not the act of a passionless man to
throw himself athwart the whole movement of the national life, to
urge an outwardly hopeless cause, to incur obloquy and to resist the
contagion of collective emotion. The impulse to avoid the hostility
of public opinion is one of the strongest in human nature, and can
only be overcome by an unusual force of direct and uncalculating
impulse; it is not cold reason alone that can prompt such an act.'

Having misrepresented my thesis, he continues: 'There is no
doubt that this provides a happy method of controversy for general
use by pacifists. They thus avoid the necessity for any tedious examination of the actual arguments used by their opponent, by
depriving these arguments at one stroke of all validity.'

If 'North Staffs' has such a love of 'tedious examination' as he
suggests, I would refer him to *The Policy of the Entente* and *Justice in*

Wartime (both published by the Labour Press), where he will find that I have set forth the detailed discussion which I presupposed in the lecture.

He proceeds to suggest that the difference between him and me is one of ethical valuation. No doubt this is true on the surface. But ethical differences usually spring from differences of impulse. 'Whole philosophies, whole systems of ethical valuation, spring up in this way: they are the embodiment of a kind of thought which is subservient to impulse, which aims at providing a quasi-rational ground for the indulgence of impulse'. 'This difference of opinion will seem to be ethical or intellectual, whereas its real basis is a difference of impulse. No genuine agreement will be reached, in such a case, so long as the difference of impulse persists.' (These again are quotations from the lecture.)

I cannot imagine what led 'North Staffs' to his final exhortation not to 'falsely simplify matters by assuming that it is a struggle between the assailants and the defenders of privilege. It is not Democracy against Privilege.' There was not a syllable in my lecture to suggest to any one who listened to it that I regarded the matter in this light. It is not democracy, but liberty, that is in danger. The persecutions of early Christians, the massacre of St. Bartholomew, the Press Gang, and Conscription for the Unmarried, have none of them been contrary to democracy. But the tyrannous power of the State, whether wielded by a monarch or by a majority, is an evil against which I will protest no matter how 'negligeable' may be the minority on whom it is exercised.

BERTRAND RUSSELL

North Staffs' Praise of War

In the *Cambridge Magazine* for February 26 North Staffs does something to bring to a clear issue the differences between him and me. These differences are rooted in character and disposition, and will not be dispelled by argument; but I will do my best towards helping to make them explicit.

North Staffs distinguishes two types of reasons: (1) Those dealing with facts; (2) those concerned with ethics. I referred him to two pamphlets, one dealing with the one, the other with the other. He bought *one* of these pamphlets, and complains that it does not deal with the topics discussed in the other. This seems unreasonable.

As regards ethical reasons, he says that I 'consistently refuse to admit that any such reasons can possibly exist'. The reception given to Bernhardi's works in this country, and the determination to maintain that Germany is wholly responsible for the war, had led me to think that this was common ground, so far as Englishmen's explicit opinions were concerned. Does North Staffs wish to associate himself with Bernhardi in the praise of war as a good in itself? If so, he will find himself in an even smaller minority than that in which I find myself. If not, I must suppose that he wishes to praise only defensive wars. To this I would reply (1) that this war is less purely defensive than most of us believe; (2) that even defensive wars are less justifiable, on the grounds of their effects, than men usually suppose them to be. Both these points have been argued at length in the pamphlets referred to.

On the abstract question of ethics which North Staffs proceeds to raise, I do certainly mean to maintain that all ethics is subjective, and that ethical agreement can only arise through similarity of desires and impulses. It is true that I did not hold this view formerly, but I have been led to it by a number of reasons, some logical, some derived from observation. Occam's Razor, or the principle that constructions are to be substituted for inferred entities whenever possible, leads me to discard the notion of absolute good if ethics can be accounted for without it. Observation of ethical valuations leads me to think that all ethical valuations can be so accounted for, and that the claim of universality which men associate with their ethical judgments embodies merely the impulse to persecution or tyranny. An ethical argument can only have practical efficacy in one of two ways: (1) by showing that the effects of some kind of action are different from what the opponent supposes; this is really a scientific, not an ethical argument; (2) by altering the desires or impulses of the opponent, not merely his intellectual judgments. I cannot imagine any argument by which it could be shown that something is intrinsically good or intrinsically bad; for this reason ethical valuations not embodying desires or impulses cannot have any importance.

For my part, I should wish to see in the world less cruelty, persecution, punishment, and moral reprobation than exists at present; to this end, I believe that a recognition of the subjectivity of ethics might conduce. But if North Staffs likes these things, and judges them to be in themselves good, I cannot prove by argument that he is mistaken; I can only say his desires and mine are different. If his

belief in the intrinsic excellence of war has some other basis, I hope
he will set it forth.

BERTRAND RUSSELL

P.S. Since writing the above I have seen North Staffs' continuation
in the *Magazine* for March 4. Most of what he says in this continuation I said in my lecture on Religion on February 9. But the
antithesis between heroic ethics and ethics devoted to life, which he
draws, is quite baseless. An ethic is rendered heroic, not by the
values which it recognizes, but by the intensity of its recognition
and the sacrifices it is willing to make to realize them. In that sense
my ethic is as 'heroic' as his; and I do not condemn *all* wars, as I
stated in 'The Ethics of War', and again in my lecture on war. But
the things which I value are very *seldom* promoted by war. I value
the kind of life which seems to me 'heroic', the kind which is
devoted to certain ends that are in one sense above life, but that
only acquire actual existence when they are embodied in life. I find
that it is not pursuit of these ends that leads to modern wars, and
that modern wars are the greatest obstacle to the achievement of
these ends. I wish North Staffs would tell us explicitly what are the
things which he values; for so long as he keeps silence about this,
the controversy remains indefinite.

17

IS THERE AN ABSOLUTE GOOD?

1922

Reprinted from *CPBR* vol. 9: 345–6. This paper remained unpublished in Russell's lifetime and he soon rejected its principal thesis. It appears to have been delivered at a special meeting of the Apostles on 4 March 1922, held in honour of Russell's friend and fellow-Apostle, Goldsworthy Lowes Dickinson. (The meeting divided on the question, 'Is There Good in Goldie?') It anticipates a thesis made famous by J. L. Mackie as the 'error theory' (Mackie 1946: 77–90 and Mackie 1977: 15–49). Moral judgements – so the story goes – are statements or propositions and hence either true or false. But there are no properties of goodness and badness (Russell rather confusingly calls them 'predicates') so judgements about good and bad are all *false*. (Unless – and this is an important proviso – they are prefaced by a '*not*'. If nothing is good because there is no such thing as goodness then everything is *not* good – and the same, of course, goes for 'bad'.) Judgements about right and wrong are false too, since to say that an action is *right* (in the sense of being *the* right thing to do) entails that it is likely to produce more good (and less bad) than any available alternative. But since there is no such thing as goodness, no action can produce more of it than any other. Hence no action can be right. Moral judgements therefore are in error and morality is based upon a metaphysical mistake. Hence the name, the 'error theory'.

Where Russell differs from Mackie is that he feels compelled to give an account of how 'good' can be meaningful even though there is no property ('predicate') which it means. Russell always believed that 'there are words which are only significant because there is something that they mean, and if there were not this something, they would be empty noises not words' (Russell 1959: 177). But when he was young, he was inclined to believe that all, or almost all, words were like this. This led to a problem. If the meaning of a word is the thing which it stands for, then if there is no such thing, the word itself is meaningless. If '*A*' is such a word, then it is impossible to say truly that there is no *A*. For if '*A*' is meaningful, which it must be if 'There is no *A*' is to be true, then there must be something which '*A*' means, namely *A*. In which case, 'There is no *A*' must be false. But if there is nothing that '*A*' means, then '*A*' is meaningless. In which case, 'There is no *A*' is meaningless too. Thus 'There is no *A*' is either false or meaningless. As Russell himself put it, 'unless "*A* is not" be an empty sound, it must be false – whatever *A* may be, it certainly is' (Russell 1937: 449, 1st edn 1903). This led Russell to distinguish between *existence*, which is a spatio-temporal affair, and *being*, which is more a matter of ticking over quietly in a metaphysical sort of way. Since they are mythical, the Homeric gods do not *exist* – they are not to be met with in space and time – but since words like 'Zeus' are meaningful, the Homeric gods do have *being*.

Russell came to reject this swollen ontology of non-existent beings. But to do away with them in good conscience he needed a theory of meaning which would allow such phrases as 'the King of France' (not to mention words like 'Zeus') to be meaningful without there having to be something that they mean. He supplied such a theory in his famous paper 'On Denoting' of 1905 (Russell 1956b: 41–56). A definite description such as 'the King of France' is an 'incomplete symbol' as it has no meaning in isolation (in the sense of a referent for which it stands) though it can function meaningfully (and may even refer) in the context of a sentence. Russell's analysis essentially consists of a set of rules for rephrasing sentences in which definite descriptions *do* occur so as to produce more perspicuous sentences in which they *do not*. This removes the temptation to suppose that there must *be* such a person as the King of France, in order for sentences about him to make sense. Thus to say that the King of France is bald, is to say that there is a thing which is King of France – where 'is King of France' is to be regarded as a (linguistic) predicate – that anything else which is King of France is identical with that thing, and that that thing is bald. This will be true if there is one, and only one, King of France who is bald, and false otherwise. In particular, it will be false but meaningful if there is no King of France. To say that there is no King of France is to say that nothing satisfies the predicate 'is King of France', or alternatively, that everything is not King of France. Thus the King does not have to have being in order for us to deny that he exists. As for Zeus, we can deal with him by construing 'Zeus' as a disguised definite description ('the thing which exemplifies the Zeus-properties described in the Iliad', for instance) and subjecting this description to the King-of-France treatment. That way, we can make sense of Homer without having to posit Homeric gods. (This is, of course, a rough and oversimplified account. Readers who want the full gory details should consult Coffa 1991: 99–112 and Hylton 1990: 237–75.)

Notice that the theory of 'On Denoting' takes *linguistic* predicates (property words or the linguistic items that appear in Russell's logic as propositional functions) pretty much for granted. Russell's account of how talk about the King of France can be meaningful without there being such a person requires that the predicate 'is King of France' makes sense. But does the predicate require a corresponding property *being King of France* in order to be meaningful? In 1905, Russell would probably have said yes, since at that time he was still something of a Platonist. However, by 1922 he had come to believe that there is at least one linguistic predicate, 'good' (or 'is good'), which can be used meaningfully, even though there is no property which constitutes its meaning. 'Good', like 'The King of France', is an incomplete symbol. It must be analysed away in context so as to remove the temptation to posit a corresponding property to account for the fact that talk of good makes sense. Thus the strategy employed in 1905 to dispose of implausible individuals is extended in 1922 to dispose of implausible properties. In effect, Russell accuses Moore of making an analogous mistake to the one that he himself committed before 'On Denoting' – that of supposing that a word cannot be meaningfully employed unless there is something – in this case some *property* – that it means.

The error theory is sometimes rejected on the grounds that if it were true we ought to give up moralizing (Blackburn 1993: 149–50 and Wright 1996: 1–3). If the idea is that we *morally* ought to give up moralizing, the contention is obviously false, since if the error theory is true, there is nothing that we morally ought to do. If the idea is that we *rationally* ought to give up moralizing, then we need an explication and defence of the norm of rationality involved. After all, there might well be *pragmatic* reasons for moralizing and even for cultivating moral beliefs. Morality might be a useful, or even a necessary, fiction, the cement of society or a prop to psychic health Still, this is not a defence that would have appealed to Russell who (as he put it to his brother) would rather have been 'mad with truth than sane with lies' (Russell 1968: 36). However, the real response to the Blackburn/Wright argument is that just because a theory has unpleasant consequences, it does not follow that it is false.

Whatever his reasons (and the possibilities are discussed in the Introduction), Russell *did* give up the error theory and reverted to a variant of emotivism. 'Good', he came to think, does not name a property, but this is not because it is an incomplete symbol, but because the sentences in which it appears do not express propositions. Hence the function of 'good' is not to describe anything or to denote some property, but to express some feeling or desire. Nevertheless, Russell's paper may have had some influence within the Society. Three years later, the young Apostle, F. P. Ramsey (the brother of a future Archbishop!), remarked in his chilling little piece 'Is There Anything to Discuss?' that 'most of us would agree that the objectivity of good was a thing we had settled and dismissed with the existence of God. Theology and Absolute Ethics are two famous subjects which we have realized to have no objects' (Ramsey 1990: 246–7). Since this agreement (that good, like God, can be dismissed) can hardly have been due to the influence of Moore, it may, perhaps, have been due to the influence of Russell.

When the generation to which I belong were young, Moore persuaded us all that there is an absolute good. Most of us drew the inference that *we* were absolutely good, but this is not an essential part of Moore's position, though it is one of its most attractive parts.

Moore's position, in essence, is this: When we judge (say) 'pleasure is good', the word 'good' has a meaning, and what it means is a certain simple and unanalysable predicate. I wish to leave out of account the question whether the predicate 'good' is simple, which is of minor importance; my point is that the word 'good' does not stand for a predicate at all, but has a meaning only in the sense in which descriptive phrases have meaning, i.e. in use, not in isolation; further that, when we define it as nearly as possible in accordance with the usage of absolutists, *all* propositions in which the word 'good' has a primary occurrence are false.

Moore is right, I think, in holding that when we say a thing is good we do not *merely* mean that we have towards it a certain feeling, of liking or approval or what not. There seems to me no doubt that our ethical judgments claim objectivity; but this claim, to my mind, makes them all false. Without the theory of incomplete symbols, it seemed natural to infer, as Moore did, that, since propositions in which the word 'good' occurs have meaning, therefore the word 'good' has meaning; but this was a fallacy. And it is upon this fallacy, I think, that the most apparently cogent of Moore's arguments rest.

I conceive the genesis of the notion of 'good' as follows: We have emotions of approval and disapproval. If $A, B, C, \ldots$ are the things towards which we have emotions of approval, we mistake the similarity of our emotions in the presence of $A, B, C, \ldots$ for perception of a common predicate of $A, B, C, \ldots$. To this supposed predicate we shall give the name 'good'. It may be that $A, B, C, \ldots$ will have several common predicates, but the irrelevant ones can be eliminated by the rule that the predicate 'good' is not to belong to anything of which we *dis*approve. Thus the process is as follows:

$A, B, C, \ldots$ are things of which we approve; $X, Y, Z, \ldots$ are things of which we disapprove. We judge: 'There is a predicate possessed by $A, B, C, \ldots$ but not by $X, Y, Z, \ldots$'. To this supposed predicate, so described, we give the name 'good'. Thus when we judge 'M is good', we mean: 'M has that predicate which is common to $A, B, C, \ldots$ but is absent in $X, Y, Z, \ldots$'. It will be seen that the emotions of approval and disapproval do not enter into the meaning of the proposition 'M is good', but only into its genesis. The fundamental proposition of ethics, according to the theory I am advocating, is: 'There is a predicate common to $A, B, C, \ldots$ but absent from $X, Y, Z, \ldots$'. I believe this proposition to be false. It follows that, if I am right, all ethical propositions are false. Their falsehood is of the same kind as the falsehood of the proposition: 'The present King of France is bald'; except that what is described in an ethical proposition is the predicate, not the subject.

Why believe this theory?

1   It is not considered by Moore, and the arguments which he brings against the rival theories he does consider do not apply against it.

2   It seems to be an empirical fact that the things people judge good are the same as those towards which they have an emotion

of approval, while the things they judge bad are those towards which they have an emotion of disapproval.

3   The emotions of approval and disapproval influence our actions, whereas purely theoretic judgments do not. Therefore in so far as ethics is concerned with what people actually do, or with how to influence action, the emotions suffice without the help of the predicates 'good' and 'bad'.

4   Since people disagree in their judgments of good and bad to just the same extent to which they differ in their feelings of approval and disapproval, the objectivity secured by ethical predicates is only theoretic, and does nothing to mitigate ethical disputes in practice.

5   Since the facts can be accounted for without the predicates 'good' and 'bad', Occam's razor demands that we should abstain from assuming them.

Apart from logical arguments, there is a mass of what one may call sentiment which leads one to entertain emotions of disapproval towards absolute good, i.e. to judge that good is bad. But I will not waste your time by developing these sentimental considerations.

18

WHAT I BELIEVE

Extract 1925

Reprinted from *Why I Am Not a Christian*, 1957: 43–4 and
48–9. Russell published two pieces in the 1920s with a
bearing on meta-ethics: *What I Believe*, which originally
appeared as a short book, and Chapter 22 of *An Outline of
Philosophy*, 1927. Both suggest some kind of emotivism
but I have preferred to reproduce *What I Believe* since it
seems to me by far the clearer of the two. Nevertheless, the
Outline deserves a few words of comment. In the *Outline*,
Russell announces that he no longer believes in the
doctrines of G. E. Moore 'that "good" is an indefinable
notion and that we know *a priori* certain general propositions about the kinds of things that are good on their own
account'. He cites Santayana as the meta-ethical
Mephistopheles who caused him to lose his faith. Russell
now thinks that 'good and bad are derivative from desire',
although he does not 'mean quite simply that the good is
the desired' (Russell 1927: 184.) What then, does 'good'
mean? No clear answer emerges. Earlier on, Russell asks
'what is meant when a person says: "You *ought* to do so-
and-so" or "I *ought* to do so-and-so"', and suggests that
'primarily such a sentence has emotional content; it means
"this is the act towards which I feel the emotion of
approval"' (Russell 1927: 181). This looks like a clumsy
attempt to express some form of emotivism. But he immediately goes on: 'But we do not wish to leave the matter
there; we want to find something more objective and
systematic and constant than a personal emotion.' After
eight pages of glittering but obscure argument, Russell
arrives at the conclusion that *the good life is one inspired by
love and guided by knowledge*, having endorsed something
like utilitarianism on the way. Is this conclusion supposed
to be objective, systematic and constant or does it merely

express a preference of Russell's which he hopes we will share? My best guess at what Russell is driving at is this: to say that something is good or that it ought to be done is to express approval (or something of the sort). Thus claims about the good are not genuinely true or false. However, Russell's ethic represents what we *would* approve of if we put our personal and parochial interests to one side and adopted the viewpoint of an impartial authority. The ethic we would endorse would be utilitarian in structure whilst the good to be promoted would be a life inspired by love and guided by knowledge. Such a life would be driven by 'compossible' desires, i.e. desires which can be reconciled with the desires of other people. Thus we would *agree* that the good life is inspired by love and guided by knowledge, even though it might not be strictly *true*. Why we should cultivate these impartial preferences and compossible desires remains something of a mystery. After all, indulging *im*compossible desires can be a positive pleasure if we happen to have the upper hand. As Russell himself remarks that 'immediately after the war, those who hated the Germans were happier than those who still regarded them as human beings'.

What I Believe, by contrast (but only by contrast), is a model of lucidity. Russell begins with one of his pet theses (familiar from Paper 14) that we cannot infer facts from values, what *is* from what (we think) *is good*. The attempt to do so suggests a certain anthropocentric conceit, best cured by a little astronomy. His second claim is that there is no outside standard (no objective ethical facts) to show that our valuations are right or wrong. *We* are the creators of value, hence we are the ultimate and irrefutable arbiters of good and evil. But how do we create value? Apparently by desiring things. This sounds remarkably like a reversion to the Russell of the 1890s, particularly the Russell of Papers 7, 9 and 10. Desire and value, so it seems, are intimately connected.

In Russell's view the good life is inspired by love and guided by knowledge. But there is no such thing as ethical knowledge except in the sense that it may be a matter of fact whether a given course of action conduces to a desired end. But whether an end is good or bad is not something that can genuinely be known. Why not? Because sentences of the form 'X is good' do not express propositions and hence are neither true nor false? Or because (as Paper 17 would have it) such sentences *do* express propositions but are, in fact, all *false*? Apparently not. 'When I say that the

morality of conduct is to be judged by its probable consequences, I mean that *I desire* to see approval given to
behaviour likely to realize social purposes which we desire'
[Pigden's italics]. This suggests that 'X is good' means that
I (the speaker) desire X. But this would reduce ethical
judgements to 'statements of a psychological state' (Paper
7). So far from making ethical knowledge impossible, it
would make it exceedingly cheap. After all, most of us
know our own minds well enough to know roughly what
we want. Indeed, judgements about what is good 'could
not err (except by the speaker's mistaking his own feelings)' (Paper 7 again). And there would be 'no subject of
debate' between opposed moralists who do seem to contradict one another (Russell 1966: 21). Ethics would become
a branch of empirical psychology, albeit a rather trivial one.

The obvious conclusion is that Russell is speaking
rather loosely. (*What I Believe* is, after all, a popular piece in
which the aim is to be vivid rather than strictly accurate.)
When he says that the good life is inspired by love and
guided by knowledge he is not *stating* that he desires
people to live such a life. He is *expressing* this desire. As he
himself was to put it later (see Papers 19 and 20), 'The
good life is inspired by love and guided by knowledge' is
really equivalent to a sentence in the optative mood –
'Would that everyone lived a life inspired by love and
guided by knowledge!', or something of the sort. This is
neither true nor false and hence is not something that can
be known. But it is worth stressing that Russell does not
state emotivism in this piece. It is what we must suppose
him to mean if he is not to contradict himself.

The philosophy of nature is one thing, the philosophy of value is
quite another. Nothing but harm can come of confusing them.
What we think good, what we should like, has no bearing whatever
upon what is, which is the question for the philosophy of nature.
On the other hand, we cannot be forbidden to value this or that on
the ground that the non-human world does not value it, nor can we
be compelled to admire anything because it is a 'law of nature'.
Undoubtedly we are part of nature, which has produced our desires,
our hopes and fears, in accordance with laws which the physicist is
beginning to discover. In this sense we are part of nature, we are
subordinated to nature, the outcome of natural laws, and their
victims in the long run.

The philosophy of nature must not be unduly terrestrial; for it, the earth is merely one of the smaller planets of one of the smaller stars of the Milky Way. It would be ridiculous to warp the philosophy of nature in order to bring out results that are pleasing to the tiny parasites of this insignificant planet. Vitalism as a philosophy, and evolutionism, show, in this respect, a lack of sense of proportion and logical relevance. They regard the facts of life, which are personally interesting to us, as having a cosmic significance, not a significance confined to the earth's surface. Optimism and pessimism, as cosmic philosophies, show the same naive humanism; the great world, so far as we know it from the philosophy of nature, is neither good nor bad, and is not concerned to make us happy or unhappy. All such philosophies spring from self-importance, and are best corrected by a little astronomy.

But in the philosophy of value the situation is reversed. Nature is only a part of what we can imagine; everything, real or imagined, can be appraised by us, and there is no outside standard to show that our valuation is wrong. We are ourselves the ultimate and irrefutable arbiters of value, and in the world of value Nature is only a part. Thus in this world we are greater than Nature. In the world of values, Nature in itself is neutral, neither good nor bad, deserving of neither admiration nor censure. It is we who create value and our desires which confer value. In this realm we are kings, and we debase our kingship if we bow down to Nature. It is for us to determine the good life, not for Nature – not even for Nature personified as God.

There have been at different times and among different people many varying conceptions of the good life. To some extent the differences were amenable to argument; this was when men differed as to the means to achieve a given end. Some think that prison is a good way of preventing crime; others hold that education would be better. A difference of this sort can be decided by sufficient evidence. But some differences cannot be tested in this way. Tolstoy condemned all war; others have held the life of a soldier doing battle for the right to be very noble. Here there was probably involved a real difference as to ends. Those who praise the soldier usually consider the punishment of sinners a good thing in itself; Tolstoy did not think so. On such a matter no argument is possible. I cannot, therefore, prove that my view of the good life is right; I can only state my view, and hope that as many as possible will agree. My view is this:

The good life is one inspired by love and guided by knowledge.

128

When I speak of knowledge as an ingredient of the good life, I am not thinking of ethical knowledge, but of scientific knowledge and knowledge of particular facts. I do not think there is, strictly speaking, such a thing as ethical knowledge. If we desire to achieve some end, knowledge may show us the means, and this knowledge may loosely pass as ethical. But I do not believe that we can decide what sort of conduct is right or wrong except by reference to its probable consequences. Given an end to be achieved, it is a question for science to discover how to achieve it. All moral rules must be tested by examining whether they tend to realize ends that we desire. I say ends that we desire, not ends that we *ought* to desire. What we 'ought' to desire is merely what someone else wishes us to desire. Usually it is what the authorities wish us to desire – parents, schoolmasters, policemen, and judges. If you say to me 'you ought to do so-and-so', the motive power of your remark lies in my desire for your approval – together, possibly, with rewards or punishments attached to your approval or disapproval. Since all behaviour springs from desire, it is clear that ethical notions can have no importance except as they influence desire. They do this through the desire for approval and the fear of disapproval. These are powerful social forces, and we shall naturally endeavour to win them to our side if we wish to realize any social purpose. When I say that the morality of conduct is to be judged by its probable consequences, I mean that I desire to see approval given to behaviour likely to realize social purposes which we desire, and disapproval to opposite behaviour. At present this is not done; there are certain traditional rules according to which approval and disapproval are meted out quite regardless of consequences. But this is a topic with which we shall deal in the next section.

The superfluity of theoretical ethics is obvious in simple cases. Suppose, for instance, your child is ill. Love makes you wish to cure it, and science tells you how to do so. There is not an intermediate stage of ethical theory, where it is demonstrated that your child had better be cured. Your act springs directly from desire for an end, together with knowledge of means. This is equally true of all acts, whether good or bad. The ends differ, and the knowledge is more adequate in some cases than in others. But there is no conceivable way of making people do things they do not wish to do. What is possible is to alter their desires by a system of rewards and penalties, among which social approval and disapproval are not the least potent. The question for the legislative moralist is, therefore: How shall this system of rewards and punishments be arranged so as to secure the maximum of what is desired by the legislative authority? If I say that the legislative authority has bad desires, I mean merely that its desires conflict with those of some section of the community to which I belong. Outside human desires there is no moral standard.

Thus, what distinguishes ethics from science is not any special kind of knowledge but merely desire. The knowledge required in ethics is exactly like the knowledge elsewhere; what is peculiar is that certain ends are desired, and that right conduct is what conduces to them. Of course, if the definition of right conduct is to make a wide appeal, the ends must be such as large sections of mankind desire. If I defined right conduct as that which increases my own income, readers would disagree. The whole effectiveness of any ethical argument lies in its scientific part, i.e. in the proof that one kind of conduct, rather than some other, is a means to an end which is widely desired. I distinguish, however, between ethical argument and ethical education. The latter consists in strengthening certain desires and weakening others. This is quite a different process, which will be separately discussed at a later stage.

We can now explain more exactly the purport of the definition of the good life [stated above]. When I said that the good life consists of love guided by knowledge, the desire which prompted me was the desire to live such a life as far as possible, and to see others living it; and the logical content of the statement is that, in a community where men live in this way, more desires will be satisfied than will be satisfied in one where there is less love or less knowledge. I do not mean that such a life is 'virtuous' or that its opposite is 'sinful', for these are conceptions which seem to me to have no scientific justification.

19

SCIENCE AND ETHICS
Chapter IX of *Religion and Science* 1935

Reprinted from *Religion and Science* by Bertrand Russell
(1935) by permission of Oxford University Press. After
flirting with emotivism for over twenty years, Russell
finally came out with an unequivocal statement of the
theory in 1935, two years after Barnes' 'A suggestion about
value' (Barnes 1933: 241), but one year before Ayer's
Language, Truth and Logic of 1936. (When Russell reviewed
Language, Truth and Logic he did not see fit to mention
Ayer's emotivism, which to many readers was the book's
most sensational feature. To Russell emotivism was not a
novelty, and hence not something to make a fuss about
(*CPBR* vol. 10: 331–3).)

Russell was a warrior in the battle between science and
religion, and *Religion and Science* is a polemical little book
in which the superstitious follies of religion are derided
and the triumphs of scientific rationality are celebrated.
(The follies of religion are real enough, but the rationality
of the science is somewhat exaggerated.) Why did Russell
choose *this* book for an explicit statement of emotivism?
Because he wanted to deal with an argument put about by
a group of liberal theologians and their scientific camp-
followers on the BBC. The idea is that *science is not enough*
and that in some sense it needs to be supplemented by religion. Specifically, science has nothing to say about *values*,
though it may be of use in bringing about valuable ends.
Russell admits that science has nothing to say about values
but denies that there is a special realm of truth or knowledge accessible to religion but not to science. To make this
stick he must develop an account of value judgements
which is non-cognitive in a double sense – it must
preclude the possibility of ethical knowledge by precluding
the possibility of truth. The error theory would do the

131

trick, but this has been rejected. Instead we get a form of emotivism. The propositional form of value judgements (or at least of judgements about what is good or bad in itself) is misleading. Really they are in the optative mood. What 'X is good in itself' *means* is 'Would that everyone desired X!' The speaker *expresses* his (or her) desire but does not *state* that he (or she) has it. The fact that the speaker desires everyone to desire X can be inferred from what the speaker says, but it is not part of what the speaker is saying (a distinction that goes back to 1893 and Paper 3). Value judgements are not autobiographical remarks even though they may provide the basis for biographical inferences. Now, value judgements are neither true nor false, and since they cannot be true, they cannot be *known*. Hence the fact that they cannot be known by scientific means does not show that there is some special realm of fact to which science does not have access. Religious teachers cannot plume themselves on their expertise in matters of value. For where there are no facts, there can be no expertise.

This new theory is remarkably similar to that of 'Is ethics a branch of empirical psychology?' (Paper 10). In that paper, the good is defined as what we (I, the speaker?) desire to desire, in that to say that X is good is to say that we (or I, the speaker) desire to desire X. In *Religion and Science* the speaker does not *state* that he (or she) desires to desire X, but he (or she) does *express* a desire that *we*, collectively, should desire X. The Russell of the 1930s, it seems, has not entirely forgotten the Russell of the 1890s.

Russell is sometimes dismissed (if he is considered at all) as a mere forerunner of later emotivists such as Ayer and Stevenson whose theories are more highly developed. But in some respects the theory of *Religion and Science* is actually *better* than that of Russell's successors.

1   In the theories of Ayer and Stevenson the emotion that is expressed is either *approval* or *disapproval*. But what is it to *approve* of X? Surely it is to think or feel that X is good or right. In which case, to say that 'X is good' is used to express approval is to say that 'X is good' is used to express the feeling that X is good – an obvious and vicious circularity. Since Russell's value judgements express *desires* rather than feelings of approval, he is immune to this objection.

2   Russell distinguishes, as Stevenson sometimes does not, between *expressing* an emotion and stating that you have it. Because he fails to make this distinction,

Stevenson in his 'First Pattern of Analysis' is led to the view that 'X is good' means, in part, the *statement* 'I approve of X' (Stevenson 1944: 20–36 and 81–110). If this were correct, and I said 'X is good', you could prove me wrong by showing that I disapproved of X. In fact, this would only show that I was a hypocrite – a point noted by Ayer (Ayer 1946: 109). It is true that Stevenson subsequently mended his ways under the influence of G. E. Moore (Stevenson 1963: 210–14), but if he had attended to Russell in the first place he would not have had any ways to mend.

3   It is sometimes suggested that if moral judgements merely express feelings of approval and disapproval, they cannot contradict one another. Since 'X is bad' and 'X is good', when said by different people, plainly *do* contradict one another, emotivism must be false. Stevenson and Ayer employ various dodges to deal with this difficulty, but whether or not they succeed, it is plain that Russell is immune. Desires can conflict if they cannot both be fulfilled – if they are not *compossible* in Russell's phrase. Thus sentences *expressing* those desires – sentences in the optative – can also contradict one another, if the desires expressed cannot both be satisfied. 'Would that everyone desired X!' ('X is good') and 'Would that everyone desired X not to be!' ('X is bad') cannot both be fulfilled (except in the event of everybody's having inconsistent desires). Thus they *do* contradict one another, even if they do not contradict one another in quite the *right way*.

4   According to Stevenson, validity is to be defined in terms of truth. This means that ethical judgements cannot figure in valid arguments since they cannot be true or false (at least with respect to their emotive meanings). (See Stevenson 1944: 154–9. I simplify for the sake of brevity.) Yet we do seem to distinguish between valid and invalid arguments in ethics. Hence Stevenson's version of emotivism is false. Russell's theory is immune to this objection too. For it is easy to define a concept of logical consequence that applies to optatives. An optative sentence B is the consequence of a set of optative sentences A and a (possibly empty) set of factual sentences C, if and only if the desires expressed in A cannot be fulfilled under the circumstances described in C unless the desire expressed by B is fulfilled too. An optative argument is valid if the conclusion is an optative consequence of

the premises, invalid otherwise. Thus there can be valid and invalid arguments in ethics and logical relations between ethical judgements.

However, there is a broadly logical objection to emotivist (and non-cognitivist) theories to which Russell is not immune. This is due to P. T. Geach (the son of one of Russell's best students) who modestly attributes it to Frege (Geach 1960 and 1965). Consider the following argument:

1   It is good as an end that people cultivate the arts.
2   If it is good as an end that people cultivate the arts, then it is good as a means that they should have the funding to do so.
     Therefore:
3   It is good as a means that people should have the funding to cultivate the arts.

In this argument, the sentence 'it is good as an end that people cultivate the arts', occurs twice. In 1 it occurs by itself as an assertion; in 2 it occurs unasserted as part of a larger sentence. The problem, in a nutshell, is this. Russell's theory gives us an account of what the *first* asserted occurrence means but not of what the *second un*asserted occurrence amounts to. I could assent to 2 without desiring (or expressing the desire) that people desire that the arts should be cultivated. Since there are *many* such unasserted contexts where value judgements appear as parts of larger sentences, Russell's theory is, to say the least, radically incomplete. Nor is this all. If Russell's theory were to be beefed up so as to provide an account of what the second occurrence means, it would still face a strong *prima facie* objection. In the revised theory, the two occurrences of 'it is good as an end that people cultivate the arts' would have to be given *different* readings. They would not mean the same. In which case, the argument in which they appear would be invalid, since it would rest on an equivocation. (Words must retain a constant meaning in an argument if validity is to be maintained.) But since the argument plainly *is* valid, the beefed-up theory would have to be false. Blackburn and Gibbard, the most prominent modern emotivists (or 'expressivists' as they are nowadays known), wrestle mightily with this problem but, in my opinion, neither comes off the victor. (See Blackburn 1984: 181–222, Blackburn 1993: 182–97, Gibbard 1990: 183–204, Hurley 1989: 175–85 and Dummett 1981: 295–363.)

Russell's theory faces two other problems. The first is that he provides no good reason to believe it. He appeals to the 'complete impossibility of finding any arguments to prove that this or that has intrinsic value'. But as he himself had argued, 'the difficulty in discovering the truth does not prove there is no truth to be discovered' (Russell 1966: 20). The second problem is that value judgements certainly *look* like propositions and are normally taken to be capable of truth and falsity. (This is less so now than it was in Russell's day, but this is partly because of the influence of non-cognitivists such as Russell.) For some reason we have disguised these optatives as indicatives, and then, taken in by this disguise, have fondly supposed them to be true or false. *Factual* error on the part of human beings is not at all surprising, but it does seem a little odd that we should have so radically misunderstood our own concepts.

Those who maintain the insufficiency of science, as we have seen in the last two chapters, appeal to the fact that science has nothing to say about 'values'. This I admit; but when it is inferred that ethics contains truths which cannot be proved or disproved by science, I disagree. The matter is one on which it is not altogether easy to think clearly, and my own views on it are quite different from what they were thirty years ago. But it is necessary to be clear about it if we are to appraise such arguments as those in support of Cosmic Purpose. As there is no consensus of opinion about ethics, it must be understood that what follows is my personal belief, not the dictum of science.

The study of ethics, traditionally, consists of two parts, one concerned with moral rules, the other with what is good on its own account. Rules of conduct, many of which have a ritual origin, play a great part in the lives of savages and primitive peoples. It is forbidden to eat out of the chief's dish, or to seethe the kid in its mother's milk; it is commanded to offer sacrifices to the gods, which, at a certain stage of development, are thought most acceptable if they are human beings. Other moral rules, such as the prohibition of murder and theft, have a more obvious social utility, and survive the decay of the primitive theological systems with which they were originally associated. But as men grow more reflective there is a tendency to lay less stress on rules and more on states of mind. This comes from two sources – philosophy and mystical religion. We are all familiar with passages in the prophets and the gospels, in which purity of heart is set above meticulous observance of the Law; and St. Paul's famous praise of charity, or love, teaches the same principle. The same thing will be found in all great mystics, Christian and non-Christian: what they value is a state of mind, out of which, as they hold, right conduct must ensue; rules seem to them external, and insufficiently adaptable to circumstances.

One of the ways in which the need of appealing to external rules of conduct has been avoided has been the belief in 'conscience', which has been especially important in Protestant ethics. It has been supposed that God reveals to each human heart what is right and what is wrong, so that, in order to avoid sin, we have only to listen to the inner voice. There are, however, two difficulties in this theory: first, that conscience says different things to different people; secondly, that the study of the unconscious has given us an understanding of the mundane causes of conscientious feelings.

As to the different deliverances of conscience: George III's conscience told him that he must not grant Catholic Emancipation, as, if he did, he would have committed perjury in taking the Coronation Oath, but later monarchs have had no such scruples. Conscience leads some to condemn the spoliation of the rich by the poor, as advocated by communists; and others to condemn exploitation of the poor by the rich, as practised by capitalists. It tells one man that he ought to defend his country in case of invasion, while it tells another that all participation in warfare is wicked. During the War, the authorities, few of whom had studied ethics, found conscience very puzzling, and were led to some curious decisions, such as that a man might have conscientious scruples against fighting himself, but not against working on the fields so as to make possible the conscription of another man. They held also that, while conscience might disapprove of all war, it could not, failing that extreme position, disapprove of the war then in progress. Those who, for whatever reason, thought it wrong to fight, were compelled to state their position in terms of this somewhat primitive and unscientific conception of 'conscience'.

The diversity in the deliverances of conscience is what is to be expected when its origin is understood. In early youth, certain classes of acts meet with approval, and others with disapproval; and by the normal process of association, pleasure and discomfort gradually attach themselves to the acts, and not merely to the approval and disapproval respectively produced by them. As time goes on, we may forget all about our early moral training, but we shall still feel uncomfortable about certain kinds of actions, while others will

give us a glow of virtue. To introspection, these feelings are mysterious, since we no longer remember the circumstances which
originally caused them; and therefore it is natural to attribute them
to the voice of God in the heart. But in fact conscience is a product
of education, and can be trained to approve or disapprove, in the
great majority of mankind, as educators may see fit. While, therefore, it is right to wish to liberate ethics from external moral rules,
this can hardly be satisfactorily achieved by means of the notion of
'conscience'.

Philosophers, by a different road, have arrived at a different position in which, also, moral rules of conduct have a subordinate place.
They have framed the concept of the Good, by which they mean
(roughly speaking) that which, in itself and apart from its consequences, we should wish to see existing – or, if they are theists, that
which is pleasing to God. Most people would agree that happiness is
preferable to unhappiness, friendliness to unfriendliness, and so on.
Moral rules, according to this view, are justified if they promote the
existence of what is good on its own account, but not otherwise. The
prohibition of murder, in the vast majority of cases, can be justified
by its effects, but the practice of burning widows on their husband's
funeral pyre cannot. The former rule, therefore, should be retained,
but not the latter. Even the best moral rules, however, will have *some*
exceptions, since no class of actions *always* has bad results. We have
thus three different senses in which an act may be ethically
commendable: (1) it may be in accordance with the received moral
code; (2) it may be sincerely intended to have good effects; (3) it may
in fact have good effects. The third sense, however, is generally
considered inadmissible in morals. According to orthodox theology,
Judas Iscariot's act of betrayal had good consequences, since it was
necessary for the Atonement; but it was not on this account laudable.

Different philosophers have formed different conceptions of the
Good. Some hold that it consists in the knowledge and love of God;
others in universal love; others in the enjoyment of beauty; and yet
others in pleasure. The Good once defined, the rest of ethics follows:
we ought to act in the way we believe most likely to create as much
good as possible, and as little as possible of its correlative evil. The
framing of moral rules, so long as the ultimate Good is supposed
known, is a matter for science. For example: should capital punishment be inflicted for theft, or only for murder, or not at all? Jeremy
Bentham, who considered pleasure to be the Good, devoted himself
to working out what criminal code would most promote pleasure,
and concluded that it ought to be much less severe than that

prevailing in his day. All this, except the proposition that pleasure is the Good, comes within the sphere of science.

But when we try to be definite as to what we mean when we say that this or that is 'the Good', we find ourselves involved in very great difficulties. Bentham's creed that pleasure is the Good roused furious opposition, and was said to be a pig's philosophy. Neither he nor his opponents could advance any argument. In a scientific question, evidence can be adduced on both sides, and in the end one side is seen to have the better case – or, if this does not happen, the question is left undecided. But in a question as to whether this or that is the ultimate Good, there is no evidence either way; each disputant can only appeal to his own emotions, and employ such rhetorical devices as shall rouse similar emotions in others.

Take, for example, a question which has come to be important in practical politics. Bentham held that one man's pleasure has the same ethical importance as another man's, provided the quantities are equal; and on this ground he was led to advocate democracy. Nietzsche, on the contrary, held that only the great man can be regarded as important on his own account, and that the bulk of mankind are only means to his well-being. He viewed ordinary men as many people view animals: he thought it justifiable to make use of them, not for their own good, but for that of the superman, and this view has since been adopted to justify the abandonment of democracy. We have here a sharp disagreement of great practical importance, but we have absolutely no means, of a scientific or intellectual kind, by which to persuade either party that the other is in the right. There are, it is true, ways of altering men's opinions on such subjects, but they are all emotional, not intellectual.

Questions as to 'values' – that is to say, as to what is good or bad on its own account, independently of its effects – lie outside the domain of science, as the defenders of religion emphatically assert. I think that in this they are right, but I draw the further conclusion, which they do not draw, that questions as to 'values' lie wholly outside the domain of knowledge. That is to say, when we assert that this or that has 'value', we are giving expression to our own emotions, not to a fact which would still be true if our personal feelings were different. To make this clear, we must try to analyse the conception of the Good.

It is obvious, to begin with, that the whole idea of good and bad has some connection with *desire*. *Prima facie*, anything that we all desire is 'good', and anything that we all dread is 'bad'. If we all agreed in our desires, the matter could be left there, but unfortunately our desires conflict. If I say 'what I want is good', my neighbour will say 'No, what *I* want.' Ethics is an attempt – though not, I think, a successful one – to escape from this subjectivity. I shall naturally try to show, in my dispute with my neighbour, that my desires have some quality which makes them more worthy of respect than his. If I want to preserve a right of way, I shall appeal to the landless inhabitants of the district; but he, on his side, will appeal to the landowners. I shall say: 'What use is the beauty of the countryside if no one sees it?' He will retort: 'What beauty will be left if trippers are allowed to spread devastation?' Each tries to enlist allies by showing that his own desires harmonize with those of other people. When this is obviously impossible, as in the case of a burglar, the man is condemned by public opinion, and his ethical status is that of a sinner.

Ethics is thus closely related to politics: it is an attempt to bring the collective desires of a group to bear upon individuals; or, conversely, it is an attempt by an individual to cause his desires to become those of his group. This latter is, of course, only possible if his desires are not too obviously opposed to the general interest: the burglar will hardly attempt to persuade people that he is doing them good, though plutocrats make similar attempts, and often succeed. When our desires are for things which all can enjoy in common, it seems not unreasonable to hope that others may concur; thus the philosopher who values Truth, Goodness and Beauty seems, to himself, to be not merely expressing his own desires, but pointing the way to the welfare of all mankind. Unlike the burglar, he is able to believe that his desires are for something that has value in an impersonal sense.

Ethics is an attempt to give universal, and not merely personal, importance to certain of our desires. I say 'certain' of our desires, because in regard to some of them this is obviously impossible, as we saw in the case of the burglar. The man who makes money on the Stock Exchange by means of some secret knowledge does not wish others to be equally well informed: Truth (in so far as he values it) is for him a private possession, not the general human good that it is for the philosopher. The philosopher may, it is true, sink to the level of the stockjobber, as when he claims priority for a discovery. But this is a lapse: in his purely philosophic capacity, he wants only to enjoy the contemplation of Truth, in doing which he in no way interferes with others who wish to do likewise.

To seem to give universal importance to our desires – which is the business of ethics – may be attempted from two points of view, that of the legislator, and that of the preacher. Let us take the legislator first.

I will assume, for the sake of argument, that the legislator is personally disinterested. That is to say, when he recognizes one of his desires as being concerned only with his own welfare, he does not let it influence him in framing the laws; for example, his code is not designed to increase his personal fortune. But he has other desires which seem to him impersonal. He may believe in an ordered hierarchy from king to peasant, or from mine-owner to black indentured labourer. He may believe that women should be submissive to men. He may hold that the spread of knowledge in the lower classes is dangerous. And so on and so on. He will then, if he can, so construct his code that conduct promoting the ends which he values shall, as far as possible, be in accordance with individual self-interest; and he will establish a system of moral instruction which will, where it succeeds, make men feel wicked if they pursue other purposes than his.[1] Thus 'virtue' will come to be in fact, though not in subjective estimation, subservience to the desires of the legislator, in so far as he himself considers these desires worthy to be universalized.

The standpoint and method of the preacher are necessarily somewhat different, because he does not control the machinery of the State, and therefore cannot produce an artificial harmony between his desires and those of others. His only method is to try to rouse in others the same desires that he feels himself, and for this purpose his appeal must be to the emotions. Thus Ruskin caused people to like Gothic architecture, not by argument, but by the moving effect of rhythmical prose. *Uncle Tom's Cabin* helped to make people think slavery an evil by causing them to imagine themselves as slaves. Every attempt to persuade people that something is good (or bad) in itself, and not merely in its effects, depends upon the art of rousing feelings, not upon an appeal to evidence. In every case the preacher's skill consists in creating in others emotions similar to his own – or

1 Compare the following advice by a contemporary of Aristotle (Chinese, not Greek): 'A ruler should not listen to those who believe in people having opinions of their own and in the importance of the individual. Such teachings cause men to withdraw to quiet places and hide away in caves or on mountains, there to rail at the prevailing government, sneer at those in authority, belittle the importance of rank and emoluments, and despise all who hold official posts' (Waley 1958: 37).

dissimilar, if he is a hypocrite. I am not saying this as a criticism of the preacher, but as an analysis of the essential character of his activity.

When a man says 'this is good in itself', he seems to be making a statement, just as much as if he said 'this is square' or 'this is sweet'. I believe this to be a mistake. I think that what the man really means is: 'I wish everybody to desire this', or rather 'Would that everybody desired this.' If what he says is interpreted as a statement, it is merely an affirmation of his own personal wish; if, on the other hand, it is interpreted in a general way, it states nothing, but merely desires something. The wish, as an occurrence, is personal, but what it desires is universal. It is, I think, this curious inter-locking of the particular and the universal which has caused so much confusion in ethics.

The matter may perhaps become clearer by contrasting an ethical sentence with one which makes a statement. If I say 'all Chinese are Buddhists', I can be refuted by the production of a Chinese Christian or Mohammedan. If I say 'I believe that all Chinese are Buddhists,' I cannot be refuted by any evidence from China, but only by evidence that I do not believe what I say; for what I am asserting is only something about my own state of mind. If, now, a philosopher says 'Beauty is good', I may interpret him as meaning either 'Would that everybody loved the beautiful' (which corres-ponds to 'all Chinese are Buddhists') or 'I wish that everybody loved the beautiful' (which corresponds to 'I believe that all Chinese are Buddhists'). The first of these makes no assertion, but expresses a wish; since it affirms nothing, it is logically impossible that there should be evidence for or against it, or for it to possess either truth or falsehood. The second sentence, instead of being merely optative, does make a statement, but it is one about the philosopher's state of mind, and it could only be refuted by evidence that he does not have the wish he says he does. This second sentence does not belong to ethics, but to psychology or biography. The first sentence, which does belong to ethics, expresses a desire for something but asserts nothing.

Ethics, if the above analysis is correct, contains no statements, whether true or false, but consists of desires of a certain general kind, namely such as are concerned with the desires of mankind in general – and of gods, angels and devils, if they exist. Science can discuss the causes of desires, and the means for realizing them, but it cannot contain any genuinely ethical sentences, because it is concerned with what is true or false.

The theory which I have been advocating is a form of the doctrine which is called the 'subjectivity' of values. This doctrine consists in maintaining that, if two men differ about values, there is not a disagreement as to any kind of truth, but a difference of taste. If one man says 'oysters are good' and another says '*I* think they are bad,' we recognize that there is nothing to argue about. The theory in question holds that all differences as to values are of this sort, although we do not naturally think them so when we are dealing with matters that seem to us more exalted than oysters. The chief ground for adopting this view is the complete impossibility of finding any arguments to prove that this or that has intrinsic value. If we all agreed, we might hold that we know values by intuition. We cannot *prove*, to a colour-blind man, that grass is green and not red. But there are various ways of proving to him that he lacks a power of discrimination which most men possess, whereas in the case of values there are no such ways, and disagreements are much more frequent than in the case of colours. Since no way can be even imagined for deciding a difference as to values, the conclusion is forced upon us that the difference is one of tastes, not one as to any objective truth.

The consequences of this doctrine are considerable. In the first place, there can be no such thing as 'sin' in any absolute sense; what one man calls 'sin' another may call 'virtue,' and though they may dislike each other on account of this difference, neither can convict the other of intellectual error. Punishment cannot be justified on the ground that the criminal is 'wicked', but only on the ground that he has behaved in a way which others wish to discourage. Hell, as a place of punishment for sinners, becomes quite irrational.

In the second place, it is impossible to uphold the way of speaking about values which is common among those who believe in Cosmic Purpose. Their argument is that certain things which have been evolved are 'good', and therefore the world must have had a purpose which was ethically admirable. In the language of subjective values, this argument becomes: 'Some things in the world are to our liking, and therefore they must have been created by a Being with our tastes, Whom, therefore, we also like, and Who, consequently, is good.' Now it seems fairly evident that, if creatures having likes and dislikes were to exist at all, they were pretty sure to like *some* things in their environment, since otherwise they would find life intolerable. Our values have been evolved along with the rest of our constitution, and nothing as to any original purpose can be inferred from the fact that they are what they are.

Those who believe in 'objective' values often contend that the view which I have been advocating has immoral consequences. This seems to me to be due to faulty reasoning. There are, as has already been said, certain ethical consequences of the doctrine of subjective values, of which the most important is the rejection of vindictive punishment and the notion of 'sin'. But the more general consequences which are feared, such as the decay of all sense of moral obligation, are not to be logically deduced. Moral obligation, if it is to influence conduct, must consist not merely of a belief, but of a desire. The desire, I may be told, is the desire to be 'good' in a sense which I no longer allow. But when we analyse the desire to be 'good' it generally resolves itself into a desire to be approved, or, alternatively, to act so as to bring about certain general consequences which we desire. We have wishes which are not purely personal, and, if we had not, no amount of ethical teaching would influence our conduct except through fear of disapproval. The sort of life that most of us admire is one which is guided by large impersonal desires; now such desires can, no doubt, be encouraged by example, education, and knowledge, but they can hardly be created by the mere abstract belief that they are good, nor discouraged by an analysis of what is meant by the word 'good'.

When we contemplate the human race, we may desire that it should be happy, or healthy, or intelligent, or warlike, and so on. Any one of these desires, if it is strong, will produce its own morality; but if we have no such general desires, our conduct, whatever our ethic may be, will only serve social purposes in so far as self-interest and the interests of society are in harmony. It is the business of wise institutions to create such harmony as far as possible, and for the rest, whatever may be our theoretical definition of value, we must depend upon the existence of impersonal desires. When you meet a man with whom you have a fundamental ethical disagreement – for example, if you think that all men count equally, while he selects a class as alone important – you will find yourself no better able to cope with him if you believe in objective values than if you do not. In either case, you can only influence his conduct through influencing his desires: if you succeed in that, his ethic will change, and if not, not.

Some people feel that if a general desire, say for the happiness of mankind, has not the sanction of absolute good, it is in some way irrational. This is due to a lingering belief in objective values. A desire cannot, in itself, be either rational or irrational. It may conflict with other desires, and therefore lead to unhappiness; it may rouse opposition in others, and therefore be incapable of gratification. But it cannot be considered 'irrational' merely because no reason can be given for feeling it. We may desire A because it is a means to B, but in the end, when we have done with mere means, we must come to something which we desire for no reason, but not on that account 'irrationally'. All systems of ethics embody the desires of those who advocate them, but this fact is concealed in a mist of words. Our desires are, in fact, more general and less purely selfish than many moralists imagine; if it were not so, no theory of ethics would make moral improvement possible. It is, in fact, not by ethical theory, but by the cultivation of large and generous desires through intelligence, happiness, and freedom from fear, that men can be brought to act more than they do at present in a manner that is consistent with the general happiness of mankind. Whatever our definition of the 'Good', and whether we believe it to be subjective or objective, those who do not desire the happiness of mankind will not endeavour to further it, while those who do desire it will do what they can to bring it about.

I conclude that, while it is true that science cannot decide questions of value, that is because they cannot be intellectually decided at all, and lie outside the realm of truth and falsehood. Whatever knowledge is attainable, must be attained by scientific methods; and what science cannot discover, mankind cannot know.

20

REPLY TO CRITICISMS
Extract 1944

Reprinted from Schilpp, P.A. ed. 1944a, *The Philosophy of Bertrand Russell*: 720–5, (Library of Living Philosophers series) by permission of Open Court Publishing Company. La Salle, Illinois, © 1944 The Library of Living Philosophers. See also *CPBR* vol. 11: 47–52. In the late 1930s Paul Arthur Schilpp (1897–1993) conceived the scheme of the Library of Living Philosophers. The idea was to ascertain (or at least clarify) what eminent philosophers meant, and what they might say to obvious objections, by putting critical questions to them while they were still alive. Each volume contains an intellectual autobiography by the eminent thinker in question, a set of critical essays by various hands and finally a set of replies to criticisms by the subject. The format has since been widely imitated.

Russell's 'Reply' reaffirms his belief in the emotivism of *Religion and Science,* and argues that emotivism is not inconsistent with moral vehemence or moral commitment. The moral vocabulary provides us with the verbal machinery to express certain preferences. Since he *has* the relevant preferences, he is surely entitled to use this machinery to express them. However, he *feels* that there is more to his belief that it would be wrong to introduce bull-fighting into America than the desire that people should not desire it. He *feels* that such a desire would be 'right' ('whatever that may mean'). It was presumably in deference to this feeling that he went on to devise the theory of *Human Society in Ethics and Politics* (Paper 21) in which he endeavours to inject a little objectivity into ethics.

Both Mr. Brightman's essay on my philosophy of religion and Mr. Buchler's on my ethics raise certain questions as to which I must first attempt to make clear what my own views are.

I am accused of inconsistency, perhaps justly, because, although I hold ultimate ethical valuations to be subjective, I nevertheless allow myself emphatic opinions on ethical questions. If there is an inconsistency, it is one that I cannot get rid of without insincerity; moreover, an inconsistent system may well contain less falsehood than a consistent one. For my own sake, as well as for that of the reader, I propose to examine this question somewhat fully.

In the first place, I am not prepared to forego my right to feel and express ethical passions; no amount of logic, even though it be my own, will persuade me that I ought to do so. There are some men whom I admire, and others whom I think vile; some political systems seem to me tolerable, others an abomination. Pleasure in the spectacle of cruelty horrifies me, and I am not ashamed of the fact that it does. I am no more prepared to give up all this than I am to give up the multiplication table.

The trouble arises through the subjectivity of ethical valuations. Let us see what this amounts to.

In practice, when two people disagree as to whether a certain kind of conduct is right, the difference of opinion can usually, though not always, be reduced to a difference as to means. This is a question in the realm of science. Suppose, for example, one person advocates capital punishment whereas another condemns it: they will probably argue as to its efficacy as a deterrent, which is a matter at least theoretically capable of being decided by statistics. Such cases raise no theoretical difficulty. But there are cases that are more difficult. Christianity, Kant, and Bentham maintain that all human beings are to count alike; Nietzsche says that most of them should be merely means to an aristocracy. He would not assent to the modern development of this doctrine, that good consists of pleasure to a German or pain to a Jew, and evil consists of pleasure to a Jew or pain to a German, but from the standpoint of ethical theory his doctrine raises the same problems as does that of the Nazis.

Let us consider two theories as to the good. One says, like Christianity, Kant, and democracy: whatever the good may be, any one man's enjoyment of it has the same value as any other man's. The other says: there is a certain sub-class of mankind – white men, Germans, gentiles, or what not – whose good or evil alone counts in an estimation of ends; other men are only to be considered as means. I shall suppose that A takes the first view, and B the second. What can either say to convict the other of error? I can only imagine arguments that would be strictly irrelevant. A might say: If you ignore the interests of a large part of mankind, they will rebel and murder you. B might say: The portion of mankind that I favour is so much superior to the rest in skill and courage that it is sure to rule in any case, so why not frankly acknowledge the true state of affairs? Each of these is an argument as to means, not as to ends. When such arguments are swept away, there remains, so far as I can see, nothing to be said except for each party to express moral disapproval of the other. Those who reject this conclusion advance no argument against it except that it is unpleasant.

The question arises: What am I to mean when I say that this or that is good as an end? To make the argument definite, let us take pleasure as the thing to be discussed. If one man affirms and another denies that pleasure is good *per se*, what is the difference between them? My contention is that the two men differ as to what they desire, but not as to what they assert, since they assert nothing. I maintain that neither asserts anything except derivatively, in the sense in which everything we say may be taken as affirming something about ourselves. If I say, 'it will rain tomorrow', I mean to make a meteorological assertion, but to a sceptical listener I only convey that I believe something about tomorrow's weather. There is a similar difference between expressing a desire and stating that I feel the desire. An ethical judgment, according to me, expresses a desire, but only inferentially implies that I feel this desire, just as a statement in the indicative expresses a belief, but inferentially implies that I have this belief.

I do not think that an ethical judgment *merely* expresses a desire; I agree with Kant that it must have an element of universality. I should interpret, 'A is good' as 'Would that all men desired A'. This *expresses* a wish, but does not *assert* one except by implication.

Mr. Buchler asks what I mean by saying that the good is primarily the desired; what I mean is that it is to be defined in terms of desire, and that to define it as the desired is a first step towards a correct definition.

Mr. Buchler maintains that when I say the good life is inspired by love and guided by knowledge, I cannot mean that I wish everybody desired men to live such a life. But let us take the question psychologically. What does the reader learn from reading this sentence? He certainly learns that I wish men lived so, and he may gather that I mean to express something more than this wish. But what is this more? I cannot see that it is anything more than the wish that others should share my wish.

I am quite at a loss to understand why any one should be surprised at my expressing vehement ethical judgments. By my own theory, I am, in doing so, expressing vehement desires as to the desires of mankind; I feel such desires, so why not express them?

What, I imagine, is mainly felt to be lacking in my ethical theory is the element of command, in fact the 'categorical imperative'. Ethics is a social force which helps a society to cohere, and every one who utters an ethical judgment feels himself in some sense a legislator or a judge, according to the degree of generality of the judgment in question. It would be easy to develop a political theory of ethics, starting from the definition: 'The good is the satisfaction of the desires of the holders of power'. In a genuine democracy, if such a thing were possible, the consequences of this definition would not be shocking to democrats. Inductively, it would cover the historical facts admirably; it would explain, for instance, why it was wicked for women to smoke until they got the vote, and then ceased to be so. It is the theory advanced by Thrasymachus in the *Republic*, and 'refuted' by the Platonic Socrates with a dose of dishonest sophistry which is large even for him. It is the theory held, though not avowed, by most schoolmasters and almost all education authorities. It may be inferred from the moral code of any community except in times of revolution. I do not, however, adopt this ethic, because I dislike the white man's burden, the inequalities of economic power, and other manifestations of the ethics of governing cliques.

All this, however, may seem beside the point. The point is that an ethical judgment ought – so it is felt – to have the same kind of objectivity as a judgment of fact. A judgment of fact – so I hold – is capable of a property called 'truth', which it has or does not have quite independently of what any one may think about it. Very many American philosophers, perhaps most, disagree with me about this, and hold that there is no such property as 'truth'. For them the problem that I am considering does not exist. But for me it is necessary to acknowledge that I see no property, analogous to 'truth', that belongs or does not belong to an ethical judgment. This, it must be admitted, puts ethics in a different category from science.

I cannot see, however, that this difference is as important as it is sometimes thought to be. Take, for example, the question of persuasion. In science there is a technique of persuasion which is so effective that controversies seldom last very long. This technique consists of an appeal to evidence, not to the emotions. But as soon as a question becomes in any way entangled in politics, theoretical methods become inadequate. Are coloured people congenitally less intelligent than white people? Are there national characteristics distinguishing individuals of the various nations? Is there any anatomical evidence that women's brains are inferior to men's? Such questions are normally decided by rhetoric, brass bands, and broken heads. Nevertheless, the detached scientist, if he exists, may, neglected and alone, persist in applying scientific methods even to questions that rouse passion.

In the matter of persuasion it is often overlooked that the advocate of scientific methods must – since persuading is a practical activity – base himself on the ethical principle that it is better to believe truth than falsehood. In my interpretation, this means that the advocate of scientific methods wishes that men believed truly, and wishes that others shared this wish. Clearly he will not, in fact, advocate scientific methods unless he has this wish. Propaganda agencies are different: they wish people to have certain beliefs, which they may themselves entertain, but which they seldom wish to see subjected to a scientific scrutiny.

Persuasion in ethical questions is necessarily different from persuasion in scientific matters. According to me, the person who judges that A is good is wishing others to feel certain desires. He will therefore, if not hindered by other activities, try to rouse these desires in other people if he thinks he knows how to do so. This is the purpose of preaching, and it was my purpose in the various books in which I have expressed ethical opinions. The art of presenting one's desires persuasively is totally different from that of logical demonstration, but it is equally legitimate.

All of this may be true, I shall be told, *provided your desires are good*; if they are evil, rhetoric in their defence is an art of the devil. But what are 'good' desires? Are they anything more than desires that you share? Certainly there *seems* to be something more. Suppose, for example, that some one were to advocate the introduction of bull-fighting in this country. In opposing the proposal, I should *feel*, not only that I was expressing my desires, but that my desires in the matter are *right*, whatever that may mean. As a matter of argument, I can, I think, show that I am not guilty of any logical inconsistency in holding to the above interpretation of ethics and at the same time expressing strong ethical preferences. But in feeling I am not satisfied. I can only say that, while my own opinions as to ethics do not satisfy me, other people's satisfy me still less.

A few matters of detail remain to be noted in Mr. Buchler's essay. He seems to think that he makes a point against me by pointing out that people often do not know what they desire. From my account of desire in *Analysis of Mind* he will see that I regard it as exceptional when people know what they desire. But their desires influence their behaviour (or, better, are exemplified in their behaviour) just as much when unconscious as when conscious.

He says that I am not concerned to make all human beings' desires coherent. I cannot understand what gave him this impression. The last chapter of *Social Reconstruction* is entirely, or almost entirely, occupied with the integration of desires, first in the individual, then in the world. The wish to harmonize desires is the chief motive of my political and social beliefs, from the nursery to the international state.

Finally, he says that I am courageous, but not judicious, and that I am lacking in *sophrosyne*. This, I think, is just. I will only add that *sophrosyne* is not a quality I wish to possess; I associate it with limited sympathies and a secure income. At one time I lived in Malaga; a few months after I ceased to do so, a large part of the civilian population were exterminated from the air while trying to escape along a narrow coastal road. Things just as bad are happening constantly. During the last war, the War Office sent for me and exhorted me to preserve a sense of humour. With great difficulty I refrained from saying that the casualty lists made me split my sides with laughter. No, I will not be serene and above the battle; what is horrible I will see as horrible, and not as part of some blandly beneficent whole.

21

A COMPROMISE
SOLUTION?

Extracts from *Human Society in Ethics and Politics* 1954

Reprinted from *Human Society in Ethics and Politics* 25–8
and 110–18. These extracts represent Russell's attempt to
inject a little objectivity into ethics whilst retaining the
belief that moral judgements are somehow based on feeling
and desire. Though the book was published in 1954, the
relevant sections were written in 1945–6 and were originally intended for inclusion in *Human Knowledge: Its Scope
and Limits* (1948). He kept them back because he was not
sure whether ethics can properly be regarded as knowledge.
These facts are significant: the first, because it gives some
clue to his strategy, and the second, because it indicates
that he was not sure whether this strategy was a success.
Human Knowledge is an endeavour to establish a mind-
independent world on the basis of private perceptions.
Human Society is an attempt to establish an ethic that is
in some degree independent of *individual* minds on the
basis of subjective sentiments. But how is this to be done,
given that Russell was strongly inclined to adopt an
emotivist analysis of moral judgements?

At the time he was writing *Human Knowledge*, Russell
was very much preoccupied with Hume, though as an epis-
temic opponent rather than as a meta-ethical ally. Nevertheless, their aims in ethics were remarkably similar. In the
Enquiries, Hume, like Russell, sought to base an objective
(or at any rate, an intersubjective) ethic on feelings and
emotions, in his case, the sentiments of approbation and
disapprobation. David Hume (1711–76) was much more of
a moral conservative than Russell, but he, too, wanted to
arrive at an ethic with a certain amount of critical bite. He
did not just want to end up endorsing current norms since,
in so far as they were influenced by religion, he regarded

them as pernicious. How did Hume propose to do it? By means of a definition and an empirical research programme.

> The hypothesis which we embrace is plain. It maintains that morality is determined by sentiment. It *defines* [my italics] virtue to be *whatever mental action or quality gives to a spectator the pleasing sentiment of approbation*; and vice the contrary. We then proceed to examine a plain matter of fact, to wit, what actions have this influence.
>
> (Hume 1975: 289)

The definition bridges the gap between the Is of the matters of fact and the Ought of what constitutes virtue. However, the matter of fact is not quite so plain as Hume suggests, since it turns out that the 'spectator' is no ordinary joe but an *ideal observer*, someone whose moral sense (which supposedly we all share) operates at optimum. For this to happen the spectator requires access to the relevant information. This means that we cannot simply predict the reactions of the spectator by observing the reactions of humankind since humankind is often misinformed. However, this whole edifice rests on a definition which Hume obviously conceives of as reporting an ordinary truth of language. It also rests on the thesis that people share the same moral sensibility which can therefore be 'idealized' to serve as the criterion for virtue.

What about Russell? His theory, like Hume's, rests on a set of 'fundamental propositions and definitions':

1   Surveying the acts which arouse emotions of approval or disapproval, we find that, as a general rule, the acts which are approved of are those believed likely to have, on the balance, effects of certain kinds, while opposite effects are expected from acts that are disapproved of.
2   Effects that lead to approval are defined as 'good', and those leading to disapproval as 'bad'.
3   An act of which, on the available evidence, the effects are likely to be better than those of any other act that is possible in the circumstances is defined as 'right'; any other act is 'wrong'. What we 'ought' to do is, by definition, the act which is right.

'These definitions and propositions, if accepted [why 'if

accepted'?], provide a coherent body of propositions which are true (or false) in the same sense as if they were propositions of science.'

Now thesis 1 is simply the Sidgwickian thesis that common-sense moralities tend to solidify around rules which are believed to have generally beneficial consequences, where the benefit is to be cashed in terms of some conception of universal human welfare. It is a rather dubious thesis especially as Russell himself has admitted that a good many communities subscribe to moralities which discount the interests of large groups of people – women, slaves, foreigners, the low-born or whatever. However, Russell seems to want to limit this Sidgwickian claim to 'civilized' communities, and it may be that if we define 'civilization' sufficiently closely we can exclude communities with blatantly partial ethics. Thesis 2 purports to be a definition of 'good effects', but it is rather unspecific since it does not state whose approval is to determine goodness – people in general, people at their impartial best, or just the enlightened and well informed? Unless the class of approvers is narrowed down, the class of approved of effects will be too large and disparate to provide us with a basis for ethical decision making. And if being *dis*approved of means that an effect is *not* good, the class of good effects may shrink away to almost nothing, unless we take care to exclude those with perverse sensibilities from our ethical jury. For most effects will be disapproved of by *somebody*. But the real problem lies with thesis 3. It is a straightforwardly utilitarian or consequentialist definition of 'right' and 'ought' and, as such, palpably false. If it were true (as Russell, in effect, had pointed out in Paper 13), it would be a tautology to say that the right thing to do is the action that seems likely to produce the best consequences. This it is not.

The solution, I suggest, is to retain 1 pretty much as is, to retain 2 with the class of approvers more carefully specified, but to replace 3 with something like:

3a The right thing to do is defined as the action which an impartial, informed and non-superstitious spectator would approve of doing.

From 1 and 3a we then derive:

3b The right thing to do is that action which seems likely to produce the best effects.

And this provides the basis for the right kind of utilitarian ethic – at least, it does so if the ethical jury in 2 has been specified in such a way as to ensure that they approve of the right effects.

The trouble is that so far from being 'true in the same sense as if they were propositions of science', definitions 2 and 3a do not seem to be true at all, at least if they are regarded as reports of linguistic usage. Tell-tale phrases such as 'if they are accepted' suggest that Russell was aware of this. Perhaps they should be understood not as accounts of how we *do* talk but as *stipulative definitions*, recording Russell's resolution to speak in a particular manner. Or perhaps they are *persuasive definitions* (a term due to Stevenson), the aim being to redirect our attitudes by giving the words 'right' and 'good' a new (or at any rate, a more specific) factual meaning whilst retaining the emotive content (the connotations of approval). Either way, the definitions can be rejected without intellectual error, along with Russell's entire ethic. And what can be rejected without intellectual error hardly deserves the name of knowledge. Russell was not at all sure that there *was* such a thing as ethical knowledge and in extreme old age, he reverted to the unhappy emotivism of Paper 20. The reason, I suspect, is that he came to see that his definitions of 'right' and 'good' were intellectually optional.

Note that Russell simply takes for granted the thesis that he felt he had to argue for at length in 1899 – that the world was not good (except, perhaps potentially) before the sixth day when God created man and the other animals (Paper 12). Note too that Russell's reasoning on this topic involves a fallacy which he seemed to have seen through in 1922. It may be that we only moralize because we have desires. But it does not follow (as Russell seems to think) that a reference to desire (or any other emotion) is built into the meaning of the moral concepts. The *genesis* of a concept does not determine its *content* (Paper 17). This relates to a point made by Wiggins about subjectivist writers in general, which applies in particular to Russell. 'What traditional subjectivists have really wanted to convey is not so much definition as commentary. Chiefly they have wanted to persuade us that . . . [in ethics] . . . there is no appeal to anything that is more fundamental than actually possible human sentiments' (Wiggins 1987: 188). Russell does have a tendency to incorporate this comment into his definitions of the moral concepts.

[The problem]

Ethics differs from science in the fact that its fundamental data are feelings and emotions, not percepts. This is to be understood strictly; that is to say, the data are the feelings and emotions themselves, not the fact that we have them. The fact that we have them is a scientific fact like another, and we become aware of it by perception, in the usual scientific way. But an ethical judgment does not state a fact; it states, though often in a disguised form, some hope or fear, some desire or aversion, some love or hate. It should be enunciated in the optative or imperative mood, not in the indicative. The Bible says 'thou shalt love thy neighbour as thyself', and a modern man, oppressed with the spectacle of international discord, may say 'would that all men loved one another'; these are pure ethical sentences, which clearly cannot be proved or disproved merely by amassing facts.

That feelings are relevant to ethics is easily seen by considering the hypothesis of a purely material universe, consisting of matter without sentience. Such a universe would be neither good nor bad, and nothing in it would be right or wrong. When, in Genesis, God 'saw that it was good' before He had created life, we must suppose that the goodness depended either upon His emotions in contemplating His work, or upon the fitness of the inanimate world as an environment for sentient beings. If the sun were about to collide with another star, and the earth were about to be reduced to gas, we should judge the forthcoming cataclysm to be bad if we considered the existence of the human race good; but a similar cataclysm in a region without life would be merely interesting. Thus ethics is bound up with life, not as a physical process to be studied by the biochemist, but as made up of happiness and sorrow, hope and fear, and the other cognate pairs of opposites that make us prefer one sort of world to another.

But when the fundamental ethical importance of feeling and desire has been admitted, it still remains a question whether there is such a thing as ethical *knowledge*. 'Thou shalt not kill' is imperative, but 'murder is wicked' seems to be indicative, and to state something true or false. 'Would that all men were happy' is optative, but 'happiness is good' has the same grammatical form as 'Socrates is mortal'. Is this grammatical form misleading, or is there truth and falsehood in ethics as in science? If I say that Nero was a bad man, am I giving information, as I should be if I said that he was a Roman Emperor, or would what I say be more accurately expressed by the words: 'Nero? Oh fie!'? This question is not an easy one, and I do not think that any simple answer is possible.

There is another closely related question, and that is as to the subjectivity of ethical judgments. If I say that oysters are good, and you say they are nasty, we both understand that we are merely expressing our personal tastes, and that there is nothing to argue about. But when Nazis say that it is good to torture Jews, and we say that it is bad, we do not feel as if we were merely expressing a difference of taste; we are even willing to fight and die for our opinion, which we should not do to enforce our view about oysters. Whatever arguments may be advanced to show that the two cases are analogous, most people will remain convinced that there is a difference somewhere, though it may be difficult to say exactly what it is. I think this feeling, though not decisive, deserves respect, and should make us reluctant to accept at all readily the view that all ethical judgments are wholly subjective.

It may be said that if hopes and desires are fundamental in ethics, then everything in ethics must be subjective, since hopes and desires are so. But this argument is less conclusive than it sounds. The data of science are individual percepts, and these are far more subjective than common sense supposes; nevertheless, upon this basis the imposing edifice of impersonal science has been built up. This depends upon the fact that there are certain respects in which the percepts of the majority agree, and that the divergent percepts of the colour-blind and the victims of hallucinations can be ignored. It may be that there is some similar way of arriving at objectivity in ethics; if so, since it must involve appeal to the majority, it will take us from personal ethics into the sphere of politics, which is, in fact, very difficult to separate from ethics.

The separation of ethics from theology is more difficult than the analogous separation in the case of science. It is true that science has only emancipated itself after a long struggle. Until the latter half of the seventeenth century, it was commonly held that a man who did not believe in witchcraft must be an atheist, and there are still people who condemn evolution on theological grounds, but very many theologians now agree that nothing in science can shake the foundations of religious belief. In ethics the situation is different. Many traditional ethical concepts are difficult to interpret, and many traditional ethical beliefs are hard to justify, except on the assumption that there is a God or a World Spirit or at least an immanent Cosmic Purpose. I do not say that these interpretations and justifications are *impossible* without a theological basis, but I do say that without such a basis they lose persuasive force and the power of psychological compulsion.

It has always been one of the favourite arguments of the orthodox that without religion men would become wicked. The nineteenth-century British freethinkers, from Bentham to Henry Sidgwick, vehemently repudiated this argument, and their repudiation gained force from the fact that they were among the most virtuous men that have ever existed. But in the modern world, which has been shocked by the excesses of totalitarians who professed themselves unbelievers, the virtues of Victorian agnostics seem less conclusive, and may even be attributed to imperfect emancipation from the Christian tradition. The whole question whether ethics, in any socially adequate form, can be independent of theology, must therefore be re-examined, with more awareness of the deep possibilities of evil than was to be found among our grandfathers, who were kept cozy by their comfortable belief in rational progress.

[A tentative solution or is there ethical knowledge?]

We come now at last to the problem to which all our previous ethical discussions have been leading. The question may be put in dry technical language, or in language showing that it involves issues of great emotional importance. Let us begin with the latter.

If we say 'cruelty is wrong', or 'you ought to love your neighbour as yourself', are we saying something which has impersonal truth or falsehood, or are we merely expressing our own preferences? If we say 'pleasure is good and pain is bad', are we making a statement, or are we merely expressing an emotion which would be more correctly expressed in a different grammatical form, say 'Hurrah for pleasure, and away dull care'? When men dispute or go to war about a political issue, is there any sense in which one side is more in the right than the other, or is there merely a trial of strength? What is meant, if anything, by saying that a world in which human beings are happy is better than one in which they are unhappy? I, for one, find it intolerable to suppose that when I say 'cruelty is bad' I am merely saying 'I dislike cruelty', or something equally subjective. What I want to discuss is whether there is anything in ethics that is not, in the last analysis, subjective.

To put the same problem in more technical language: When we examine what purport to be ethical statements, we find that they differ from statements asserting matters of fact by the presence of one or both of two terms, 'ought' and 'good', or their synonyms. Are these terms, or equivalents of them, part of any minimum vocabulary of ethics? Or are they definable in terms of desires and emotions and feelings? And, if so, do they have essential reference to the desires and emotions and feelings of the person using the words, or have they a reference to the general desires and emotions and feelings of mankind? There are words such as 'I', 'here', 'now', which have a different meaning for each different person who uses them, or even on each different occasion when they are used. Such words I call 'egocentric'. Our question is: Are ethical terms egocentric?

In discussing the above questions I shall repeat in abbreviated form arguments which have occurred in earlier chapters, but this time we must arrive at decisions, and not, as before, leave many questions open.

One possible theory is that 'ought' is indefinable, and that we know by ethical intuition one or more propositions about the kinds of acts that we ought, or ought not, to perform. There is no *logical* objection to this theory, and I am not prepared to reject it decisively. It has, however, a grave drawback, namely, that there is no general agreement as to what sorts of acts ought to be performed, and that the theory affords no means of deciding who is in the right where there is disagreement. It thus becomes, in practice though not in theory, an egocentric doctrine. If A says 'you ought to do this' and B says 'No, you ought to do that', you only know that these are their opinions, and you have no means of knowing which, if either, is right. You can only escape from this conclusion by saying dogmatically: 'Whenever there is a dispute as to what ought to be done, I am in the right, and those who disagree with me are mistaken'. But as those who disagree will make a similar claim, ethical controversy will become merely a clash of rival dogmas. These considerations lead us to abandon 'ought' as the fundamental ethical term. Let us see whether we can do any better with the concept 'good'.

We shall call something 'good' if it has value on its own account, independently of its effects. Perhaps, since the term 'good' is ambiguous, we shall do well to substitute the term 'intrinsic value'. Thus the theory that we are now to examine is the theory that there is an indefinable which we are calling 'intrinsic value', and that we know, by a different kind of ethical intuition from that considered in connection with 'ought', that certain kinds of things possess intrinsic value. The term has a negative, to which we will give the name

158

'disvalue'. A possible ethical intuition of the sort appropriate to our present theory would be: 'Pleasure has intrinsic value, and pain has intrinsic disvalue'. We shall now define 'ought' in terms of intrinsic value: an act 'ought' to be performed if, of those that are possible, it is the one having the most intrinsic value. To this definition we must add the principle: 'The act having most intrinsic value is the one likely to produce the greatest balance of intrinsic value over intrinsic disvalue, or the smallest balance of intrinsic disvalue over intrinsic value'. An intrinsic value and an intrinsic disvalue are defined as equal when the two together have zero intrinsic value.

This theory, like its predecessor, is not logically refutable. It has the advantage, over the theory which makes 'ought' fundamental, that there are much fewer disagreements as to what has intrinsic value than as to what ought to be done. And when we examine disagreements as to what ought to be done, we find, usually, though perhaps not always, that they are derived from disagreements as to the effects of actions. A savage may believe that infringing a tabu causes death; some sabbatarians believe that working on Sunday leads to defeat in war. Such considerations suggest that moral rules are really based on an estimate of consequences even when they seem to be absolute. And if we judge the morality of an act by its consequences, we seem driven to adopt some such definition of 'ought' as that suggested at the end of the last paragraph. Our present theory is, therefore, a definite improvement upon the theory which makes 'ought' indefinable.

There are, however, still objections, some analogous to the former ones, and some of a new kind. Although there is more agreement as to intrinsic value than as to rules of conduct, there are still some disagreements that are serious. One of these is as to vindictive punishment. Is there intrinsic value in inflicting pain upon those whose acts have intrinsic disvalue? Believers in hell must answer in the affirmative, and so must all those who believe that the purpose of the criminal law should not be merely deterrent and reformatory. Some stern moralists have maintained that pleasure has no intrinsic value, but I do not think they were quite sincere in this, as they maintained at the same time that the virtuous will be happy in heaven. The question of vindictive punishment is more serious, because, as in the case of disagreement about moral rules, there is no way in which the matter can be argued: if you think it good and I think it bad, neither of us can advance any reasons whatever in support of our belief.

There is a consideration of quite another kind, which, while not conclusive, tends to throw doubt on the view that intrinsic value is indefinable. When we examine the things to which we are inclined to attach intrinsic value, we find that they are all things that are desired or enjoyed. It is difficult to believe that anything would have value in a universe devoid of sentience. This suggests that 'intrinsic value' may be definable in terms of desire or pleasure or both.

If we say 'pleasure is good and pain is bad', do we mean anything more than 'we like pleasure and dislike pain'? It seems as if we must mean something more than this, but this is certainly a part of what we mean. We cannot attribute intrinsic value to everything that is desired, because desires conflict, for instance in a war, where each side desires its own victory. We could perhaps evade this difficulty by saying that only states of mind have intrinsic value. In that case, if A and B compete for something which only one of them can have, we shall say that there is intrinsic value in the pleasure of the victor, whichever he may be. There is now nothing which one of the two judges to have intrinsic value, while the other judges that the same thing has intrinsic disvalue. A may admit that the pleasure which B would derive from victory would have intrinsic value, but may argue that B's victory is nevertheless to be prevented if possible, on account of its effects. Thus we shall now consider the definition: 'Intrinsic value' means 'the property of being a state of mind desired by the person who experiences it'. This differs very little from the view that the good is pleasure. We come even nearer to the good as pleasure if we substitute 'enjoyed' for 'desired' in the above definition.

I do not think the statement 'the good is pleasure' is quite correct, but I think that most of the difficulties of ethics are the same when this statement is adopted as when we adopt one which seems to me more exact. I shall, therefore, for the sake of simplicity, adopt hypothetically, for the moment, the hedonistic definition of the good. It remains to examine how this definition can be connected with our ethical feelings and convictions.

Henry Sidgwick, in his *Methods of Ethics*, argued at length that all moral rules that are generally recognized can be deduced from the principle that we ought to aim at maximizing pleasure; he even contended that this principle accounts for the occasional exceptions that moral rules are admitted to have. There are occasions when most people would say that it is right to tell a lie, or to break a promise, or to steal or kill; all these the hedonist's principle explains. I think that, as regards the moral code of civilized communities, Sidgwick's contention is broadly true; at any rate, I am not prepared to argue against it, subject to these limitations.

What, on this theory, shall we say about praise and blame? Blame, when it is deliberate, is both an emotion and a judgment: I feel a dislike of the act that I blame, and I judge that I do right in feeling this dislike. The emotion is just a fact, and raises no theoretical issue, but the judgment is a more difficult matter. I certainly do not *mean*, when I judge an act to be right, that it is the act best calculated to maximize pleasure, for, if I did, it would be logically impossible to dispute hedonism, which it is not. Perhaps the judgment is not really a judgment, but another emotion, namely, an emotion of approval towards my likes or dislikes. According to this view, when I deliberately, and not impulsively, blame an act, I dislike the act, and feel towards my dislike an emotion of approval.

Another person, who disagrees with me about ethics, may disapprove of my approval; he will express his feeling in what *seems* to be a judgment, saying 'you ought not to have blamed that act', or something equivalent. But on our present theory he is still expressing an emotion; neither he nor I is making any assertion, and therefore our conflict is only practical, not theoretical.

If we define 'right', the matter is different. We can then have a *judgment* 'this is right'. If our definition is not to have paradoxical results, our definition of 'right' must be such that usually, when an act is right according to our definition, it is one towards which we feel the emotion of approval, and when it is wrong, it is one towards which we feel disapproval. We are thus led to seek for some common property of as many as possible of the acts commonly approved (or disapproved). If *all* had such a common property, we should have no hesitation in defining this as 'right'. But we do not find anything quite so convenient as this. What we do find is that most of the acts towards which people feel the emotion of approval have a certain common property, and that the exceptional acts, which have not this property, tend to be no longer approved of when people have become clearly aware of their exceptional character. We may then say, in a sense, that approval of such acts is mistaken.

We can now set up a series of fundamental propositions and definitions in Ethics.

1   Surveying the acts which arouse emotions of approval or disapproval, we find that, as a general rule, the acts which are approved of are those believed likely to have, on the balance, effects of certain kinds, while opposite effects are expected from acts that are disapproved of.

2   Effects that lead to approval are defined as 'good', and those leading to disapproval as 'bad'.
3   An act of which, on the available evidence, the effects are likely to be better than those of any other act that is possible in the circumstances, is defined as 'right'; any other act is 'wrong'. What we 'ought' to do is, by definition, the act which is right.
4   It is right to feel approval of a right act and disapproval of a wrong act.

These definitions and propositions, if accepted, provide a coherent body of ethical propositions, which are true (or false) in the same sense as if they were propositions of science.

It is clear that the difficulties are mainly concerned with the first proposition of the above series. We must therefore examine it more closely.

We have seen in previous chapters that different societies in different ages have given approval to a wide diversity of acts. Primitive communities, at a certain stage of development, approved of cannibalism and human sacrifice. Spartans approved of homosexuality, which to Jews and Christians was an abomination. Until the late seventeenth century, almost everybody approved of the burning of reputed witches, which we now regard as senseless cruelty. But these differences were rooted in differences of belief as to the effects of actions. Human sacrifice was supposed to promote fertility. The Spartans thought that homosexuality promoted courage in battle. We might still approve of the execution of witches, if we believed that they had the maleficent powers with which they were credited in the Middle Ages. The difference between ourselves and other ages in these respects is attributable to a difference between our beliefs and theirs as to the effects of actions. The actions which they condemned were such as, in their opinion, would have certain effects, and we agree with them in thinking that such effects are to be avoided if possible.

We are thus led to the conclusion that there is more agreement among mankind as to the effects at which we should aim than as to the kinds of acts that are approved. I think the contention of Henry Sidgwick, that the acts which are approved of are those that are likely to bring happiness or pleasure, is, broadly speaking, true. Not infrequently, an ancient tabu, which it was formerly thought disastrous to infringe, may survive, through the force of custom and tradition, long after the beliefs which gave rise to it have been forgotten. But in such cases the tabu has a precarious life, and is apt to be thrown over by those who come across, by travel or by study, customs different from those in which they have been brought up.

I do not think, however, that pleasure is quite the nearest that we can come to the common quality of the great majority of approved actions. I think we must include such things as intelligence and aesthetic sensibility. If we were really persuaded that pigs are happier than human beings, we should not on that account welcome the ministrations of Circe. If miracles were possible, and we could choose exactly the life that we should prefer, most of us would prefer a life in which we could, at least part of the time, enjoy the delicate delights of art and intellect, to one consisting wholly of houris, wines, and hot baths – partly, no doubt, from fear of satiety, but not wholly. We do not, in fact, value pleasures in proportion to their intensity; some pleasures seem to us inherently preferable to others.

If it is admitted that the great majority of approved acts are such as are believed to have certain effects, and if it is found, further, that exceptional acts, which are approved without having this character, tend to be no longer approved when their exceptional character is realized, then it becomes possible, in a certain sense, to speak of ethical error. We may say that it is 'wrong' to approve of such exceptional acts, meaning that such approval does not have the effects which mark the great majority of approved acts, and which we have agreed to take as the criterion of what is 'right'.

Although, on the above theory, ethics contains statements which are true or false, and not merely optative or imperative, its basis is still one of emotion and feeling, the emotion of approval and the feeling of enjoyment or satisfaction, the former being involved in the definition of 'right' and 'wrong', the latter in that of 'intrinsic value'. And the appeal upon which we depend for the acceptance of our ethical theory is not the appeal to the facts of perception, but to the emotions and feelings which have given rise to the concepts of 'right' and 'wrong', 'good' and 'bad'.

22

LAST PERPLEXITIES
Reply to Monro and introduction to
Hume 1946–60

This selection consists of two extracts: a paragraph from
'Notes on Philosophy, January 1960', in *Philosophy*, 1960,
35: 146–7 (*CPBR* vol. 11: 310–11) and a paragraph from a
paper entitled 'Hume' (*CPBR* vol. 11: 240) which
remained unpublished in Russell's lifetime. The January
1960 issue of the journal *Philosophy* was largely devoted to
Russell's work and included a substantial essay by D. H.
Monro (then of the University of Sydney) entitled 'Russell's
Moral Theories'. Russell's 'Notes on Philosophy, January
1960' is a reply to this issue. It is rather brief, perhaps
because he was preoccupied with his anti-nuclear
campaigns, and the section dealing with Monro's article is
naturally even briefer. In it, he reverts to the view of 1944
– that is, he finds the arguments for the 'subjectivity of
ethical values' compelling, though he cannot quite believe
that the only thing wrong with wanton cruelty is that he
does not like it (see Paper 20 above). So much for the 'body
of ethical propositions, true (or false) in the same sense as
[the] propositions of science' defended in *Human Society*!
(Paper 21.) So when did Russell reject the theory of *Human
Society* and why did he do so? The 'When?' is more difficult
to answer than the 'Why?' since Russell was always rather
ambivalent about the theory of *Human Society*. Indeed, the
'Hume' piece reproduced below suggests that even when
he was writing *Human Society* he had his doubts. 'Hume'
was originally intended as the introduction to a collection
of Hume's writings to be entitled *The Living Thoughts of
David Hume Presented by Bertrand Russell*, a publishing
project which never saw the light of print (*CPBR* vol. 11:
234). But the intended introduction was written in 1946
at precisely the period when Russell was working on
Human Knowledge and the earlier portions of *Human Society*.

In it he argues that Hume's theory 'is subject to the obvious difficulty that one man may approve of one action and another of another, so that morality, like taste, becomes purely subjective'. (In fact, Hume had an answer to this difficulty which Russell does not discuss.) But if we substitute 'effects' for 'actions', Russell's theory is subject to the same obvious difficulty. Perhaps because he realized this, Russell very soon reverted to emotivism. Within one month of the publication of *Human Society* he published a review of A. J. Ayer's *Philosophical Essays* (1954) entitled 'Light versus Heat' in which he singles out Ayer's defence of emotivism for special praise:

> There is one [essay] on 'The Analysis of Moral Judgements', with which I find myself in pretty complete agreement. [Ayer] takes the view that ethical judgements are not statements of fact, but is careful to add: 'It must not be inferred from this that I am treating them with disrespect.'
>
> (*CPBR* vol. 11: 175)

This suggests that the theory of *Human Society* was something of an aberration and that for the last forty years of his life Russell was, in the main, a reluctant emotivist. In 1960 he received a book from a Mr Harold Osborn entitled *Humanism and Moral Theory* which was evidently designed to provide humanistic ethics with some sort of objective basis. Russell thanked him for the present but regretted to say that the book had not solved his ethical perplexities. Indeed, it confirmed him in his opinion that 'any system of ethics which claims objectivity can only do so by means of a concealed ethical premise, which, if disputed, cannot be demonstrated' (Feinberg and Kasrils 1969: 130). This is precisely what is wrong with the meta-ethic of *Human Society*.

Reply to D. H. Monro 1960

The only thing further that I have to say concerns Mr. Monro's article on my moral theories. I am not, myself, satisfied with what I have read or said on the philosophical basis of ethics. I cannot see how to refute the arguments for the subjectivity of ethical values, but I find myself incapable of believing that all that is wrong with wanton cruelty is that I don't like it. I have no difficulty in practical moral judgments, which I find that I make on a roughly hedonistic basis, but, when it comes to the philosophy of moral judgments, I am impelled in two opposite directions and remain perplexed. I have already expressed this perplexity in print, and I should deeply rejoice, if I could find or be shown a way to resolve it, but as yet I remain dissatisfied.

Extract from 'Hume' 1946

Ever since the time of Kant, who conceived that he had found an answer to Hume, philosophers have regarded Hume primarily as the man who threw doubt on causation and the validity of induction, but in his own day it was not so that he was regarded. His big book, *The Treatise of Human Nature*, which he wrote when he was young and unknown, attracted no attention. He therefore, for a while, abandoned philosophy and devoted himself to the writing of essays and history. Even in the *Treatise* it is only one-third of the book that is concerned with theoretical philosophy; the other two-thirds are concerned with morals and the passions, as to which his observations are both sensible and kindly. Locke had maintained that ethical propositions are capable of theoretical demonstration, like those of mathematics. Hume will have none of this; his theory, he says, 'maintains that morality is determined by sentiment. It defines virtue to be whatever mental action or quality gives to a spectator the pleasing sentiment of approbation; and vice the contrary.' This theory is subject to the obvious difficulty that one man may approve of one action and another of another, so that morality, like taste, becomes purely subjective. Hume, however, finds nothing objectionable in this consequence of his theory. He attaches great importance to benevolence as a source of good actions, and has more belief in its prevalence than is possible in our age of mass atrocities. He valued himself more as a moralist than as a purely theoretical philosopher. He tells us that his *Enquiry Concerning the Principles of Morals* is his best work. I do not think any modern philosopher would agree with this estimate, not because of any defect in his ethical writings, but only because they do not give scope for that acuteness of sceptical analysis, which caused him to perceive problems of which previous philosophers had been unconscious.

Part III

REASON AND THE PASSIONS

23

REASON: THE SLAVE OF
THE PASSIONS

Extract from *Human Society in Ethics and
Politics* 1954

Reprinted from the Preface to *Human Society* 7–11. David
Hume is famous, among other things, for the sensational-
sounding claim that reason is the slave of the passions
(Hume 1978: 415, *Treatise*, II, iii, 3). What he means by
this is that beliefs by themselves do not motivate – that
they require the aid of desires or emotions if they are to
have an influence on the will. Since reason – the faculty
which generates beliefs – cannot generate new desires, it
cannot determine which ends we are to pursue. Russell
held to this doctrine throughout most of his career. He
believed it in 1894 when he wrote 'Cleopatra and Maggie
Tulliver?' (Paper 8) and he believed it in 1954 when he was
putting the finishing touches to *Human Society*. He also
believed it during most of the intervening sixty years; in
1916 when he wrote Paper 16, in 1925 when he wrote
What I Believe (Paper 18) and in 1935 when he wrote
Religion and Science (Paper 19). However, in *Human Society*
the thesis is much more explicit. I reproduce this piece
because I suspect that this Humean doctrine had a major
influence on Russell's ethics. In particular it may help to
explain his reluctant allegiance to emotivism. If Hume's
writings are put to the torture, it is possible to extract the
following argument for some form of non-cognitivism.

1   Genuine beliefs do not motivate by themselves – they
     require the aid of pre-existing passions or desires.
     (Slavery of Reason thesis.)
2   Moral 'beliefs' *do* motivate by themselves.
     Therefore:
3   Moral 'beliefs' are not genuine beliefs.

If Russell had something like this at the back of his mind,

it might explain why he found emotivism so compelling. If moral 'beliefs', unlike genuine beliefs, motivate, this must be because to 'believe' a moral judgement is not to assent to a proposition but to adopt a desire or to register an emotion.

I hope also that this book, which is concerned throughout with human passions and their effect upon human destiny, may help to dispel a misunderstanding not only of what I have written, but of everything written by those with whom I am in broad agreement. Critics are in the habit of making a certain accusation against me which seems to imply that they approach my writings with a preconception so strong that they are unable to notice what, in fact, I say. I am told over and over again that I over-estimate the part of reason in human affairs. This may mean that I think either that people are, or that they ought to be, more rational than my critics believe them to be. But I think there is a prior error on the part of my critics, which is that they, not I, irrationally over-estimate the part which reason is capable of playing, and this comes I think from the fact that they are in complete confusion as to what the word 'reason' means.

'Reason' has a perfectly clear and precise meaning. It signifies the choice of the right means to an end that you wish to achieve. It has nothing whatever to do with the choice of ends. But opponents of reason do not realize this, and think that advocates of rationality want reason to dictate ends as well as means. They have no excuse for this view in the writings of rationalists. There is a famous sentence: 'Reason is and ought only to be, the slave of the passions.' This sentence does not come from the works of Rousseau or Dostoevsky or Sartre. It comes from David Hume. It expresses a view to which I, like every man who attempts to be reasonable, fully subscribe. When I am told, as I frequently am, that I 'almost entirely discount the part played by the emotions in human affairs,' I wonder what motive-force the critic supposes me to regard as dominant. Desires, emotions, passions (you can choose whichever word you will), are the only possible causes of action. Reason is not a cause of action but only a regulator. If I wish to travel by plane to New York, reason tells me that it is better to take a plane which is going to New York than one which is going to Constantinople. I suppose that those who think me unduly rational, consider that I ought to become so agitated at the airport as to jump into the first plane that I see, and when it lands me in Constantinople I ought to curse the people among whom I find myself for being Turks and not Americans. This would be a fine, full-blooded way of behaving, and would, I suppose, meet with the commendation of my critics.

One critic takes me to task because I say that only evil passions prevent the realization of a better world, and goes on triumphantly to ask, 'are all human emotions necessarily evil?' In the very book that leads my critic to this objection, I say that what the world needs is Christian love, or compassion. This, surely, is an emotion, and, in saying that this is what the world needs, I am not suggesting reason as a driving force. I can only suppose that this emotion, because it is neither cruel nor destructive, is not attractive to the apostles of unreason.

Why, then, is there this violent passion which causes people, when they read me, to be unable to notice even the plainest statement, and to go on comfortably thinking that I say the exact opposite of what I do say? There are several motives which may lead people to hate reason. You may have incompatible desires and not wish to realize that they are incompatible. You may wish to spend more than your income and yet remain solvent. And this may cause you to hate your friends when they point out the cold facts of arithmetic. You may, if you are an old-fashioned schoolmaster, wish to consider yourself full of universal benevolence, and at the same time derive great pleasure from caning boys. In order to reconcile these two desires you have to persuade yourself that caning has a reformatory influence. If a psychiatrist tells you that it has no such influence on some peculiarly irritating class of young sinners, you will fly into a rage and accuse him of being coldly intellectual. There is a splendid example of this pattern in the furious diatribe of the great Dr. Arnold of Rugby against those who thought ill of flogging.

There is another, more sinister, motive for liking irrationality. If men are sufficiently irrational, you may be able to induce them to serve your interests under the impression that they are serving their own. This case is very common in politics. Most political leaders acquire their position by causing large numbers of people to believe that these leaders are actuated by altruistic desires. It is well understood that such a belief is more readily accepted under the influence of excitement. Brass bands, mob oratory, lynching, and war, are stages in the development of the excitement. I suppose the advocates of unreason think that there is a better chance of profitably deceiving the populace if they keep it in a state of effervescence. Perhaps it is my dislike of this sort of process which leads people to say that I am unduly rational.

But I would put to these men a dilemma: since reason consists in a just adaptation of means to ends, it can only be opposed by those who think it a good thing that people should choose means which cannot realize their professed ends. This implies either that they should be deceived as to how to realize their professed ends, or that their real ends should not be those that they profess. The first is the case of a populace misled by an eloquent *fuehrer*. The second is that of the schoolmaster who enjoys torturing boys, but wishes to go on thinking himself a benevolent humanitarian. I cannot feel that either of these grounds for opposing reason is morally respectable.

There is another ground upon which some people oppose what they imagine to be reason. They think that strong emotions are desirable, and that no one who feels a strong emotion will be reasonable about it. They seem to think that any person who feels strongly must lose his head and behave in a silly manner which they applaud because it shows him to be passionate. They do not, however, think in this way when self-deception would have consequences that they would dislike. No one, for example, holds that a general ought to hate the enemy so passionately as to become hysterical and incapable of rational planning. It is not, in fact, the case that strong passions prevent a just estimate of means. There are people, like the Comte de Monte Cristo, who have burning passions leading them straight to the right choice of means. Do not tell me that that worthy man's aims were irrational. There is no such thing as an irrational aim except in the sense of one that is impossible of realization. Nor are cold calculators always conventionally wicked. Lincoln calculated coldly in the American Civil War and was roundly abused by the Abolitionists who, as apostles of passion, wished him to adopt measures that looked vigorous but would not have led to emancipation.

I suppose the essence of the matter is this: that I do not think it a good thing to be in that state of insane excitement in which people do things that have consequences directly opposite to what they intend, as, for example, when they get themselves killed in running across a street because they could not stop to notice the traffic. Those who praise such behaviour must either wish to practise successful hypocrisy or be the victims of some self-deception which they cannot bear to surrender. I am not ashamed of thinking ill of both these states of mind, and if it is for thinking ill of them that I am accused of excessive rationality, I plead guilty. But if it is supposed that I dislike strong emotion, or that I think anything except emotion can be a cause of action, then I most emphatically deny the charge. The world that I should wish to see is one where emotions are strong but not destructive, and where, because they are acknowledged, they lead to no deception either of oneself or of others. Such a world would include love and friendship and the pursuit of art and knowledge. I cannot hope to satisfy those who want something more tigerish.

Part IV

THE FUNCTION OF MORALITY

24

THE DEVELOPMENT OF
MORALS
1907

Reprinted from *CPBR* vol. 12: 336–40, originally published in *The Independent Review*, 12 (February 1907). This paper is a review of *Morals in Evolution*, by the political philosopher L. T. Hobhouse (1864–1929), a leading light among the New Liberals, a group of thinkers who sought to combine an old-fashioned respect for the liberties of the individual with a new-fangled faith in social engineering and welfarist legislation. However, Hobhouse tried to justify this, on the whole, laudable ethic by presenting it as the outcome of an evolutionary process. Russell was scathing in print but even more scathing in private. The book 'seems to me, roughly speaking worthless. It might be called "from cannibalism to the Liberal Party" – a sort of advance of the human race, like "from log cabin to White House"' (Letter to Margaret Llewelyn Davies, 24 November 1906, *CPBR* vol. 12: 334). Why was Russell so savage? First of all, Hobhouse's argument would seem to embody an inference from Is to Ought, from facts about what people have believed to the moral thesis that Hobhouse's ethic is correct (or at any rate, an improvement on what has gone before). But if Hume is to be believed, such inferences are invalid (Hume 1978: 469). Even if history *does* reveal a pattern of development, a sustained tendency to move from the values of cannibals to those of the Liberal Party, this does not show that we should adopt the values of the Liberal Party rather than those of the cannibals. Thus far, Russell's argument is merely Humean. But Moore's moral realism furnishes an additional objection which can be expressed as a dilemma. Either the development of morals is progressive or it is not. If it *is* progressive, what this means is that successive moral systems have been closer and closer approximations to the truth. Thus to know that the sequence has been progressive, we must already have a rough idea of what the moral truth is. In which case, the history of morals is redundant. If the development of morals is *not* progressive, then the fact that the ethic of the Liberal Party comes last in the sequence does not count in its favour. Hobhouse's book is worthless either way (or, at best, of merely historical interest). But the history of morals is of less interest to a moral realist, like the Russell of 1906, than to the moral sceptic that he subsequently became. In later life Russell was much exercised by the social functions of morality, some of which are decidedly sinister. As Marx says, 'the ruling ideas of each age have ever been the ideas of its ruling class' principally because the ruling class takes care to promote the moral ideas which justify its rule (McLellan 1977: 236). Worse, morality breeds a spirit of vindictiveness. As Russell was to put it in his eighties, 'the purpose of morals is to enable people to inflict suffering without compunction' (Russell 1961: 184). To a moral realist of a Moorean stamp these facts are sad but are not of any theoretical significance. It may be that morality as an institution has had all sorts of bad effects, but this is because the moralities people have believed in are false. The solution is to convince them of the moral truth, then all will be well. But if you no longer believe in the existence of a moral truth this blithe solution no longer works. A humane person may begin to wonder whether morality as an institution needs to be reformed or even done away with. To answer this question, a history of its workings is essential.

Morals in Evolution: A Study in Comparative Ethics. By L. T. Hobhouse. 2 vols. London: Chapman and Hall, 1906. Pp. xvii, 375; vii, 294.

In this work, Mr. Hobhouse traces the development of moral ideas from the rudest savages to the present day, or perhaps rather further. His first volume tells what men have thought it right to do, while his second tells why they have thought so; that is to say, his first volume tells what standard of conduct has, at various times and places, been expected of men, while his second deals with the ethical, religious or magical beliefs which have made men consider such conduct desirable. The first volume is divided into chapters dealing with different subjects, such as property and marriage, each of which separately is traced through its whole development. The second volume is divided according to the various ethical systems dealt with, and is therefore more or less progressive, putting the most developed systems last.

The parts of the book which deal with savages and early civilizations are, to my mind, the more interesting, if only on account of the curious facts which always make anthropology pleasing. Thus we learn that Babylonian sorcerers used to invoke the coal-scuttle under the title 'child of Ea', and that there are tribes which do not know that human beings have fathers. It is curious, too, to see how far the European's idea of the savage has travelled since the time when he was the 'noble savage' and had all the virtues that civilized man is apt to lack. Thus we read of a Red Indian, telling of his ideas of hospitality, who said: 'If a white man . . . enters one of our cabins we all treat him as I do you. We dry him if he is wet, we warm him if he is cold, and give him meat and drink that he may allay his hunger and thirst; and we spread soft furs for him to rest and sleep on. We demand nothing in return. But if I go into a white man's house at Albany and ask for victuals and drink, they say, "Where is your money?" And if I have none, they say, "Get out, you Indian dog!"' But this Indian, as was to be expected, lived in the eighteenth century. What one learns further about American aborigines is less idyllic. Thus among the Creek Indians, 'the women were wont to make payment in tobacco for the privilege of whipping prisoners as they passed.' Elsewhere: 'prisoners are tortured in sufficient numbers to atone for those similarly dealt with by their enemies; and it is stated that children are encouraged to take part in the process in order to instil hardness and vindictive feelings into their minds' – a view of education which suggests the usual defence of public schools. By some savages, we find, 'prisoners are not merely killed and eaten on the spot, but are taken home, well treated and fattened for the slaughter, possibly provided with a wife and encouraged to breed a family for the same purpose.' 'What! shall I starve as long as my sister has children whom she can sell?' was the reply of a negro to Burton. Such facts are encouraging when one feels inclined to doubt the reality of progress.

Many interesting facts about early civilizations are told by Mr. Hobhouse, notably extracts from the code of Hammurabi, which gives an astonishing insight into Babylonian society 2000 years before Christ. Many of the anticipations of Christianity mentioned in the book are very remarkable. The following is not Christian or Jewish, but is Nebuchadnezzar's hymn to Marduk on ascending the throne:

O Eternal ruler! Lord of the Universe! . . .
It is Thou who hast created me,
And Thou hast entrusted to me sovereignty over mankind.
According to Thy mercy, O Lord, which Thou bestowest
upon all,
Cause me to love Thy supreme rule.
Implant the fear of Thy divinity in my heart.

Among the most interesting of sages are those of China. It is hard to grow very enthusiastic about Confucius, although he invented the Golden Rule; but his disciple Mencius is refreshing, if only for his remark on Generals: 'There are men who say, "I am skilful at marshalling troops; I am skilful at conducting a battle." They are great criminals.'[1] The following story of Mencius is also interesting:

> When Mencius saw King Seuen much touched by the frightened appearance of an ox being led to the sacrifice, and ordering that a sheep should be substituted for it, he told him very justly that it was because 'you saw the oxen and had not seen the sheep.' A superior man, he went on, cannot eat the animals whose dying cries he has heard, and so he keeps away from his cook-room.

When we come to the Greeks and the moderns, the book becomes less satisfactory, since it is impossible, within Mr. Hobhouse's limits, to give anything like an adequate discussion, and we therefore get mainly either an outline of what every one knows, or an account so compressed that it can hardly be followed unless one has read fuller accounts elsewhere.

The main result of the inquiries into forms of social organization, marriage, property, class-relations and relations between communities, which constitute Mr. Hobhouse's first volume, is that there is a tendency to emphasize society at one pole, and the individual at the other, as against minor groups such as the clan or the commune. This conclusion carries internationalism with it as the natural goal of development, since all aggregations short of humanity as a whole

---

1 It is notable that Chinese anti-militarism goes too far even for Mr Hobhouse, who suggests it is largely due to cowardice.

tend to lose their force. But although this view of development results in the main, there are, as Mr. Hobhouse admits, great difficulties the moment we come to special questions. In regard to marriage, for example, shall we regard the Catholic indissolubility of marriage or the American freedom of divorce as representing a more advanced stage? Both exist at the same date and in equally civilized countries. It might be argued that the American system is a reversion, not an advance, for great freedom of divorce existed before the rise of Catholicism. But this question will be answered by every one according to his opinion on divorce, and it seems that the history of the subject can afford no guidance. Indeed it may be urged that the function of history in forming moral opinion is rather more limited than Mr. Hobhouse appears to think. The fact that things have developed in a certain direction is no evidence that it would not have been better if they had developed otherwise, nor that it would be good they should develop further in the same direction. Thus there is a tendency for civilized societies in early stages to move towards absolute monarchy; but few people now-a-days think absolute monarchy a good form of government for the most civilized communities. The study of past moral systems is useful as showing that society can survive under institutions which to us seem monstrous, and as illustrating the part played by custom and irrational prejudice in almost all beliefs. In this way, it instils wholesome doubts and promotes a careful examination of our views, and thus may suggest grounds *against* many cherished ethical dogmas; but it is quite incapable of giving grounds *for* any opinion as to what is desirable. Such an opinion can only validly come from our own perception of what is good, not from the distilled essence of the views of previous ages.

This is illustrated towards the end of Mr. Hobhouse's book, when he comes to giving his own views on ethics. These views are recommended partly by some rather summary philosophical argumentation, partly as the natural outcome of previous systems. Mr. Hobhouse's ethics is not that of Mill, although his *Theory of Knowledge* is an able defence of Mill against idealist critics; in fact, his ethics is rather that of the critics than that of Mill. He rejects the view that happiness is the good, and also criticizes the utilitarians for regarding the good of society as merely the aggregate of the goods enjoyed by separate people. The end, he says, is not happiness but 'the spiritual growth in which happiness is found'. (II, p. 246.) 'We need a standard of value which must prove its genuineness by the same test which we apply to speculative principles. It must give harmony, order, coherence to our efforts and our judgments, while its negation must leave them disordered and discordant.' (II, p. 249.) 'In modern thought the principle of human development under whatever name becomes in a new sense the pivot upon which ethical conceptions turn.' (II, p. 251.) 'For rationalism the moral basis lies in the unfolding of the full meaning of the moral order, as that through which the human spirit grows.' (II, p. 274.) There is a difficulty in understanding what Mr. Hobhouse means by these views, because development and growth presumably consist in travelling towards the good, or from good to better, and are therefore not themselves capable of being used to explain what the good is.

Another difficulty in Mr. Hobhouse's views is to discover what part in religion he would assign to beliefs as to the nature of the universe or of God. 'Instead of religion being the basis of ethics,' he says, 'ethics becomes the test to which religion must submit.' (II, p. 252.) If this means merely that we ought not to *worship* anything which is not good, there is nothing to be said against it; but if it means that our *beliefs* on religious subjects are to be influenced by our beliefs as to what is good, then it presupposes that we already know for certain that the universe is good – a paradoxical view for which no evidence is offered by Mr. Hobhouse. That this view is held by him appears also from his remark (II, p. 48.) that the Greek philosophers first taught the world, what it has too often forgotten, that goodness and God are identical. This presumably means that power and goodness are united, for 'God', in the sense in which it was used before the Greeks, seems to mean merely a person of extraordinary power. Mr. Hobhouse, therefore, must suppose that the controlling forces of the world are good. The question whether this is so is not without importance, and it is a pity he has not indicated his reasons for his view. 'There is', he says, 'no real Ahriman that strives with Ormuzd. Evil is merely the automatic result of the inorganic.' (II, p. 281.) But is there not equally no real Ormuzd? And is not good equally the automatic result of the inorganic? This is the view which science *prima facie* suggests, and Mr. Hobhouse alleges no reason against it.

Owing to the plan of Mr. Hobhouse's book, there is much material about early customs, out of which one expects his conclusions to grow; but the conclusions, when we reach them, seem unconnected with this material, and therefore have to be given so shortly as to seem obscure and arbitrary. Yet one cannot doubt that he regards his anthropological data as merely means to an end, namely to his conclusions as to ethics and politics; and the book is rendered unsatisfactory by the very insufficient connection between his data and his conclusions. The only possible connection – and this is not made out – would be that, given the opinions of the Australians, the Red Indians, the Babylonians, etc., the opinions of Mr. Hobhouse are those which would naturally come next in order of development. But it is also given that the opinions of the Australians, the Red Indians, the Babylonians, etc., are palpable nonsense. What use, one wonders, may posterity make of this datum?

It is true that Mr. Hobhouse does lip-service to these sceptical suggestions. Thus he says: 'Nothing is more certain, if the rationalist doctrine is true, than [that] doctrine itself will grow, and as growth implies, will change.' (II, p. 257.) But he feels sure that the truth is to be got by a *growth* from the present doctrine. This, indeed, is implied in the word *evolution*, which, where no reason has been shown why growth rather than radical change is the road to truth, is really a question-begging term. For aught that appears to the contrary, the wheat and the tares may be a more appropriate analogy; here, though the wheat is to grow, the tares are to be destroyed. Nor can one be sure, at any stage, that the wheat is already sown; it may be that all that is now growing is tares. I do not mean that complete scepticism is the only rational attitude in ethics, but I do mean that knowledge in ethics cannot be attained by merely studying changes of opinion. And to call these changes 'evolution' or 'growth' or 'development' is to assume that we know that the changes constitute a progress, i.e. that we know which stages are better and which worse. But if we already know this, it is merely an unnecessary *detour* to deduce it from the course of events. None of us believe human sacrifice to be bad because it is by savages that it is practised; on the contrary, being already convinced that human sacrifice is bad, we infer progress from the fact that the practice has died out. The whole subject of evolution is full of opportunities for question-begging arguments, and to such arguments, I believe, its apparent power of giving guidance for the future is almost wholly due.

25

WHAT IS MORALITY?

1922

Reprinted from *CPBR* vol. 9: 348–50, originally published
in *The Nation and Athenaeum*, 32 (11 November 1922):
254–5. This piece is nominally a review of a book by B. M.
Laing (1887–1960), who lectured in philosophy at
Sheffield (hence the references to Yorkshire industrialism).
But rather than reviewing Laing, Russell seems much more
interested in developing his own ideas which he prudently
puts in the mouth of an *advocatus diaboli* (devil's advocate).
At the beginning of the War he had written to Alexander
that 'the universal outburst of righteousness in all nations
since the war began' had given him 'a disgust of all ethical
notions, which evidently are chiefly useful as an excuse for
murder' (*CPBR* vol. 8: 56). However, as an anti-War
activist he was compelled to make use of these noxious
notions in his own propaganda. Since he was busy trying to
save the bacon of the conscientious objectors and reverse
the foreign policy of the British Empire, it would have
been rather too much if he had added to his burdens by
taking on the institution of morality as well. Nor was his
moralizing insincere. As we have already seen (Papers 20
and 22), Russell, the self-righteous moralist, was often at
odds with Russell, the moral sceptic. However, the idea
that morality often acts as a device for *contracting* (rather
than extending) our natural sympathies was one he
retained to the end of his life. The second count in his
critique of morality is the obvious (if *marxisante*) thought
that moral beliefs and institutions often subserve the interests of the ruling class. Moreover, in 1922, when he wrote
this paper, Russell may have been moved by the thought
that since all moral judgements are false, the moralist is
essentially a purveyor of fictions – for this was the year of
'Is there an absolute good?' (Paper 17). Now, if morality is

compounded of falsehoods, fosters cruelty and often serves as a prop to predatory elites, perhaps we would be better off without it. Perhaps humanity could get by on the basis of natural sympathies, enlightened self-interest and means–end calculations. Russell suggests this in a half-humorous manner and does not endorse it himself. This is partly due to caution, but partly, I suspect, because he was genuinely ambivalent. Not so, Ian Hinckfuss and Richard Garner, who have both taken up the cause of what might be called 'humanistic amoralism' (Hinckfuss 1987 and Garner 1994). Hinckfuss, sadly, had to tone down the title of his book for publication, but what he originally proposed was 'To Hell with Morality!'

A Study in Moral Problems. By B.M. Laing. London: George Allen & Unwin; New York: Macmillan, 1922. Pp. 279.

The impression made by this book is that Professor Laing must have had originally a very definitely academic outlook upon human problems, but that contact with real life – in the war and in Yorkshire industrialism – has been gradually directing his attention towards new sets of facts which university tradition ignores. There is room for the process to go further, and to lead to a less traditional statement of the problems confronting modern moralists than that with which Professor Laing begins:

> Throughout the following chapters there runs one central problem, and upon it all the arguments converge. It is the problem of the relation between human action and natural law. It is an old one and one that has been dealt with by eminent thinkers: Kant and Lotze are but two. On account of the development of science with its insistence upon the reign of universal law, it has become in modern times a very important problem because of its bearing upon moral and social effort. The freedom that is somehow implied in morality has to be reconciled with the rigidity and uniformity that characterize natural law. That problem must be and is here regarded as a fundamental one, because it lies at the basis of all the more specific moral problems like evil, social conflicts, conflicts of values, the instability and uncertainty of moral progress and moral achievement.

There is, however, a question prior to those raised in this passage,

and it is one which Professor Laing recognizes, but does not sufficiently discuss. It is the question: Is there, in any objective sense,
such a thing as morality or immorality? Or is the conception of
morality merely part of the police force by which dominant groups
seek to enforce their authority? The combination of psychoanalysis
with Marxian political theory has forced this question insistently
upon many people. Psychoanalysis shows that the basis of a passion
is by no means always, or even usually, what the patient thinks it is;
and Marx suggests that all morality is derived from class-interest.
This latter view, in its strict economic form, is undoubtedly too
narrow; but when we include other groups, national, religious, etc.,
it becomes far more plausible. Without committing ourselves to
this opinion, let us see what could be said for it by an advocate.

In the first place (he would say), if you wish to understand the
nature of the moral sentiments, you should study the occasions on
which they are most strongly aroused. At the outbreak of the war,
there was an extraordinary wave of moral sentiment in all the
belligerent countries; we felt a moral horror of the Germans because
of the invasion of Belgium, and they felt an exactly equal moral
horror of us because of our blockade – at any rate those were the
reasons assigned. *The Times* feels moral horror of the Bolsheviks
whenever it is proposed that something should be done to diminish
the misery in Russia. Anarchists feel moral horror of the tyrants
whom they assassinate. Judges are full of moral fervour when they
condemn men to be flogged. The Charity Organization Society is
full of moral condemnation of the undeserving poor, and Socialists
who advocate confiscation are full of moral condemnation of the
undeserving rich.

From these facts, our moral *advocatus diaboli* draws the conclusion
that morality is a device for inhibiting our natural sympathies on
occasions when we wish to inflict pain, whether from motives of self-
preservation, ambition, or sheer cruelty. He will say that sympathy
conflicts with egoism, and that morality enables us to camouflage the
victory of egoism as really a higher form of sympathy. He will point
out that the conception of sin is anterior, historically and anthropo-
logically, to the conception of virtue, and that to this day the
occasions when we feel most moral are the occasions when we are
administering punishment. He will go on to say that, if the moralists
really desired a happier world, as they say they do, they would work
for the abolition of morality, since, if it were extinct, sympathy would
have free play, and men would not torture each other so much as they
do. But he would not press this *argumentum ad hominem*, since his

position debars him from the tempting conclusion that all moralists are immoral and that he is moral when he inflicts pain upon them.

There are, of course, answers to this position, whether valid or invalid. But although Professor Laing's first chapter is headed 'Grounds for Scepticism in Moral Theory and Practice', we do not find in his pages any argument capable of refuting a moral sceptic. Within its limitations, however, the book has many merits. Against the views which it rejects it gives, as a rule, good grounds; and the views which it advocates are, on almost all points, enlightened and rational. It rejects the view that morality consists mainly of sacrifice:

> Morality has been interpreted as if it were a moloch, as if the moral life for ever demanded sacrifices from human beings and the sacrifice of some values for others. Morality has hitherto had this character, but ethical theory has never questioned whether it need have this character or why it does have this character. The result has been that ethics has done little more than endeavour to give a reasoned justification of what the average person's moral beliefs and aspirations are; and in doing so it has accepted all the unquestioned assumptions of the ordinary moral consciousness. Its attitude is analogous to what the attitude of natural science would be if the latter accepted all the popular beliefs regarding natural phenomena, and tried merely to make them systematic.

This is well said. Again, in discussing the theory that the rivalry of States is due to over-population, the author says:

> The struggle over primary ends between States is due not to the lack of the means of subsistence in these States, but to the need of finding fresh populations to absorb these means of subsistence; and unless fresh markets and fresh consumers are found, the respective States will suffer internally. A mere restriction of population will thus only serve to reduce the numbers of consumers.

It would be easy to criticize this view, which hardly gives the whole truth. At the same time, it is to be observed that Germany had no population problem in the years before the war (the former emigration had ceased); that France has none now; and that China, where the problem is worst, is the least militaristic of great nations. The population problem is used as an excuse for militarism, but is not a *vera causa*.

The book is good in detail, but would be better if the author's own views were stated more trenchantly and clearly, and if less respect were paid to the ethical doctrines which are traditional in university philosophy.

Interlude 1

A NEW MORALITY VERSUS *NO* MORALITY

In 1922, we find Russell flirting with humanistic amoralism. But by 1929 he had changed his tune. He concludes another review with the following declaration:

> Undoubtedly the world needs a new morality, and not merely a revolt against the old one. At present in America many of those who have thrown off the old taboos have put nothing whatever in their place, and for this they are hardly to blame, since the moralists with very few exceptions have made no attempt to think out a new morality, the essence of which must be that it is creative and positive, not restrictive and negative. All morality is an embodiment of our emotions towards our fellow creatures. Traditional morality is an embodiment mainly of jealousy and tyranny. Until we learn to produce human beings in whom these are not the dominant attitudes towards their fellow creatures, we shall not get an *improvement* in morals, though we may get a *change* through a new direction of malevolence.
>
> (*CPBR* vol. 10: 394)

Note that what the world needs, according to Russell, is a *new* morality and not, as in 1922, *no* morality. He may be a moral reformer but he is no longer (if he ever was) a nihilist or humanistic amoralist. Why did Russell change his mind? Not, I think, because he was moved by the excesses of morally liberated Americans. Some other reason must be sought for such a major shift.

To begin with, the meta-ethic Russell had adopted by 1929 made moralizing a rather more respectable business than it appeared to be in 1922. In 1922 he thought that judgements about good and bad were *false*, since there were no such properties. And he thought judgements about right and wrong were false too, since no action could be more productive of good than any other, which is what rightness requires. But by 1929 this had changed. In so far as moral judgements are concerned with the means to agreed on ends, they can be straightforwardly true or false. It is true that judgements about ends embody our emotions and desires, but since the moral vocabulary is there to express our emotions and desires, there is nothing wrong with using it for its express purpose. Hence being a moralist does not entail being a deceiver, and accepting a morality does not entail being a dupe. However, I am not at all sure whether the switch to emotivism explains the propensity to moralize (even in a way that is not jealous and tyrannical) or whether the propensity to moralize explains the switch to emotivism.

Another factor, I suggest, is this. By 1929, Russell had been a parent for eight years and a school teacher for one. The need for a morality, whether new or otherwise, would have been borne in on him by experience. For it is difficult even to *imagine* raising children so as to be reasonably civilized beings, without instilling some kind of moral code. Russell's code, we may hope, was more benign and life-enhancing than most, but it was still a morality rather than an amorality. (Indeed, this is evident from his books.) Amoralists such as Garner and Hinckfuss sometimes talk as if all that is required for a civilized society are friendly feelings, means–end calculations and a spirit of give-and-take. But friendly feelings (not to mention a spirit of give-and-take) need to be cultivated, and one of the ways to cultivate them is to suggest that they are the right sorts of feelings to have. 'The instinctive desires of children,' says Russell, 'are vague; education and opportunity can turn them into many different channels' (Russell 1926: 75). Although in 1926 he thought the 'raw material of instinct' was 'ethically neutral' (*loc. cit.*) by 1932, he had come to think that these raw instincts could easily be diverted into channels which were somewhat suspect.

> If children are never interfered with by adults, the bigger children are likely to establish a tyranny over the smaller ones so that the liberty which is supposed to be the watch-word of the school will exist only for an aristocracy of the physically strong.
>
> (Russell 1932: 61)

Thus Russell's experiences with children may have led him to doubt whether people in general have enough natural sympathy to sustain the kind of co-operative society that humanistic amoralists desire.

Allen Wood argues that *Marx* was (in my terminology) both an error theorist and a humanistic amoralist. But he raises the following problem. 'If all morality is an illusion, then a clear-sighted person must be able to go through life entirely without moral beliefs, moral emotions, moral reactions. But is it possible to do this?' (Wood 1991: 522). Even if it is *not* possible for a person to get through life without moral beliefs etc., this does not show that the error theory is false. An illusion does not cease to be an illusion just because it is indispensable. But if we cannot get by without moral beliefs and feelings, then Marx's amoralist utopia – like other amoralist utopias – is unworkable and humanistic amoralism is not a practical proposition. Russell's own writings show that it is diffi-cult even to *think* about a utopia – let alone to set one up – without bringing in something like a morality. In his preparatory notes for *The Principles of Social Reconstruction* (written in 1916 and sent to D. H. Lawrence) he starts off in fine style:

> *Morality* is disapproval of the community for those who act against the holders of power. Hence enemies in war are wicked by definition. Morality is essentially part of the criminal law: it is a means of bringing self-interest into harmony with the interests of others. But when this is seen, it loses its efficacy, since it depends on belief in absolute 'wickedness'. Certain interests uphold it: (1) that it supports those in possession, since aggression is wicked, (2) that it provides an excuse for hatred and punishment which are pleasures, (3) that it gives occasion for self-esteem, since we ourselves are very virtuous.
>
> Something more positive than morality must take its place, since morality is dissolved by thought.
>
> (*CPBR* vol. 12: 288)

So far, this is pretty strong stuff, but this radical-sounding rejection of morality is not properly thought through. Instead, it peters out in a meditation on punishment, which Russell proposes to replace by the threat of ostracism. Apparently, potential criminals, like the gentlemen of Russell's day, are to be kept in line by the threat of expulsion from their clubs. 'In a decent community the penalties against cheating at cards would be quite sufficient'. (Note the word 'decent'.) We then find that 'Justice and Liberty are what remains of morality' (quite a substantial remainder!), and that 'these the statesman must respect'. (Whence this moral 'must'?) Russell goes on to treat us to his views on sex and marriage, from which it transpires that even more remains of morality than Justice and Liberty. 'Sex relations', it seems, are 'bad without love, also without children', 'sex relations without a common life are bad' (because 'they emphasize sex too much') and sex relations entered into on either side 'for other than sexual reasons' are not merely bad, but 'vile' (*CPBR* vol. 13: 289–91). These notes do not reveal Russell at his best, but they *do* show how difficult it is to be a consistent amoralist. And, of course, what might be called *the practicality problem* is even more severe if I am right about the raising of children. If it is impossible – or even very difficult – to bring up children without bringing them up moral, then the amoral society could only exist if people were carefully de-moralized on reaching adulthood. It is not obvious that this would be worth the effort.

But though an amoral society may be an impossibility, it *is* possible for *groups* to reject morality. The Bolsheviks claimed to have emancipated themselves from morality, and though their emancipation was no doubt incomplete (their rhetoric often suggests that the rejection of morality is somehow *noble*), they did make a fist of living down to their professed lack of moral principle. The result was a human catastrophe.

The Bolsheviks were not analytical philosophers and their pronouncements on meta-ethics are not completely clear. But they were obviously moral sceptics of a fairly radical kind. 'In what sense do we reject ethics, reject morality?' asks Lenin. 'We reject any morality based on extra-human and extra-class concepts. We say that this is deception, dupery, stultification . . . there is no such thing as a morality that stands outside human society; that is a fraud' (Lenin 1920: 416–17). This sounds remarkably like the error theory combined with some variant of amoralism. When he adds that 'to us morality is subordinated to the interests of the proletariat's class struggle', this is clearly intended as a *stipulative* definition. For a communist, the moral words are to be defined with respect to the class struggle. But this is a linguistic (as well as a moral) innovation. The communist definitions are not supposed to conform with common usage. Lenin, therefore, is an *error theorist* about the current moral concepts and an *amoralist* in that he rejects any demands arising from these bourgeois delusions. Why then, should Lenin's audience, the young men and women of the Komsomol, commit themselves to communism? What Lenin relies on is a sentiment of sympathy. There is much scornful talk of those who do not give a rap for anyone else, and it is clear that his remarks are addressed to those who are *not* like this. Now this *is* humanistic amoralism, though it is modified in its effects by Lenin's bizarre factual opinions and ferocious passions. Bukharin's views were remarkably similar, as were Trotsky's. (See Paper 26, Pipes 1994: 328–9, Trotsky 1973: 13–26 and Cohen 1980: 168.) This meta-ethic was used to defend the terroristic acts of the Bolshevik state. After all, if nothing is really wrong, it cannot be wrong to shoot hostages. Indeed, shooting hostages may actually be *right* if we define 'right actions' as those which advance the cause of the proletariat or the classless society.

The human catastrophe that resulted staggers the imagination. Pipes suggests that in the first five years of the Bolshevik regime (i.e. under *Lenin*, not Stalin) *10.7 million people* died a premature death (Pipes 1994: 508–9). (Indeed, the number may rise to 23 million if we take the natural rate of increase of the population into account.) Of these a substantial fraction – hundreds of thousands, perhaps millions – were directly killed on Bolshevik orders, either in the Terror or during the numerous peasant revolts.

In 1916, Russell wrote that he wished to see 'less cruelty, persecution, punishment and moral reprobation than exists at present'. To this end, he thought 'a recognition of the subjectivity of ethics might conduce' (Paper 16). But the Bolsheviks were much given to cruelty, persecution, punishment and moral reprobation even though they recognized 'the subjectivity of ethics'. As Russell himself was to put it, Bolshevik Russia 'seemed to me one vast prison in which the jailers were cruel bigots' (Russell 1956a: 8).

In 1922, Russell's *advocatus diaboli* wrote that 'if moralists really desired a happier world', 'they would work for the abolition of morality' (Paper 25). But the Bolsheviks professed to be free from moral scruples and happiness (to put it mildly) did not result.

Russell was well aware of these facts, as Paper 26 demonstrates. Perhaps this explains why, by 1929, he no longer sought to abolish morality altogether (if, indeed, he ever did) but only to replace the current code with something more humane.

26

A RUSSIAN COMMUNIST
PHILOSOPHER

1926

Reprinted from *CPBR* vol. 9: 364–71, originally published in *The New Leader*, 13, 45, 20 August 1926: 3–5. This piece is a review of Bukharin's *Historical Materialism*. Nikolai Ivanovich Bukharin (1888–1938) was one of the leaders of the Bolshevik revolution and a member of Lenin's Politbureau. He was the principal architect of the New Economic Policy, which allowed the peasants to keep, and even to sell, some of their surplus produce. (Formerly, under 'War Communism', everything in excess of the bare necessities had been requisitioned by the state.) I regret to say that he sometimes sinned against the canons of Bolshevik amoralism by arguing that it was *wrong* to mistreat the peasants (Cohen 1980: 167–8). During the late 1920s he and Stalin were the co-rulers of Russia but Stalin reversed his policies and procured his downfall during the period of 'Collectivization'. Thereafter Stalin played a cat-and-mouse game with him until he was finally arrested, forced to admit to imaginary crimes, and shot. Bukharin tried to subvert his show trial by admitting his crimes in general (as presumably he had agreed to do) but denying them in detail. (His plea, in effect, was: 'Yes I was head of an anti-Soviet conspiracy, but no, I did not conspire to commit any anti-Soviet acts.') This would discredit his own testimony and suggest that it was forced. Unfortunately, his audience, both foreign and domestic, lacked the logical acumen to understand this subtle ploy.

In this paper Russell does not waste time on Bukharin's meta-ethic. Instead he argues that Bukharin's pretensions to a scientific understanding of society are essentially fraudulent. Thus policies based on this understanding are unlikely to work. In particular, it is foolish to inflict present pains for the sake of future gains – to shoot hostages for the sake of the classless society, for example – if there is no good reason to suppose that the gains will come about. Of course, this argument is consistent with Russell's brand of utilitarianism, but it should also appeal to a humanistic amoralist – at least, it should do so if his (or her) concern for human welfare is at all genuine. From a scientific point of view, Leninism is at best dubious, and at worst bosh. The Bolsheviks' rigid adherence to such a worthless theory cries out for explanation. Russell's *advocatus diaboli* argues that 'morality is a device for inhibiting our natural sympathies on occasions when we wish to inflict pain'. It seems that for professed amoralists, there are factual theories which can have much the same effect.

Historical Materialism: A System of Sociology. By Nikolai Bukharin. London: George Allen & Unwin, 1926. Pp. xv, 218.

Bukharin's *Historical Materialism* is a very useful book to everyone who wishes to understand the philosophy upon which the Soviet Government is based. It may be taken as authoritative, in view of the position of Bukharin, who, as the cover reminds us, is editor-in-chief of *Pravda*.

Bolshevism is misunderstood, in this country, by friends and enemies equally. This book will not be read by the latter, but the former will do well to read it before deciding that, in the main, they are in agreement with Moscow. As Trotsky has somewhat trenchantly reminded us, our Labour Movement (not excluding the I.L.P.) differs from the Communist Party in Russia by the fact that it has no philosophy. Outside politics, there is no proposition upon which the members of the I.L.P. are all agreed. To most British minds this seems to be of no consequence, but for my part I believe the Bolsheviks are right in thinking a coherent philosophy important. That being the case, I propose to concentrate on Bukharin's philosophy, and say very little about his politics and economics, which are familiar to readers of the *New Leader*.

He begins by laying it down that men's opinions on politics and economics (and also, as we afterwards learn, on religion, philosophy, art, and practically everything else) are the result of economic causes. He then asks:

If the social sciences have a class character, in what way is proletarian science superior to bourgeois science, for the working class also has its interests, its aspirations, its practice, while the bourgeoisie has a practice of its own? Both classes must be considered as interested parties. . . . One of these classes has one kind of eye-glasses, red ones, the other class has a different kind, white ones. Why are red glasses better than white ones?

His answer is that all human institutions are liable to change, but the defenders of the old have to conceal this fact from others and from themselves; therefore, their bias demands more distortion of facts than is demanded by the advocates of change. This is a valid argument at all times against those who think that they have established a truth for eternity, like Catholic theologians; but most defenders of the capitalist system are not concerned with eternity – their children and grandchildren usually represent the extreme limit of their purview. Therefore, so far as Bukharin's argument shows, the question whether the bias of the capitalist or that of the Communist is the more misleading turns on the question whether capitalism will last less or more than (say) another sixty years. He expressly rules out ethical considerations; at the place indicated by dots in the above quotation, he says, 'It is not sufficient to say that one class is good, high-minded, concerned with the welfare of humanity, while the other is greedy, eager for profits, etc.'

Consequently, as between two disputants, one of whom advocates capitalism *for the present*, while the other advocates 'Socialism in our time', the question which is right will be reduced to the question which is going to be victorious in the near future. Until the future has disclosed the answer to that question we cannot, on Bukharin's principles, know which had the most distorting bias. This seems an unsatisfactory conclusion. And we must face the possibility that the future will bring neither capitalism nor Socialism, but something which no one has yet thought of. All this, however, concerns only Bukharin's Introduction.

The body of the book begins by a statement of the metaphysic of materialistic determinism.

Everything in nature, therefore, from the movements of the planets down to the little grain or mushroom, is subject to a certain uniformity or, as it is generally put, to a certain *natural law*. We observe the same condition in social life also, i.e., in the life of human society.

It is a mistake to think of the laws governing human society in terms of *goal* or *purpose*, because, though men have purposes, these purposes have causes, so that the explanation by causes is the fundamental one. Some people have maintained that the essence of human society consists in its capacity for making laws, but, even if this were true,

> Would it follow that we may never ask ourselves *why* people regulate these relations at a certain time and in a certain place in one way, while they order them quite differently in another place and at another time? For example, the bourgeois German Republic in 1919 and 1920 regulated social relations by shooting the workers; the Soviet Proletarian Republic regulates these relations by shooting counter-revolutionary capitalists. . . . Would it be sufficient simply to say that the purposes are different? Everyone will see at once that this would not be sufficient, for everyone will ask: but why, why should 'men' in one case set themselves one goal, and in another case a different goal? This brings us face to face with the answer: because in the one case the proletariat is in power, in the other case the bourgeoisie; the bourgeoisie desires one thing, because the conditions of its life cause it to have one set of desires; but the conditions of the life of the workers cause them to have a different set of wishes, etc.

He concludes that, in the social sciences as elsewhere, 'scientific explanations are causal explanations'.

It will be seen that there is no place for ethics in this system. We act as we do because natural laws control us, just as they control the planets. The ethical notions of a class are caused like everything else, and there is no sense in asking whether one class has 'better' ethical notions than another. The only question is whether it is going to win in the struggle for power. Accordingly we find Bukharin pouring scorn on humanitarianism, philanthropy, etc.

> In the old discussions between Marxists and Social-Revolutionaries the latter usually formulated the question from the point of view of philanthropy, 'ethics,' 'compassion' for the 'weaker brother,' and similar rubbish of a ruling class intellectual nature. . . . The Marxists, however, were not concerned with lachrymose sentiments or philanthropy,

but with a precise study of class peculiarities, with *finding out* what class would lead in the impending struggle for socialism.

In addition to determinism, i.e. the doctrine that everything is determined by previous causes, Bukharin also advocates materialism, in the sense that the fundamental causes of events, even of human events, are always to be found in the physical world. In his own words: 'Mind cannot exist without matter, while matter may very well exist without mind; matter existed before mind; mind is a special property of matter organised in a special manner.' Any other metaphysic is condemned, along with belief in God, as a bourgeois device. 'Of course, the senile bourgeoisie, now drooling about God like a soft-brained old man, regards materialism with hatred. It is easy to see that materialism necessarily will be the revolutionary theory of the young revolutionary class, the proletariat.'

He is not complimentary to people who believe in God.

> To drag in this poor old man (i.e., God) who constitutes perfection, according to his worshipers [*sic*], and who is obliged to create, together with Adam, lice and prostitutes, murderers and lepers, hunger and poverty, syphilis and vodka, as a punishment for sinners whom he created and who commit sins by his desire, and to continue playing this comedy for ever in the eyes of a delighted universe – to drag in God is a necessary step for idealist theory. But from the point of view of science it means reducing this 'theory' to an absurdity.

Bukharin takes us next through a curious region in Marxian Theory, the region where Hegel's influence survives. In a chapter called 'Dialectic Materialism', he explains that Marx wished to discover the laws of change in societies, and that he found these laws to result from contradictions implicit in the structure of the societies. He says in italics: 'Historical "growth" is the development of contradictions.' This is exactly Hegel's view; Bukharin quotes with approval Hegel's dictum: 'Contradiction is the power that moves things.' He also states that 'two philosophers particularly, the ancient Heraclitus and the modern Hegel, have formulated the law of change'.

Marx was at first a disciple of Hegel, and retained in later life a belief in the dialectic method invented by that philosopher. In this method, development is by logical jumps from one form of society into its opposite, to be replaced later by a synthesis of the two. But development is not boundless; in Hegel, it ended with the Prussian State; in Marx, it went one step farther, to the establishment of Communism. From that point on, the world was to be happy ever after; there were to be no revolutions against the Prussian State in Hegel, and there are to be none against the Communist State in Bukharin. Hegel and Bukharin are agreed in considering that the Government which they serve represents the ultimate goal of human evolution.

This whole aspect of Marxism seems curiously out of place in the modern world, and not of a piece with the rest of its doctrines. Hegel's use of contradiction was based upon his belief in logic, which, in turn, was justified by the view that thought is the ultimate reality in the world. But when matter is taken as the ultimate reality, it is inconsistent to retain a view of development which rests upon the notion that Reason is supreme.

Marx's adoption of the Hegelian dialectic method must be regarded as an historical accident, due to the facts that he was a student when Hegel's influence was at its height, and that he had practically completed his system before the publication of Darwin's *Origin of Species*. There remains to this day in Marxism a certain dislike of the ideas associated with biological evolution. This is partly because the dialectic method afforded a reason for revolutions, whereas evolution has been supposed (quite falsely) to show 'the inevitability of gradualness'. Bukharin himself points out that the post-Darwinian theory of mutations has reintroduced development by sudden jumps. But there is still nothing biological in his outlook; and this must be attributed to the fact that Marx's thinking was done before evolution came to the fore.

Bukharin, following Marx, holds not only that all causation in human affairs is ultimately derived from physical laws, but also that it shows itself entirely through economics, and more especially through methods of production. Politics, philosophy, religion, and art are all determined by the prevailing productive technique. For example, seven pages (pp. 189–96) are devoted to showing the dependence of music upon economic factors.

Now, this point, which is of the essence of the Marxian philosophy, does not follow from materialistic determination, though Bukharin and others maintain that it does. There are many other theories of social changes which are equally materialistic, e.g. some maintain that the collapse of Rome was due to malaria; many writers consider climate a vital factor in determining national character; Freudians maintain that sex, not the economic motive, is fundamental in human affairs.

None of these theories can be refuted by means of general considerations; each must be investigated in the light of detailed facts. Psycho-analysis is not mentioned in Bukharin's book, but some materialistic alternatives to economic determination are mentioned. They are all rejected after a very summary discussion. One feels that the real reason for their rejection is that they do not lead to proletarian optimism: no theory can be tolerated which does not prove that there is a good time coming for the proletariat. Of course, such an unscientific motive cannot be avowed, but it is, nevertheless, clearly operative, e.g. in the discussion of the population question (pp. 123–6).

Some further steps are necessary to complete the philosophy of Communism. Following the Hegelian dialectic method, it is argued that every economic system other than Communism must develop internal contradictions, which will show themselves as conflicts between classes; in these conflicts the class whose self-interest is in line with the materialistically inevitable development of society will win; that class at the present day is the proletariat. Strife is part of the essential principle by means of which development takes place; therefore, pacifism is logically absurd, except as a device of the possessing classes to prevent revolution – e.g. the divine right of kings in seventeenth-century England, and the inviolability of contracts under the American Constitution.

Since religion and philosophy are expressions of class interests, the proletarian State is to enforce Marxian views of both, if necessary by religious persecution. It is useless to hope that religion will disappear of itself:

> Nothing 'disappears of itself' in society; as early as the days of Marx, we find the latter, in a brilliant essay . . . poking fun at the view of 'religion a private matter.' Marx considers this slogan to mean merely that the workers must demand of the bourgeois State that it shall not poke its police nose into things that do not concern it; but it by no means signifies that the workers are to be 'tolerant' of all the remnants of the wretched past, of all the powers of reaction.

It is hard to see why, on Bukharin's view, the religious opinions of the proletarian should not concern the bourgeois policeman.

We may sum up Bukharin's Historical Materialism in the following series of propositions:

I   Every event in the world is the outcome of previous events in accordance with physical laws. This applies to human events as much as to the movements of the planets.

II   In human affairs, physical causes operate through the method of production, when we are considering large-scale social phenomena. The method of production determines the politics, laws, religion and art of a society in their broad outlines.

III Every method of production other than that of Communism involves a division of classes with antagonistic desires. In the consequent strife, the subordinate class ultimately wins, owing to technical developments in production; this leads to a new epoch, with a new method.

IV The victory of the proletariat leads to Communism, which abolishes the division of classes, and therefore the conflict between the interests of different people, and therefore the State, which is the organ of the ruling class. The proletarian revolution, like every other, is the inevitable outcome of physical laws; there is no need to think of it as ethically desirable, which is the bourgeois point of view condemned in the Social Revolutionaries.

Of these propositions, I am willing to accept the first as probable, though not as certain. I have stated it in language slightly different from Bukharin's, so as to free it from the notion of matter as a 'substance', which modern physics seems to me to render obsolete. But I do not think this has any important *practical* consequences in the present connection.

The second proposition, however, which infers economic from physical determinism, is much more questionable. Of course, it is true that economic causes determine a great deal, but to say that they determine everything is to say something which does not follow from physical determinism, and which history, to my mind, does not bear out. Contrast the religious mysticism of India with the elegant scepticism of China: these flourished in closely similar economic circumstances. Why did geometry arise among the Greeks rather than among the Phoenicians or any of the other commercial peoples of the Eastern Mediterranean? Why did Copernicus and Columbus flourish when they did? Because people took to reading Greek, which, so far as economic considerations were concerned, they could have done several centuries earlier. Why did the industrial revolution come when it did? Because of science: the intellectual advance was the cause of the economic transformation, not vice versa. Thus even when we confine ourselves to large-scale social phenomena, economic determinism is only a half-truth.

The third proposition, advanced as applying to the future, is very rash. In America at the present time, the immense majority of the proletariat are quite content with the capitalist system; the American Federation of Labour is more anti-Bolshevik than Mr. Baldwin. Perhaps capitalism may in time succeed in contenting all the powerful sections of wage-earners. Nothing could be more likely to lead to this result than a study of the Communist philosophy: men will concede much if the alternative is ruin or death. In human affairs, a prediction is very likely to be rendered false by the mere fact that it is made, since it puts men on their guard. The view that there will inevitably be a civil war between capitalists and proletarians, in which the former will be defeated, assumes that capitalists will inevitably miscalculate their chances of victory; if not, they will buy safety by such surrenders as may be necessary. And if the proletarian party are not *certain* of victory, they may be induced to accept concessions short of complete Communism.

All these possibilities are illustrated by the United States. In England, the corresponding possibilities were realized by the nineteenth-century surrender of the aristocracy to the bourgeoisie.

The fourth proposition is also doubtful. In a country with a highly developed industrial population, like our own, it is probable that the State would play a smaller part, and the Trade Unions a larger part, than in Russia; something like a federation of industries might result, instead of the State Socialism necessitated by Russian conditions.

Nor is it true that Communism puts an end to economic conflict. Take laziness: one man's shirking would do very little to diminish the national dividend, so that each individual will have a motive for trying to do as little work as possible. To prevent this, it will still be necessary to retain the machinery of compulsion. Again, some men will prefer longer hours and more goods, others shorter hours and more leisure; this might easily become the basis of political conflicts.

Take again the question of population. Even if America and Japan were both Communistic, I do not for a moment believe that Americans would welcome Japanese immigration; yet the pressure of population in Japan might keep this question as urgent as it is today.

Finally: we do not know enough about the laws of social phenomena to be able to predict the future with any certainty, even in its broadest outlines. Some new discovery or invention may alter everything. Imagine how utterly wide of the mark any prediction would have been that was made some time before the industrial revolution. For this reason, it is unwise to adopt any policy involving great immediate suffering for the sake of even a great gain in the distant future, because the gain may never be realized.

The above gives the outline of the reasons which lead me to be unable to accept the Bolshevik philosophy, in spite of sympathy with its aims and admiration for its systematic completeness.

27

POWER AND MORAL CODES

Extracts from Chapter 15 of *Power: A New Social Analysis* 1938

Reprinted from *Power*: 237–63. In some ways this paper would be better placed in Part II, since the second half contains excellent accounts both of Russell's meta-ethic and of his normative theory. The meta-ethic of *Power* is much the same as that of *Religion and Science*, a variant of emotivism. Judgements about what is good and bad are in the optative mood and hence neither true nor false. Judgements about right and wrong can be construed as true or false so long as the ends to be promoted by right action are agreed upon. In normative ethics, Russell remains a good utilitarian, but since we cannot calculate the consequences of every act, he thinks we need a code to guide our conduct; thus far, the theory of *Religion and Science*. However, what really interests Russell in this paper is the contrast between *positive* morality (roughly 'morality as an institution') and *personal* morality, the morality of the prophet, the rebel or the non-conformist. He still takes a dim view of positive morality since it tends to sanctify the powers that be, and to license (and even encourage) vindictiveness towards outgroups. However, it also promotes social cohesion which is definitely a plus as 'men are so little gregarious by nature that anarchy is a constant danger'. Accordingly, there is no more talk of abolishing morality in *Power* though Russell obviously has hopes to reform it. And although Russell is still a believer in the 'subjectivity of value' he is no longer so sure that if it were widely recognized this would automatically lead to 'less cruelty, persecution, and punishment'. In Chapter 6, he argues that one of the principal problems facing the world is that of 'naked power'. 'Most of the great abominations of history are connected with naked power', he declares, and 'if human life is to be, for the mass of mankind, anything better than a dull misery punctuated by periods of sharp horror, there must be as little naked power as possible' (Russell 1938: 106). Now, power is naked if those who are subject to it do not recognize it as morally legitimate. Since the subjects do not consent, the rulers must rely on force. Naked power occurs when the subjects do not subscribe to the morality handed down by the rulers. This can happen for two reasons: either (1) because the subjects subscribe to a *different* morality (as when the rulers are foreign conquerors or the subjects are heretics); or (2) because the subjects – perhaps under the influence of something like 'the subjectivity of values' – cease to have strong moral beliefs.

> A form of power which has been traditional becomes naked as soon as the tradition ceases to be accepted. It follows that periods of free thought and vigorous criticism tend to develop into periods of naked power. So it was in Greece and so it was in Renaissance Italy.

Thus moral criticism of the kind Russell indulged in, whether at the normative or the meta-ethical level, can have disastrous results, leading to a collapse of traditional authority and a calamitous slide into a period of naked power. Things get really bad, according to Russell, when the doctrine of Thrasymachus (the anti-hero of Plato's *Republic*) becomes widely accepted and people come to believe that 'justice is the advantage of the stronger' (meaning the rulers or the ruling class).

> Whenever this view is generally accepted, rulers cease to be subject to moral restraints, since what they do is not felt to be shocking except by those who suffer directly. Rebels equally . . . need not be afraid that . . . ruthlessness will make them unpopular.
>
> (Russell 1938: 99–100)

It is notable that the opinions of Lenin and Bukharin were remarkably similar to those of Thrasymachus. To be precise, they seem to have thought *either* that morality is compounded of falsehoods (though falsehoods which tend to favour the interests of the ruling class) *or* that it can be defined as what serves the interests of the proletariat (or if you are a bourgeois, of the bourgeoisie). Thus the actions of (say) Franco in massacring his socialist opponents may have been *wrong* from the Bolshevik point of view, but they were not *shocking*, since he was merely doing what, according to his own definition of 'right', was the right thing to do. But the real problem is that Russell's own position is precious close to that of Thrasymachus. His writings are studded with Thrasymachean remarks ('*morality* is disapproval of the community for those who act against the holders of power') though these are usually not intended to be taken quite literally. Even the theory of *Power* implies that what *passes* for justice will often *be* to the advantage of the stronger, though this is not what 'justice' *means*. For these reasons, Russell is anxious to develop a conception of *personal*, as opposed to *positive*, morality so that when belief in positive morality decays as a result of 'vigorous criticism', there is no descent into a chaos of (non-humanistic) amoralism. He also needs a meta-ethic that gives some sort of legitimacy to personal morality and provides an alternative to the positivism of Thrasymachus. In fact, his brand of emotivism does just this, as the opinions of the subjects are, at any rate, no less legitimate than those of the rulers, since both express desires. Finally, he needs to suggest a *normative* ethic which allows people to criticize ancient injustice without undermining government as such. Utilitarianism does the job nicely, since the good utilitarian will obey any reasonably humane government that allows him (or her) to work for legal and constitutional change.

Morality, at any rate since the days of the Hebrew prophets, has had two divergent aspects. On the one hand, it has been a social institution analogous to law; on the other hand, it has been a matter for the individual conscience. In the former aspect, it is part of the apparatus of power; in the latter, it is often revolutionary. The kind which is analogous to law is called 'positive' morality; the other kind may be called 'personal'. I wish in this chapter to consider the relations of these two kinds of morality to each other and to power.

Positive morality is older than personal morality, and probably older than law and government. It consists originally of tribal customs, out of which law gradually develops. Consider the extraordinarily elaborate rules as to who may marry whom, which are found among very primitive savages. To us, these seem merely rules, but presumably to those who accept them they have the same moral compulsive force as we feel in our rules against incestuous unions. Their source is obscure, but is no doubt in some sense religious. This part of positive morality appears to have no relation to social inequalities; it neither confers exceptional power nor assumes its existence. There are still moral rules of this sort among civilized people. The Greek Church prohibits the marriage of godparents of the same child, a prohibition which fulfils no social purpose, either good or bad, but has its source solely in theology. It seems probable that many prohibitions which are now accepted on rational grounds were originally superstitious. Murder was objectionable because of the hostility of the ghost, which was not directed only against the murderer, but against his community. The community therefore had an interest in the matter, which they could deal with either by punishment or by ceremonies of purification. Gradually purification came to have a spiritual signification, and to be identified with repentance and absolution; but its original ceremonial character is still recalled by such phrases as 'washed in the blood of the Lamb'.

This aspect of positive morality, important as it is, is not the one with which I wish to deal. I wish to consider those aspects of accepted ethical codes in which they minister to power. One of the purposes – usually in large part unconscious – of a traditional morality is to make the existing social system work. It achieves this purpose, when it is successful, both more cheaply and more effectively than a police force does. But it is liable to be confronted with a revolutionary morality, inspired by the desire for a redistribution of power. I want, in this chapter, to consider, first, the effect of power on moral codes, and then the question whether some other basis can be found for morality.

The most obvious example of power-morality is the inculcation of obedience. It is (or rather was) the duty of children to submit to parents, wives to husbands, servants to masters, subjects to princes, and (in religious matters) laymen to priests; there were also more specialized duties of obedience in armies and religious orders. Each of these duties has a long history, running parallel with that of the institution concerned.

Let us begin with filial piety. There are savages at the present day who, when their parents grow too old for work, sell them to be eaten. At some stage in the development of civilization, it must have occurred to some man of unusual forethought that he could, while his children were still young, produce in them a state of mind which would lead them to keep him alive in old age; presumably he was a man whose own parents were already disposed of. In creating a party to support his subversive opinion, I doubt whether he appealed merely to motives of prudence; I suspect that he invoked the Rights of Man, the advantages of a mainly frugiferous diet, and the moral blamelessness of the old who have worn themselves out labouring for their children. Probably there was at the moment some emaciated but unusually wise elder, whose advice was felt to be more valuable than his flesh. However this may be, it came to be felt that one's parents should be honoured rather than eaten. To us, the respect for fathers in early civilizations seems excessive, but we have to remember that a very powerful deterrent was needed to put an end to the lucrative practice of having them eaten. And so we find the Ten Commandments suggesting that if you fail to honour your father and mother you will die young, the Romans considering parricide the most atrocious of crimes, and Confucius making filial piety the very basis of morality. All this is a device, however instinctive and unconscious, for prolonging parental power beyond the early years when children are helpless. The authority of parents has of course been reinforced by their possession of property, but if filial piety had not existed young men would not have allowed their fathers to retain control of their flocks and herds after they had become feeble.

The same sort of thing happened in regard to the subjection of women. The superior strength of male animals does not, in most cases, lead to continual subjection of the females, because the males have not a sufficient constancy of purpose. Among human beings, the subjection of women is much more complete at a certain level of civilization than it is among savages. And the subjection is always reinforced by morality. A man, says St. Paul, 'is the image and glory of God: but the woman is the glory of the man. For the man is not of the woman; but the woman of the man. Neither was the man created for the woman; but the woman for the man' (I Corinthians, xi. 7–9). It follows that wives ought to obey their husbands, and that unfaithfulness is a worse sin in a wife than in a husband. Christianity, it is true, holds, in theory, that adultery is equally sinful in either sex, since it is a sin against God. But this view has not prevailed in practice, and was not held even theoretically in pre-Christian times. Adultery with a married woman was wicked, because it was an offence against her husband; but female slaves and war-captives were the legitimate property of their master, and no blame attached to intercourse with them. This view was held by pious Christian slave-owners, though not by their wives, even in nineteenth-century America.

The basis of the difference between morality for men and morality for women was obviously the superior power of men. Originally the superiority was only physical, but from this basis it gradually extended to economics, politics, and religion. The great advantage of morality over the police appears very clearly in this case, for women, until quite recently, genuinely believed the moral precepts which embodied male domination, and therefore required much less compulsion than would otherwise have been necessary.

Kings, until George I, were objects of religious veneration.

> There's such divinity doth hedge a king,
> That treason can but peep the thing it would,
> Acts little of his will.

The word 'treason', even in republics, has still a flavour of impiety. In England, government profits much by the tradition of royalty. Victorian statesmen, even Mr. Gladstone, felt it their duty to the Queen to see to it that she was never left without a Prime Minister. The duty of obedience to authority is still felt by many as a duty towards the sovereign. This is a decaying sentiment, but as it decays government becomes less stable, and dictatorships of the Right or the Left become more possible.

Bagehot's *English Constitution* – a book still well worth reading – begins the discussion of the monarchy as follows:

> The use of the Queen, in a dignified capacity, is incalculable. Without her in England, the present English Government would fail and pass away. Most people when they read that the Queen walked on the slopes at Windsor – that the Prince of Wales went to the Derby – have imagined that too much thought and prominence were given to little things. But they have been in error; and it is nice to trace how the actions of a retired widow and an unemployed youth become of such importance.
>
> The best reason why Monarchy is a strong government is, that it is an intelligible government. The mass of mankind understand it, and they hardly anywhere in the world understand any other. It is often said that men are ruled by their imaginations; but it would be truer to say that they are governed by the weakness of their imaginations.

This is both true and important. Monarchy makes social cohesion easy, first, because it is not so difficult to feel loyalty to an individual as to an abstraction, and secondly, because kingship, in its long history, has accumulated sentiments of veneration which no new institution can inspire. Where hereditary monarchy has been abolished, it has usually been succeeded, after a longer or short time, by some other form of one-man rule: tyranny in Greece, the Empire in Rome, Cromwell in England, the Napoleons in France, Stalin and Hitler in our own day. Such men inherit a part of the feelings formerly attached to royalty. It is amusing to note, in the confessions of the accused in Russian trials, the acceptance of a morality of submission to the ruler such as would be appropriate in the most ancient and traditional of absolute monarchies. But a new dictator, unless he is a very extraordinary man, can hardly inspire *quite* the same religious veneration as hereditary monarchs enjoyed in the past.

Wherever there is a traditional monarchy, rebellion against the government is an offence against the king, and is regarded by the orthodox as a sin and an impiety. Kingship acts therefore, broadly speaking, as a force on the side of the *status quo*, whatever that may be. Its most useful function, historically, has been the creation of a widely diffused sentiment favourable to social cohesion. Men are so little gregarious by nature that anarchy is a constant danger, which kingship has done much to prevent. Against this merit, however, must be set the demerit of perpetuating ancient evils and increasing the forces opposed to desirable change. This demerit has, in modern times, caused monarchy to disappear over the greater part of the earth's surface.

The power of priests is more obviously connected with morals than any other form of power. In Christian countries, virtue consists in obedience to the will of God, and it is priests who know what the will of God commands. The precept that we ought to obey God rather than man is, as we saw, capable of being revolutionary; it is so in two sets of circumstances, one, when the State is in opposition to the Church, the other, when it is held that God speaks directly to each individual conscience. The former state of affairs existed before Constantine, the latter among the Anabaptists and Independents. But in non-revolutionary periods, when there is an established and traditional Church, it is accepted by positive morality as the intermediary between God and the individual conscience. So long as this acceptance continues, its power is very great, and rebellion against the Church is thought more wicked than any other kind. The Church has its difficulties none the less, for if it uses its power too flagrantly men begin to doubt whether it is interpreting the will of God correctly; and when this doubt becomes common, the whole ecclesiastical edifice crumbles, as it did in Teutonic countries at the Reformation.

There are, however, more complicated results of opposition to priestly power. The Church being the official guardian of the moral code, its opponents are likely to revolt in morals as well as in doctrine and government. They may revolt, like the Puritans, into greater strictness, or, like the French Revolutionaries, into greater laxity; but in either case morals come to be a private matter, not, as before, the subject of official decisions by a public body.

It must not be supposed that personal morality is in general worse than official priestly morality, even when it is less severe. There is some evidence than when, in the sixth century B.C., Greek sentiment was becoming strongly averse from human sacrifice, the oracle at Delphi tried to retard this humanitarian reform, and to keep alive the old rigid practices. Similarly in our own day, when the State and public opinion consider it permissible to marry one's deceased wife's sister, the Church, in so far as it has power, maintains the old prohibition.

Morality, where the Church has lost power, has not become genuinely personal except for a few exceptional people. For the majority, it is represented by public opinion, both that of neighbours in general, and that of powerful groups such as employers. From the point of view of the sinner, the change may be slight, and may also be for the worse. Where the individual gains is not as sinner, but as judge: he becomes part of an informal democratic tribunal, whereas, where the Church is strong, he must accept the rulings of Authority. The Protestant whose moral feelings are strong usurps the ethical functions of the priest, and acquires a quasi-governmental attitude towards other people's virtues and vices, especially the latter:

> Ye've naught to do but mark and tell
> Your neighbours' faults and folly.

This is not anarchy; it is democracy.

The thesis that the moral code is an expression of power is, as we have seen, not wholly true. From the exogamous rules of savages onward, there are, at all stages of civilization, ethical principles which have no visible relation to power – among ourselves, the condemnation of homosexuality may serve as an example. The Marxist thesis, that the moral code is an expression of *economic* power, is even less adequate than the thesis that it is an expression of power in general. Nevertheless, the Marxist thesis is true in a very great many instances. For example: in the Middle Ages, when the most powerful of the laity were landowners, when bishoprics and monastic orders derived their income from land, and when the only investors of money were Jews, the Church unhesitatingly condemned 'usury', i.e. all lending of money at interest. This was a debtor's morality. With the rise of the rich merchant class, it became impossible to maintain the old prohibition: it was relaxed first by Calvin, whose clientele was mainly urban and prosperous, then by the other Protestants, and last of all by the Catholic Church.[1] Creditor's morality became the fashion, and nonpayment of debts a heinous sin. The Society of Friends, practically if not theoretically, excluded bankrupts until very recently.

Duty to enemies is a difficult conception. Clemency was recognized as a virtue in antiquity, but only when it was successful, that is to say, when it turned enemies into friends; otherwise, it was condemned as a weakness. When fear had been aroused, no one expected magnanimity: the Romans showed none towards Hannibal or the followers of Spartacus. In the days of chivalry, a knight was expected to show courtesy to a knightly captive. But the conflicts of knights were not very serious; not the faintest mercy was shown to the Albigenses. In our day, almost equal ferocity has been shown towards the victims of the white terrors in Finland, Hungary, Germany, and Spain, and hardly any protests have been aroused except among political opponents. The terror in Russia, likewise, has been condoned by most of the Left. Now, as in the days of the Old Testament, no duty to enemies is acknowledged in practice when they are sufficiently formidable to arouse fear. Positive morality, in effect, is still only operative within the social group concerned, and is therefore still, in effect, a department of government. Nothing short of a world government will cause people of pugnacious disposition to admit, except as a counsel of perfection, that moral obligations are not confined to a section of the human race.

---

1   On this subject cf. Tawney (1929) *Religion and the Rise of Capitalism.*

I have been concerned hitherto, in this chapter, with positive morality, and, as has become evident, it is not enough. Broadly speaking, it is on the side of the powers that be, it does not allow a place for revolution, it does nothing to mitigate the fierceness of strife, and it can find no place for the prophet who proclaims some new moral insight. Certain difficult questions of theory are involved, but before considering them let us remind ourselves of some of the things that only opposition to positive morality could achieve.

The world owes something to the Gospels, though not so much as it would if they had had more influence. It owes something to those who denounced slavery and the subjection of women. We may hope that in time it will owe something to those who denounce war and economic injustice. In the eighteenth and nineteenth centuries, it owed much to the apostles of tolerance; perhaps it will again in some happier age than ours. Revolutions, against the mediaeval Church, the Renaissance monarchies, and the present power of plutocracy, are necessary for the avoidance of stagnation. Admitting, as we must, that mankind needs revolution and individual morality, the problem is to find a place for these things without plunging the world into anarchy.

There are two questions to be considered: First, what is the wisest attitude for positive morality from its own standpoint, to take to personal morality? Second, what degree of respect does personal morality owe to positive morality? But before discussing either of these, something must be said as to what is meant by personal morality.

Personal morality may be considered as a historical phenomenon, or from the standpoint of the philosopher. Let us begin with the former.

Almost every individual that has ever existed, so far as history is aware, has had a profound horror of certain kinds of acts. As a rule, these acts are held in abhorrence, not only by one individual, but by a whole tribe or nation or sect or class. Sometimes the origin of the abhorrence is unknown, sometimes it can be traced to a historical personage who was a moral innovator. We know why Mohammedans will not make images of animals or human beings; it is because the Prophet forbade them to do so. We know why orthodox Jews will not eat hare; it is because the Mosaic Law declares that the hare is unclean. Such prohibitions, when accepted, belong to positive morality; but in their origin, at any rate when their origin is known, they belonged to private morality.

Morality, for us, however, has come to mean something more than ritual precepts, whether positive or negative. In the form in which it is familiar to us it is not primitive, but appears to have a number of independent sources – Chinese sages, Indian Buddhists, Hebrew prophets, and Greek philosophers. These men, whose importance in history it is difficult to overestimate, all lived within a few centuries of each other, and all shared certain characteristics which marked them out from their predecessors. Lao-Tse and Chuang-Tse deliver the doctrine of the Tao as what they know of their own knowledge, not through tradition or the wisdom of others; and the doctrine consists not of specific duties, but of a way of life, a manner of thinking and feeling, from which it will become plain, without the need of rules, what must be done on each occasion. The same may be said of the early Buddhists. The Hebrew prophets, at their best, transcend the Law, and advocate a new and more inward kind of virtue, recommended not by tradition, but by the words 'thus saith the Lord'. Socrates acts as his daemon commands, not as the legally constituted authorities desire; he is prepared to suffer martyrdom rather than be untrue to the inner voice. All these men were rebels in their day, and all have come to be honoured. Something of what was new in them has come to be taken as a matter of course. But it is not altogether easy to say what this something is.

The minimum that must be accepted by any thoughtful person who either adheres to a religion having a historical origin, or thinks that some such religion was an improvement on what went before, is this: that a way of life which was in some sense better than some previous way of life was first advocated by some individual or set of individuals, in opposition to the teaching of State and Church in their day. It follows that it cannot always be wrong for an individual to set himself up in moral questions, even against the judgment of all mankind up to his day. In science, every one now admits the corresponding doctrine; but in science the ways of testing a new doctrine are known, and it soon comes to be generally accepted, or else rejected on other grounds than tradition. In ethics, no such obvious ways exist by which a new doctrine can be tested. A prophet may preface his teaching by 'thus saith the Lord', which is sufficient for him; but how are other people to know that he has had a genuine revelation?

We must face the question: What is meant by an ethical doctrine, and in what ways, if any, can it be tested?

Historically, ethics is connected with religion. For most men, authority has sufficed: what is laid down as right or wrong by the Bible or the Church *is* right or wrong. But certain individuals have, from time to time, been divinely inspired: they have known what was right or wrong because God spoke directly to them. These individuals, according to orthodox opinion, all lived a long time ago, and if a modern man professes to be one of them it is best to put him in an asylum, unless, indeed, the Church sanctions his pronouncements. This, however, is merely the usual situation of the rebel become dictator, and does not help us to decide what are the legitimate functions of rebels.

Can we translate ethics into non-theological terms? Victorian freethinkers had no doubt that this was possible. The utilitarians, for instance, were highly moral men, and were convinced that their morality had a rational basis. The matter is, however, rather more difficult than it appeared to them.

Let us consider a question suggested by the mention of the utilitarians, namely: Can a rule of conduct ever be a self-subsistent proposition of ethics, or must it always be deduced from the good or bad effects of the conduct in question? The traditional view is that certain kinds of acts are sinful, and certain others virtuous, independently of their effects. Other kinds of acts are ethically neutral, and may be judged by their results. Whether euthanasia or marriage with a deceased wife's sister should be legalized is an ethical question, but the gold standard is not. There are two definitions of 'ethical' questions, either of which will cover the cases to which this adjective is applied. A question is 'ethical' (1) if it interested the ancient Hebrews, (2) if it is one on which the Archbishop of Canterbury is the official expert. It is obvious that this common use of the word 'ethical' is wholly indefensible.

Nevertheless, I find, speaking personally, that there are kinds of conduct against which I feel a repugnance which seems to me to be moral, but to be not obviously based upon an estimate of consequences. I am informed by many people that the preservation of democracy, which I think important, can only be secured by gassing immense numbers of children and doing a number of other horrible things. I find that, at this point, I cannot acquiesce in the use of such means. I tell myself that they will not secure the end, or that, if they do, they will incidentally have other effects so evil as to outweigh any good that democracy might do. I am not quite sure how far this argument is honest: I think I should refuse to use such means even if I were persuaded that they would secure the end and that no others

215

would. *Per contra*, psychological imagination assures me that nothing that I should think good can possibly be achieved by such means. On the whole, I think that, speaking philosophically, all acts ought to be judged by their effects; but as this is difficult and uncertain and takes time, it is desirable, in practice, that some kinds of acts should be condemned and others praised without waiting to investigate consequences. I should say, therefore, with the utilitarians, that the right act, in any given circumstances, is that which, on the data, will probably produce the greatest balance of good over evil of all the acts that are possible; but that the performance of such acts may be promoted by the existence of a moral code.

Accepting this view, ethics is reduced to defining 'good' and 'bad', not as means, but as ends in themselves. The utilitarian says that the good is pleasure and the bad is pain. But if some one disagrees with him, what arguments can he produce?

Consider various views as to the ends of life. One man says 'the good is pleasure'; another, 'the good is pleasure for Aryans and pain for Jews'; another, 'the good is to praise God and glorify Him for ever'. What are these three men asserting, and what methods exist by which they can convince each other? They cannot, as men of science do, appeal to facts: no facts are relevant to the dispute. Their difference is in the realm of desire, not in the realm of statements about matters of fact. I do not assert that when I say 'this is good' I mean 'I desire this'; it is only a particular kind of desire that leads me to call a thing good. The desire must be in some degree impersonal; it must have to do with the sort of world that would content me, not only with my personal circumstances. A king might say: 'Monarchy is good, and I am glad I am a monarch.' The first part of this statement is indubitably ethical, but his pleasure in being a monarch only becomes ethical if a survey persuades him that no one else would make such a good king.

I have suggested on a former occasion (in *Religion and Science* [Paper 19]) that a judgment of intrinsic value is to be interpreted, not as an assertion, but as an expression of desire concerning the desires of mankind. When I say 'hatred is bad', I am really saying: 'Would that no one felt hatred'. I make no assertion; I merely express a certain type of wish. The hearer can gather that I feel this wish, but that is the only *fact* that he can gather, and that is a fact of psychology. There are no facts of ethics.

The great ethical innovators have not been men who *knew* more than others; they have been men who *desired* more, or, to be more accurate, men whose desires were more impersonal and of larger scope than those of average men. Most men desire their own happiness; a considerable percentage desire the happiness of their children; not a few desire the happiness of their nation; some, genuinely and strongly, desire the happiness of all mankind. These men, seeing that many others have no such feeling, and that this is an obstacle to universal felicity, wish that others feel as they do; this wish can be expressed in the words 'happiness is good'.

All great moralists, from Buddha and the Stoics down to recent times, treated the good as something to be, if possible, enjoyed by all men equally. They did not think of themselves as princes or Jews or Greeks; they thought of themselves merely as human beings. Their ethic had always a twofold source: on the one hand, they valued certain elements in their own lives; on the other hand, sympathy made them desire for others what they desired for themselves. Sympathy is the universalizing force in ethics; I mean sympathy as an emotion, not as a theoretical principle. Sympathy is in some degree instinctive: a child may be made unhappy by another child's cry. But limitations of sympathy are also natural. The cat has no sympathy for the mouse; the Romans had no sympathy for any animals except elephants; the Nazis have none for Jews, and Stalin had none for kulaks. Where there is limitation of sympathy there is a corresponding limitation in the conception of the good: the good becomes something to be enjoyed only by the magnanimous man, or only by the superman, or the Aryan, or the proletarian, or the Christadelphian. All these are cat-and-mouse ethics.

The refutation of a cat-and-mouse ethic, where it is possible, is practical, not theoretical. Two adepts at such an ethic, like quarrelsome little boys, each begin: 'Let's play I'm the cat and you're the mouse.' 'No, no', they each retort, 'you shan't be the cat, I will'. And so, more often than not, they become the Kilkenny cats. But if one of them succeeds completely, he may establish his ethic; we then get Kipling and the White Man's Burden, or the Nordic Race, or some such creed of inequality. Such creeds, inevitably, appeal only to the cat, not to the mouse; they are imposed on the mouse by naked power.

Ethical controversies are very often as to means, not ends. Slavery may be attacked by the argument that it is uneconomic; the subjection of women may be criticized by maintaining that the conversation of free women is more interesting; persecution may be deplored on the ground (wholly fallacious, incidentally) that the religious convictions produced by it are not genuine. Behind such arguments, however, there is generally a difference as to ends. Sometimes, as in Nietzsche's criticism of Christianity, the difference of ends becomes nakedly apparent. In Christian ethics, all men count alike; for Nietzsche, the majority are only a means to the hero. Controversies as to ends cannot be conducted, like scientific controversies, by appeals to facts; they must be conducted by an attempt to change men's feelings. The Christian may endeavour to rouse sympathy, the Nietzschean may stimulate pride. Economic and military power may reinforce propaganda. The contest is, in short, an ordinary contest for power. Any creed, even one which teaches universal equality, may be a means to the domination of a section; this happened, for instance, when the French Revolution set to work to spread democracy by force of arms.

Power is the means, in ethical contests as in those of politics. But with the ethical systems that have had most influence in the past, power is not the end. Although men hate one another, exploit one another, and torture one another, they have, until recently, given their reverence to those who preached a different way of life. The great religions that aimed at universality, replacing the tribal and national cults of earlier times, considered men as men, not as Jew or Gentile, bond or free. Their founders were men whose sympathy was universal, and who were felt, on this account, to be possessed of a wisdom surpassing that of temporary and passionate despots. The result was not all that the founders could have wished. At an *auto-da-fe*, the mob had to be prevented by the police from attacking the victims, and was furious if one whom it had hoped to see burnt alive succeeded, by a tardy recantation, in winning the privilege of being strangled first and burnt afterwards. Nevertheless, the principle of universal sympathy conquered first one province, then another. It is the analogue, in the realm of feeling, of impersonal curiosity in the realm of intellect; both alike are essential elements in mental growth. I do not think that the return to a tribal or aristocratic ethic can be of long duration; the whole history of man since the time of Buddha points in the opposite direction. However passionately power may be desired, it is not power that is thought good in moments of reflective meditation. This is proved by the characters of the men whom mankind have thought most nearly divine.

The traditional moral rules that we considered at the beginning of this chapter – filial piety, wifely submission, loyalty to kings, and so on – have all decayed completely or partially. They may be succeeded, as in the Renaissance, by an absence of moral restraint, or, as in the Reformation, by a new code in many ways more strict than those that have become obsolete. Loyalty to the State plays a much larger part in positive morality in our time than it did formerly; this, of course, is the natural result of the increase in the power of the State. The parts of morals that are concerned with other groups, such as the family and the Church, have less control than they used to have; but I do not see any evidence that, on the balance, moral principles or moral sentiments have less influence over men's actions now than in the eighteenth century or the Middle Ages.

Let us end this chapter with a summary analysis. The moral codes of primitive societies are generally believed, in those societies, to have a supernatural origin; in part, we can see no reason for this belief, but to a considerable extent it represents the balance of power in the community concerned: the gods consider submission to the powerful a duty, but the powerful must not be so ruthless as to rouse rebellion. Under the influence of prophets and sages, however, a new morality arises, sometimes side by side with the old one, sometimes in place of it. Prophets and sages, with few exceptions, have valued things other than power – wisdom, justice, or universal love, for example – and have persuaded large sections of mankind that these are aims more worthy to be pursued than personal success. Those who suffer by some part of the social system which the prophet or sage wishes to alter have personal reasons for supporting his opinion; it is the union of their self-seeking with his impersonal ethic that makes the resulting revolutionary movement irresistible.

We can now arrive at some conclusion as to the place of rebellion in social life. Rebellion is of two sorts: it may be purely personal, or it may be inspired by desire for a different kind of community from that in which the rebel finds himself. In the latter case, his desire can be shared by others; in many instances, it has been shared by all except a small minority who profited by the existing system. This type of rebel is constructive, not anarchic; even if his movement leads to temporary anarchy, it is intended to give rise, in the end, to a new stable community. It is the impersonal character of his aims that distinguishes him from the anarchic rebel. Only the event can decide, for the general public, whether a rebellion will come to be thought justified; when it is thought to have been justified, previously existing authority would have been wise, from its own point of view, in not offering a desperate resistance. An individual may perceive a way of life, or a method of social organization, which more of the desires of mankind could be satisfied than under the existing method. If he perceives truly, and can persuade men to adopt his reform, he is justified. Without rebellion, mankind would stagnate, and injustice would be irremediable. The man who refuses to obey authority has, therefore, in certain circumstances, a legitimate function, provided his disobedience has motives which are social rather than personal. But the matter is one as to which, by its very nature, it is impossible to lay down rules.

Part V

CONTEMPLATION AND THE GOOD LIFE

Interlude 2

SPINOZA AND THE ETHIC OF IMPERSONAL SELF-ENLARGEMENT

In some respects, Russell's normative ethic is less interesting than his various meta-ethics or his views on applied ethics. He was, as we have seen, a utilitarian of sorts, who believed that the right thing to do is what, on the available evidence, seems likely to produce the best balance of good over evil consequences. Since we cannot perform the requisite calculations in every case, we need codes of conduct, though these should be taken with a pinch of salt and reassessed from time to time in the light of new information. This is sensible and humane but dull. Russell's conception of the good – the end to be promoted – is a bit more interesting. To begin with, although he valued human happiness, he did not see this in crudely hedonistic terms. However pleasurable the life of a pig may be, Russell would not have preferred the life of a pig to that of a human being. Russell also valued *passion* and a life which allowed for spontaneous (but 'creative') impulses. These views distinguish him from the classical utilitarians whom he otherwise admired. However, the *really* distinctive features of Russell's ethic were derived from Benedictus de Spinoza (1632–77), who remained a philosophical hero even though Russell rejected most of his metaphysics. There was something about Spinoza's attitude to life that Russell regarded as profoundly right (Spinoza 1951). Kenneth Blackwell calls this 'the ethic of impersonal self-enlargement' (Blackwell 1985: 17). According to this ideal, the best life is lived in awareness of the Other. This includes other selves (since Russell considered a purely selfish life unfulfilling, and a life without history – which involves *knowledge* of other selves – drab) but also the *wholly* other – the non-human universe of large impersonal forces, the wind, the sea, the mountains and the stars and even (if they exist) the entities of mathematics. He felt that the self is enlarged by the contemplation of the not-self and that the person whose concerns are limited to their own states of mind has confined themselves within a spiritual prison. By the same token, a philosophy that reduces reality to an emanation of the self reduces the self by denying it access to the Other. All this may sound unduly elevated, but in practice what this means is that the good person takes an interest in other people (including people who may not be connected with them) and in the world at large. Russell sometimes talks about contemplation in this connection, but this should not be understood as a purely passive process. The contemplative mind does not just sit and stare (though Russell was not averse to this kind of contemplation) but actively seeks to know the Other through science, history and other forms of enquiry.

Part V contains three pieces which develop these themes. The first is from 'Prisons', a rather solemn and pontifical piece that Russell wrote under the influence of his lover, Lady Ottoline Morrell (1873–1938). Like much of the material he wrote for Lady Ottoline, it is a joke-free zone, but I include it because the metaphor of self-enlargement is developed with peculiar clarity. The second is an extract from *The Impact of Science on Society* of 1952, which relates his ethical attitude to his belief in scientific realism, and in particular, his rejection of pragmatism. The third, from his *History of Western Philosophy*, is an attempt to explain what the Spinozistic attitude amounts to in personal terms and why it is supposed to help in cases of affliction and sorrow.

28

THE GOOD OF THE INTELLECT

Extract from 'Prisons' 1911

Reprinted from *CPBR* vol. 12: 105–6. This paper is from the drafts of 'Prisons', a book that Russell planned but never published. That Russell did not inflict this book on the world is partly due to the damning criticisms of Evelyn Whitehead (1865–1961) to whom we all owe a vote of thanks. It was not the ideas she objected to but the style: 'She says it is dull – the most damning criticism there is', and that 'the emotions spoken of are not spoken of so as to be felt' (letter quoted in *CPBR* vol. 12: 99). Though Russell's relationship with Lady Ottoline led to an awakening of the senses and the spirit, his feelings were often expressed in a pompous and elevated diction which it is painful to read. But though Russell was later to clothe his ideal in more attractive words he was seldom so explicit as in the present piece.

All the goods men seek consist in *some* form of union of Self and not-Self. The union sought by the life of instinct, which belongs to the particular soul, starts from the Self and consists in domination over the not-Self. Thus where this good is attained, the not-Self is made smaller than the Self, and the Self sets bounds to the greatness of its goods. The union sought by the life of reason, which belongs to the universal soul, starts from the not-Self and consists in knowledge, love and service of the not-Self; by this union, the boundaries of the self are enlarged, and the greatness of the not-Self becomes the greatness of the Self. The good of the intellect is *knowledge*. This good, though not perhaps the greatest of the three goods of reason, is the foundation and condition of the others. The intellect must first achieve knowledge of the not-Self before feeling and will can give love and service. The intellect, like every other passion, may be instinctive or rational. It is instinctive when, starting from what it already is, it desires to subdue the known world to its pre-existing faculties. It is rational when, by impartial contemplation, it attains to knowledge of what is other than itself. The instinctive contemplation desires to assimilate the world to man. 'Man is the measure of all things' it says; 'truth is man-made; space, time and the eternal truths are properties of the mind; if there be anything not created by the mind, it is unknowable and of no account for us'. Thus contemplation is fettered to Self; what is called knowledge is not a union with the not-Self, but a set of prejudices, habits, desires making an impenetrable veil between us and the world beyond. The man who finds pleasure in such a theory of knowledge is like the man who never leaves the domestic circle for fear his word might not be law.

The rational contemplation, on the contrary, finds its satisfaction in every enlargement of the not-Self, in everything that magnifies the objects contemplated and thereby the subject contemplating. Everything, in contemplation, that is personal and private – everything that depends upon habit, education, self-interest, desire – distorts the object, and thereby impairs the union which the intellect seeks. By thus making a barrier between the subject and the object, such personal and private things become a prison to the intellect. The free intellect will see as God might see, without a *here* and *now*, without hopes and fears, without the trammels of customary beliefs and traditional prejudices, calmly, dispassionately, in the sole and exclusive desire for knowledge – knowledge as impersonal, as purely contemplative as it is possible for man to attain. Hence also the free intellect will value more the abstract and universal knowledge into which the accidents of private history do not enter, than the knowledge brought by the senses, and dependent, as such knowledge must be, upon an exclusive and personal point of view and a body whose sense-organs distort as much as they reveal.

29

ON THE ETHICAL IMPORTANCE OF SCIENTIFIC REALISM

Extract from *The Impact of Science on Society* 1952

Reprinted from *The Impact of Science on Society*, chap. iv: 72–7. This paper shows that Russell's distaste for anti-realist and instrumentalist philosophies of science is connected with his ideal of impersonal self-enlargement. Of course Russell does not attempt to derive an Is (as that pragmatism *is* false) from an Ought (as that we ought to enlarge the Self through contemplation of the Other), but he does suggest that there is something morally suspect, as well as wrong-headed, about attempts to reduce the vast forces of nature to useful predictive devices enabling human beings to achieve their puny ends. Despite occasional flirtations with phenomenalism, Russell retained this attitude throughout most of his life. The first part of this paper was written in the 1950s, whilst the second dates back to 1907.

The philosophy which has seemed appropriate to science has varied from time to time. To Newton and most of his English contemporaries science seemed to afford proof of the existence of God as the Almighty Lawgiver: He had decreed the law of gravitation and whatever other natural laws had been discovered by Englishmen. In spite of Copernicus, Man was still the *moral* centre of the universe, and God's purposes were mainly concerned with the human race. The more radical among the French *philosophes*, being politically in conflict with the Church, took a different view. They did not admit that laws imply a lawgiver; on the other hand, they thought that physical laws could explain human behaviour. This led them to materialism and denial of free will. In their view, the universe has no purpose and man is an insignificant episode. The vastness of the universe impressed them and inspired in them a new form of humility to replace that which atheism had made obsolete. This point of view is well expressed in a little poem by Leopardi and expresses, more nearly than any other known to me, my own feeling about the universe and human passions:

THE INFINITE[1]

Dear to me always was this lonely hill
And this hedge that excludes so large a part
Of the ultimate horizon from my view.
But as I sit and gaze, my thought conceives
Interminable vastnesses of space
Beyond it, and unearthly silences,
And profoundest calm; whereat my heart almost
Becomes dismayed. And as I hear the wind
Blustering through these branches, I find myself
Comparing with this sound that infinite silence;
And then I call to mind eternity,
And the ages that are dead, and this that now
Is living, and the noise of it. And so
In this immensity my thought sinks drowned:
And sweet it seems to shipwreck in this sea.

But this has become an old-fashioned way of feeling. Science used to be valued as a means of getting to know the world; now, owing to the triumph of technique, it is conceived as showing how to change the world. The new point of view, which is adopted in practice throughout America and Russia, and in theory by many modern philosophers, was first proclaimed by Marx in 1845, in his *Theses on Feuerbach*. He says:

The question whether objective truth belongs to human thinking is not a question of theory, but a practical question. The truth, i.e. the reality and power, of thought must be demonstrated in practice. The contest as to the reality or non-reality of a thought which is isolated from practice, is a

1 Translation by R. C. Trevelyan from *Translations from Leopardi*, Cambridge University Press, 1941.

purely scholastic question. . . . Philosophers have only *interpreted* the world in various ways, but the real task is to alter
it.

From the point of view of technical philosophy, this theory has been
best developed by John Dewey, who is universally acknowledged as
America's most eminent philosopher.

This philosophy has two aspects, one theoretical and the other
ethical. On the theoretical side, it analyses away the concept
'truth', for which it substitutes 'utility'. It used to be thought
that, if you believed Caesar crossed the Rubicon, you believed
truly, because Caesar did cross the Rubicon. Not so, say the
philosophers we are considering: to say that your belief is 'true' is
another way of saying that you will find it more profitable than
the opposite belief. I might object that there have been cases of
historical beliefs which, after being generally accepted for a long
time, have in the end been admitted to be mistaken. In the case of
such beliefs, every examinee would find the accepted falsehood of
his time more profitable than the as yet unacknowledged truth.
But this kind of objection is swept aside by the contention that a
belief may be 'true' at one time and 'false' at another. In 1920 it
was 'true' that Trotsky had a great part in the Russian Revolution;
in 1930 it was 'false'. The results of this view have been admirably
worked out in George Orwell's *1984*.

This philosophy derives its inspiration from science in several
different ways. Take first its best aspect, as developed by Dewey. He
points out that scientific theories change from time to time, and
that what recommends a theory is that it 'works'. When new
phenomena are discovered, for which it no longer 'works', it is
discarded. A theory – so Dewey concludes – is a tool like another; it
enables us to manipulate raw material. Like any other tool, it is
judged good or bad by its efficiency in this manipulation, and like
any other tool, it is good at one time and bad at another. While it is
good it may be called 'true', but this word must not be allowed its
usual connotations. Dewey prefers the phrase 'warranted assert-
ibility' to the word 'truth'.

The second source of the theory is technique. What do we want
to know about electricity? Only how to make it work for us. To
want to know more is to plunge into useless metaphysics. Science is
to be admired because it gives us power over nature, and the power
comes wholly from technique. Therefore an interpretation which
reduces science to technique keeps all the useful part, and dismisses

only a dead weight of mediaeval lumber. If technique is all that interests you, you are likely to find this argument very convincing.

The third attraction of pragmatism – which cannot be wholly separated from the second – is love of power. Most men's desires are of various kinds. There are the pleasures of sense; there are aesthetic pleasures and pleasures of contemplation; there are private affections; and there is power. In an individual, any one of these may acquire predominance over the others. If love of power dominates, you arrive at Marx's view that what is important is not to understand the world, but to change it.

Traditional theories of knowledge were invented by men who loved contemplation – a monkish taste, according to modern devotees of mechanism. Mechanism augments human power to an enormous degree. It is therefore this aspect of science that attracts the lovers of power. And if power is all you want from science, the pragmatist theory gives you just what you want, without accretions that to you seem irrelevant. It gives you even more than you could have expected, for if you control the police it gives you the god-like power of *making truth*. You cannot make the sun cold, but you can confer pragmatic 'truth' on the proposition 'the sun is cold' if you can ensure that everyone who denies it is liquidated. I doubt whether Zeus could do more.

This engineer's philosophy, as it may be called, is distinguished from common sense and from most other philosophies by its rejection of 'fact' as a fundamental concept in defining 'truth'. If you say, for example, 'the South Pole is cold', you say something which, according to traditional views, is 'true' in virtue of a 'fact', namely that the South Pole is cold. And this is a fact, not because people believe it, or because it pays to believe it; it just *is* a fact. Facts, when they are not about human beings and their doings, represent the limitations of human power. We find ourselves in a universe of a certain sort, and we find out what sort of a universe it is by observation, not by self-assertion. It is true that we can make changes on or near the surface of the earth, but not elsewhere. Practical men have no wish to make changes elsewhere, and can therefore accept a philosophy which treats the surface of the earth as if it were the whole universe. But even on the surface of the earth our power is limited. To forget that we are hemmed in by facts which are for the most part independent of our desires is a form of insane megalomania. This kind of insanity has grown up as a result of the triumph of scientific technique. Its latest manifestation is Stalin's refusal to believe that heredity can have the temerity to ignore

Soviet decrees, which is like Xerxes whipping the Hellespont to teach Poseidon a lesson.

'The pragmatic theory of truth (I wrote in 1907) is inherently connected with the appeal to force. If there is a non-human truth, which one man may know while another does not, there is a standard outside the disputants, to which, we may urge, the dispute ought to be submitted; hence a pacific and judicial settlement of disputes is at least theoretically possible. If, on the contrary, the only way of discovering which of the disputants is in the right is to wait and see which of them is successful, there is no longer any principle except force by which the issue can be decided. . . . In international matters, owing to the fact that the disputants are often strong enough to be independent of outside control, these considerations become more important. The hopes of international peace, like the achievement of internal peace, depend upon the creation of an effective force of public opinion formed upon an estimate of the rights and wrongs of disputes. Thus it would be misleading to say that the dispute is decided by force, without adding that force is dependent upon justice. But the possibility of such a public opinion depends upon the possibility of a standard of justice which is a cause, not an effect, of the wishes of the community; and such a standard of justice seems incompatible with the pragmatist philosophy. This philosophy, therefore, although it begins with liberty and toleration, develops, by inherent necessity, into the appeal to force and the arbitrament of the big battalions. By this development it becomes equally adapted to democracy at home and to imperialism abroad. Thus here again it is more delicately adjusted to the requirements of the time than any other philosophy which has hitherto been invented.

'To sum up: Pragmatism appeals to the temper of mind which finds on the surface of this planet the whole of its imaginative material; which feels confident of progress, and unaware of non-human limitations to human power; which loves battle, with all the attendant risks, because it has no real doubt that it will achieve victory; which desires religion, as it desires railways and electric light, as a comfort and a help in the affairs of this world, not as providing non-human objects to satisfy the hunger for perfection. But for those who feel that life on this planet would be a life in prison if it were not for the windows into a greater world beyond; for those to whom a belief in man's omnipotence seems arrogant; who desire rather the stoic freedom that comes of mastery over the passions than the Napoleonic domination that sees the kingdoms of this world at its feet – in a word, to men who do not find man an adequate object of their worship, the pragmatist's world will seem narrow and petty, robbing life of all that gives it value, and making man himself smaller by depriving the universe which he contemplates of all its splendour.'

30

THE SPINOZISTIC
OUTLOOK

Extract from the *History of Western Philosophy* 1946

Reprinted from the *History of Western Philosophy*, 560–2.
Russell has just been arguing that Spinoza's method and
his metaphysics are both fundamentally wrong. Nevertheless something of value remains in his ethical stance.
This paper endeavours to explain what that something is.
Here the emphasis is on the personal and the practical side
of Russell's Spinozistic ethic rather than the moral significance of a belief in an external world.

But when we come to Spinoza's ethics, we feel – or at least I feel –
that something, though not everything, can be accepted even when
the metaphysical foundation has been rejected. Broadly speaking,
Spinoza is concerned to show how it is possible to live nobly even
when we recognize the limits of human power. He himself, by his
doctrine of necessity, makes these limits narrower than they are; but
when they indubitably exist, Spinoza's maxims are probably the
best possible. Take, for instance, death: nothing that a man can do
will make him immortal, and it is therefore futile to spend time in
fears and lamentations over the fact that we must die. To be
obsessed by the fear of death is a kind of slavery; Spinoza is right in
saying that 'the free man thinks of nothing less than of death'. But
even in this case, it is only death in general that should be so
treated; death of any particular disease should, if possible, be
averted by submitting to medical care. What should, even in this
case, be avoided, is a certain kind of anxiety or terror; the necessary
measures should be taken calmly, and our thoughts should, as far as
possible, be then directed to other matters. The same considerations
apply to all other purely personal misfortunes.

But how about misfortunes to people whom you love? Let us

think of some of the things that are likely to happen in our time to inhabitants of Europe or China. Suppose you are a Jew, and your family has been massacred. Suppose you are an underground worker against the Nazis, and your wife has been shot because you could not be caught. Suppose your husband, for some purely imaginary crime, has been sent to forced labour in the Arctic, and has died of cruelty and starvation. Suppose your daughter has been raped and then killed by enemy soldiers. Ought you, in these circumstances, to preserve a philosophic calm?

If you follow Christ's teaching, you will say 'Father, forgive them, for they know not what they do.' I have known Quakers who could have said this sincerely and profoundly, and whom I admired because they could. But before giving admiration one must be very sure that the misfortune is felt as deeply as it should be. One cannot accept the attitude of some among the Stoics, who said, 'What does it matter to me if my family suffer? I can still be virtuous.' The Christian principle, 'Love your enemies,' is good, but the Stoic principle, 'Be indifferent to your friends,' is bad. And the Christian principle does not inculcate calm, but an ardent love even towards the worst of men. There is nothing to be said against it except that it is too difficult for most of us to practise sincerely.

The primitive reaction to such disasters is revenge. When Macduff learns that his wife and children have been killed by Macbeth, he resolves to kill the tyrant himself. This reaction is still admired by most people, when the injury is great, and such as to arouse moral horror in disinterested people. Nor can it be wholly condemned, for it is one of the forces generating punishment, and punishment is sometimes necessary. Moreover, from the point of view of mental health, the impulse to revenge is likely to be so strong that, if it is allowed no outlet, a man's whole outlook on life may become distorted and more or less insane. This is not true universally, but it is true in a large percentage of cases. But on the other side it must be said that revenge is a very dangerous motive. In so far as society admits it, it allows a man to be the judge in his own case, which is exactly what the law tries to prevent. Moreover it is usually an excessive motive; it seeks to inflict more punishment than is desirable. Torture, for example, should not be punished by torture, but the man maddened by lust for vengeance will think a painless death too good for the object of his hate. Moreover – and it is here that Spinoza is in the right – a life dominated by a single passion is a narrow life, incompatible with every kind of wisdom. Revenge as such is therefore not the best reaction to injury.

Spinoza would say what the Christian says, and also something more. For him, all sin is due to ignorance; he would 'forgive them, for they know not what they do.' But he would have you avoid the limited purview from which, in his opinion, sin springs, and would urge you, even under the greatest misfortunes, to avoid being shut up in the world of your sorrow; he would have you understand it by seeing it in relation to its causes and as a part of the whole order of nature. As we saw, he believes that hatred can be overcome by love: 'Hatred is increased by being reciprocated, and can on the other hand be destroyed by love. Hatred which is completely vanquished by love, passes into love; and love is thereupon greater, than if hatred had not preceded it.' I wish I could believe this, but I cannot, except in exceptional cases where the person hating is completely in the power of the person who refuses to hate in return. In such cases, surprise at being not punished may have a reforming effect. But so long as the wicked have power, it is not much use assuring them that you do not hate them, since they will attribute your words to the wrong motive. And you cannot deprive them of power by non-resistance.

The problem for Spinoza is easier than it is for one who has no belief in the ultimate goodness of the universe. Spinoza thinks that, if you see your misfortunes as they are in reality, as part of the concatenation of causes stretching from the beginning of time to the end, you will see that they are only misfortunes to you, not to the universe, to which they are merely passing discords heightening an ultimate harmony. I cannot accept this; I think that particular events are what they are, and do not become different by absorption into a whole. Each act of cruelty is eternally a part of the universe; nothing that happens later can make that act good rather than bad, or can confer perfection on the whole of which it is a part.

Nevertheless, when it is your lot to have to endure something that is (or seems to you) worse than the ordinary lot of mankind, Spinoza's principle of thinking about the whole, or at any rate about larger matters than your own grief, is a useful one. There are even times when it is comforting to reflect that human life, with all that it contains of evil and suffering, is an infinitesimal part of the life of the universe. Such reflections may not suffice to constitute a religion, but in a painful world they are a help towards sanity and an antidote to the paralysis of utter despair.

BIBLIOGRAPHY

Aiken, L. W. (1963) *Bertrand Russell's Philosophy of Morals*, New York: Humanities Press.

Ayer, A. J. (1946) *Language, Truth and Logic*, 2nd edn, New York: Dover.

Ayer, A. J. (1954) *Philosophical Essays*, London: Macmillan.

Baldwin, Thomas (1990) *G.E. Moore*, London: Routledge.

Barnes, W. H. F. (1933) 'A suggestion about value', *Analysis* 1: 45–6. (Reprinted in Sellars, Wilfrid and Hospers, John (eds) (1970) *Readings in Ethical Theory*, 2nd edn, Englewood Cliffs, NJ: Prentice Hall.)

Blackburn, Simon (1984) *Spreading the Word*, Oxford: Oxford University Press.

Blackburn, Simon (1993) *Essays in Quasi-Realism*, New York: Oxford University Press.

Blackwell, K. (1985) *The Spinozistic Ethics of Bertrand Russell*, London: Allen & Unwin.

Bradley, F. H. (1927) *Ethical Studies*, 2nd edn, Oxford: Oxford University Press.

Bradley, F. H. (1930) *Appearance and Reality*, 9th impression, Oxford: Oxford University Press.

Brink, David O. (1989) *Moral Realism and the Foundations of Ethics*, Cambridge: Cambridge University Press.

Coffa, Alberto C. (1991) *The Semantic Tradition from Kant to Carnap: To the Vienna Station*, Wessels, L. (ed.), Cambridge: Cambridge University Press.

Cohen, S. (1980) *Bukharin and the Bolshevik Revolution*, Oxford: Oxford University Press.

Dawkins, R. (1989) *The Selfish Gene*, 2nd edn, Oxford: Oxford University Press.

Dummett, M. (1981) *Frege: The Philosophy of Language*, 2nd edn, London: Duckworth.

Durrant, R. G. (1970) 'Identity of properties and the definition of "good"', *Australasian Journal of Philosophy* 48(3): 360–1.

Feinberg, B. and Kasrils, R. (eds) (1969) *Dear Bertrand Russell*, London: Allen & Unwin.

Foot, P. (ed.) (1967) *Theories of Ethics*, Oxford: Oxford University Press.

Garner, Richard (1994) *Beyond Morality*, Philadelphia: Temple University Press.

Geach, P. T. (1956) 'Good and evil', *Analysis* 17: 33–42. (Reprinted in Foot, P. (ed.) (1967) *Theories of Ethics*, Oxford: Oxford University Press, 68–73.)

Geach, P. T. (1960) 'Ascriptivism', *Philosophical Review* 69(3): 2. (Reprinted in Geach, P. T. (1972) *Logic Matters*, Oxford: Blackwell, 250–4; all references are to this reprint.)

Geach, P. T. (1965) 'Assertion', *Philosophical Review* 74(4): 4. (Reprinted in Geach, P. T. (1972) *Logic Matters*, Oxford: Blackwell, 254–69; all references are to this reprint.)

Geach, P. T. (1972) *Logic Matters*, Oxford: Blackwell.

Gibbard, Alan (1990) *Wise Choices, Apt Feelings: A Theory of Normative Judgement*, Oxford: Oxford University Press.

Godwin, W. (1971) *Enquiry Concerning Political Justice*, Codell Carter, K. (ed.), Oxford: Oxford University Press.

Grayling, A. (1996) *Russell*, Oxford: Oxford University Press.

Green, T. H. (1883) *Prolegomena to Ethics*, Bradley, A. C. (ed.), Oxford: Oxford University Press.

Green, T. H. (1986) *Lectures on Political Obligation and Other Writings*, Harris, P. and Morrow, J. (eds), Cambridge: Cambridge University Press.

Griffin, N. (ed.) (1992) *The Selected Letters of Bertrand Russell: vol. 1 The Private Years 1884–1914*, Harmondsworth: Allen Lane.

Hare, R. M. (1952) *The Language of Morals*, Oxford: Oxford University Press.

Hinckfuss, Ian (1987) *The Moral Society: Its Structure and Effects*, Canberra: Department of Philosophy, Australian National University.

Hooker, Brad (ed.) (1996) *Truth in Ethics*, Oxford: Blackwell.

Hume, David (1975) *Enquiries Concerning Human Understanding and Concerning the Principles of Morals*, 3rd edn, Nidditch, P. H. and Selby-Bigge, L. A. (eds), Oxford: Oxford University Press.

Hume, David (1978) *A Treatise of Human Nature*, 2nd edn, Selby-Bigge, L. A. and Nidditch, P. H. (eds), Oxford: Oxford University Press.

Hurley, S. L. (1989) *Natural Reasons: Personality and Polity*, Oxford: Oxford University Press.

Hylton, Peter (1990) *Russell, Idealism and the Emergence of Analytic Philosophy*, Oxford: Oxford University Press.

Kant, Immanuel (1959) *Foundations of the Metaphysics of Morals*, Beck, L. W. (trans.), Indianapolis: Bobbs-Merrill.

Keynes, John Maynard (1972) *Essays in Biography*, London: Macmillan/ Cambridge University Press.

Kitcher, P. (1985) *Vaulting Ambition*, Cambridge, MA: MIT Press.

Langford, C. H. (1942) 'The notion of analysis in Moore's philosophy', in Schilpp, P. A. (ed.) *The Philosophy of G.E. Moore*, Evanston, IL: Northwestern University Press, 321–42.

Lee, D. (ed.) (1980) *Wittgenstein's Lectures, Cambridge 1930–31*, Oxford: Blackwell.

Lenin, V. I. (1920) 'The Tasks of the Youth Leagues', in Lenin, V. I. *Selected Works, vol. 3* (1975) Moscow: Progress Publishers, 410–23.

Lenin, V. I. (1975) *Selected Works, vol. 3*, revised edn, Moscow: Progress Publishers.

Levy, P. (1981) *Moore: G.E. Moore and the Cambridge Apostles*, Oxford: Oxford University Press.

Lewis, David (1989) 'Dispositional theories of value II', *Proceedings of the Aristotelian Society* suppl. vol. 63: 129–32.

Mackie, J. L. (1946) 'The refutation of morals', *Australasian Journal of Psychology and Philosophy* 24 (1–2): 77–90.

Mackie, J. L. (1976) 'Sidgwick's pessimism', *Philosophical Quarterly* 26(105). (Reprinted in Mackie, J. L. (1985) *Persons and Values*, Mackie, J. and P. (eds), Oxford: Oxford University Press, 77–90; all references are to this reprint.)

Mackie, J. L. (1977) *Ethics: Inventing Right and Wrong*, Harmondsworth: Penguin.

Mackie, J. L. (1978) 'The law of the jungle: moral alternatives and the principles of evolution', *Philosophy* 53: 206. (Reprinted in Mackie, J. L. (1985) *Persons and Values*, Mackie, J. and P. (eds), Oxford: Oxford University Press, 120–31; all references are to this reprint.)

Mackie, J. L. (1985) *Persons and Values*, Mackie, J. and P. (eds), Oxford: Oxford University Press.

Maxwell, Grover (1974) 'The later Bertrand Russell: philosophical revolutionary', in Nakhnikian, G. (ed.) *Bertrand Russell's Philosophy*, London: Duckworth.

McLellan, D. (ed.) (1977) *Karl Marx: Selected Writings*, Oxford: Oxford University Press.

McTaggart, J. McT. Ellis (1893) *The Further Determination of the Absolute*, Cambridge, privately printed. (Reprinted in McTaggart, J. McT. Ellis (1931) *Philosophical Studies*, Keeling, S. V. (ed.), London: Edward Arnold, 210–72. (Reissued (1996), Bristol: Thoemmes Press.)

McTaggart, J. McT. Ellis (1931) *Philosophical Studies*, Keeling, S. V. (ed.), London: Edward Arnold. (Reissued (1996), Bristol: Thoemmes Press.)

Misak, C. J. (1995) *Verificationism: Its History and Prospects*, London: Routledge.

Monk, Ray (1996) *Bertrand Russell: The Spirit of Solitude, 1872–1921*, London: Jonathan Cape.

Monk, Ray and Palmer, Anthony (eds) (1996) *Bertrand Russell and the Origins of Analytic Philosophy*, Bristol: Thoemmes Press.

Monro, D. H. (1960) 'Russell's moral theories', *Philosophy* 35 (January): 30–50. (Reprinted in Pears, D. F. (ed.) (1972) *Bertrand Russell: A Collection of Critical Essays*, Garden City, NY: Anchor Books.)

Moore, G. E. (1912) *Ethics*, London: Williams & Norgate.

Moore, G. E. (1942) 'A reply to my critics', in Schilpp, P. A. (ed.) *The Philosophy of G.E. Moore*, Evanston, IL: Northwestern University Press, 533–678.

Moore, G. E. (1991) *The Elements of Ethics*, Regan, T. (ed.), Philadelphia: Temple University Press.

Moore, G. E. (1993) *Principia Ethica*, revised edn, Baldwin, T. (ed.), Cambridge: Cambridge University Press.

Moorehead, Caroline (1992) *Bertrand Russell: A Biography*, London: Sinclair-Stevenson.

Nietzsche, F. (1954) *The Portable Nietzsche*, Kaufmann, W. (trans.), Harmondsworth: Penguin.

Parfit, D. (1984) *Reasons and Persons*, Oxford: Oxford University Press.

Pigden, Charles (1989) 'Logic and the autonomy of ethics', *Australasian Journal of Philosophy* 67(2): 127–51.

Pigden, Charles (1990) 'Geach on "good"', *Philosophical Quarterly* 40(159): 129–54.

Pigden, Charles (1991) 'Naturalism', in Singer, P. (ed.) *A Companion to Ethics*, Oxford: Blackwell.

Pigden, Charles (1996a) 'Bertrand Russell: a neglected ethicist', in Monk, R. and Palmer, A. (eds) *Bertrand Russell and the Origins of Analytic Philosophy*, Bristol: Thoemmes Press, 331–60.

Pigden, Charles (1996b) 'Bertrand Russell: meta-ethical pioneer', *Philosophy of the Social Sciences* 26(2): 181–204.

Pipes, R. (1990) *The Russian Revolution: 1899–1919*, London: Harvill.

Pipes, R. (1994) *Russia Under the Bolshevik Regime: 1919–1924*, London: HarperCollins.

Prior, A. N. (1960) 'The autonomy of ethics', *Australasian Journal of Philosophy* 38: 199–206.

Ramsey, F. P. (1990) *Philosophical Papers*, Mellor, D. H. (ed.), Cambridge: Cambridge University Press.

Ross, W. D. (1930) *The Right and the Good*, Oxford: Oxford University Press.

Russell, Bertrand (1912) *The Problems of Philosophy*, London: Williams & Norgate. (Reissued (1967) Oxford: Oxford University Press.)

Russell, Bertrand (1916) *The Principles of Social Reconstruction*, London: Allen & Unwin.

Russell, Bertrand (1917) *Mysticism and Logic*, London: Allen & Unwin. (Reissued with a new introduction by Slater, J. (1994), London: Routledge.)

Russell, Bertrand (1920) *The Practice and Theory of Bolshevism*, London: Allen & Unwin. (Reissued with an introduction by Coates, K. (1995), Nottingham: Spokesman.)

Russell, Bertrand (1925) *What I Believe*, London: Kegan Paul.

Russell, Bertrand (1926) *On Education Especially in Early Childhood*, London: Allen & Unwin.

Russell, Bertrand (1927) *An Outline of Philosophy*, London: Allen & Unwin. (Revised edition, with introduction by Slater, J. (1995), London: Routledge.)

Russell, Bertrand (1929) *Marriage and Morals*, London: Allen & Unwin.

Russell, Bertrand (1930) *The Conquest of Happiness*, London: Allen & Unwin.

Russell, Bertrand (1932) *Education and the Social Order*, London: Allen & Unwin.

Russell, Bertrand (1935) *Religion and Science*, London: Home University Library. (Reissued (1961), Oxford: Oxford University Press.)

Russell, Bertrand (1937) *The Principles of Mathematics*, 2nd edn, London: Allen & Unwin. (Reissued with new introduction by Slater, J. (1992), London: Routledge.)

Russell, Bertrand (1938) *Power: A New Social Analysis*, London: Allen & Unwin. (Reprinted with a new introduction by Willis, K. (1995), London: Routledge.)

Russell, Bertrand (1944) 'Reply to Criticisms', in Schilpp, P. A. (ed.) *The Philosophy of Bertrand Russell*, Evanston, IL: Northwestern University Press, 681–741.

Russell, Bertrand (1946) *History of Western Philosophy*, London: Allen & Unwin.

Russell, Bertrand (1948) *Human Knowledge: Its Scope and Limits*, London: Allen & Unwin.

Russell, Bertrand (1949) *Authority and the Individual*, London: Allen & Unwin. (Reissued with a new introduction by Willis, K. (1995), London: Routledge.)

Russell, Bertrand (1950) *Unpopular Essays*, London: Allen & Unwin. (Revised edition with a new introduction by Willis, K. (1995), London: Routledge.)

Russell, Bertrand (1952) *The Impact of Science on Society*, London: Allen & Unwin.

Russell, Bertrand (1954) *Human Society in Ethics and Politics*, London: Allen & Unwin. (Reissued with a new introduction by Slater, J. (1992) London: Routledge.)

Russell, Bertrand (1956a) *Portraits from Memory*, London: Allen & Unwin. (Now available from Spokesman, Nottingham.)

Russell, Bertrand (1956b) *Logic and Knowledge*, Marsh, R. C. (ed.), London: Allen & Unwin.

Russell, Bertrand (1957) *Why I Am Not a Christian*, Edwards, P. (ed.), London: Allen & Unwin.

Russell, Bertrand (1959) *My Philosophical Development*, London: Allen & Unwin. (Revised edition with an introduction by Baldwin, T. (1995), London: Routledge; all references are to the revised edition.)

Russell, Bertrand (1960) 'Notes on Philosophy, January 1960', *Philosophy* 35 (April 1960): 146–7.

Russell, Bertrand (1961) *Fact and Fiction*, London: Allen & Unwin. (Reissued with a new introduction by Slater, J. (1994), London: Routledge.)

Russell, Bertrand (1966) *Philosophical Essays*, 2nd edn, London: Allen & Unwin.

Russell, Bertrand (1967) *The Autobiography of Bertrand Russell. Vol. 1 1872–1914*, London: Allen & Unwin.

Russell, Bertrand (1968) *The Autobiography of Bertrand Russell. Vol. II, 1914–1944*, London: Allen & Unwin.

Russell, Bertrand (1969) *The Autobiography of Bertrand Russell. Vol. III, 1944–1967*, London: Allen & Unwin.

Russell, Bertrand (1973) *Essays in Analysis*, Lackey, D. (ed.), London: Allen & Unwin.

Russell, Bertrand (1983) *The Collected Papers of Bertrand Russell. Vol. 1, Cambridge Essays 1888–1899*, Blackwell, K., Brink, A., Griffin, N., Rempel, R. and Slater, J. (eds), London: Allen & Unwin.

Russell, Bertrand (1985) *The Collected Papers of Bertrand Russell. Vol. 12, Contemplation and Action 1902–1914*, Rempel, R., Brink, A. and Moran, M. (eds), London: Allen & Unwin.

Russell, Bertrand (1986) *The Collected Papers of Bertrand Russell. Vol 8, The Philosophy of Logical Atomism and Other Essays*, Slater, J. (ed.), London: Allen & Unwin.

Russell, Bertrand (1987) *Bertrand Russell on Ethics, Sex and Marriage*, Seckel, A. (ed.), Buffalo, NY: Prometheus.

Russell, Bertrand (1988a) *The Collected Papers of Bertrand Russell. Vol. 9, Essays on Language, Mind, and Matter*, Slater, J. and Frohman, B. (eds), London: Allen & Unwin.

Russell, Bertrand (1988b) *The Collected Papers of Bertrand Russell. Vol. 13, Prophecy and Dissent 1914–1916*, Rempel, R., Frohman, B., Lippincot, M. and Moran, M. (eds), London: Unwin Hyman.

Russell, Bertrand (1992) *The Collected Papers of Bertrand Russell. Vol. 6, Logical and Philosophical Papers 1909–1913*, Slater, J. and Frohman, B. (eds), London: Routledge.

Russell, Bertrand (1994) *The Collected Papers of Bertrand Russell. Vol. 4, Foundations of Logic 1903–1905*, Urquhart, A. and Lewis, A. C. (eds), London: Routledge.

Russell, Bertrand (1995) *The Collected Papers of Bertrand Russell. Vol. 14, Prophecy and Dissent 1916–1918*, Rempel, R., Greenspan, L., Haslam, B., Lewis, A. C., and Lippincot, M. (eds), London: Routledge.

Russell, Bertrand (1996) *The Collected Papers of Bertrand Russell. Vol. 10, A Fresh Look at Empiricism 1927–42*, Slater, J. (ed.), London: Routledge.

Russell, Bertrand (1997) *The Collected Papers of Bertrand Russell. Vol. 11, Last Philosophical Testament 1943–1968*, Slater, J. (ed.) with the assistance of Peter Kollner, London: Routledge.

Russell, Bertrand and Whitehead, A. N. (1910) *Principia Mathematica*, Cambridge: Cambridge University Press. (Abridged edn to *56 (1962), Cambridge: Cambridge University Press.)

Ryan, Alan (1988) *Bertrand Russell: A Political Life*, Harmondsworth: Penguin.

Sainsbury, Mark (1979) *Russell*, London: Routledge.

Santayana, George (1970) 'Hypostatic ethics' (from his *Winds of Doctrine*, 1912), reprinted in Sellars, Wilfrid and Hospers, John (eds) *Readings in Ethical Theory*, 2nd edn, Englewood Cliffs, NJ: Prentice Hall, 130–7.

Schacht, Richard (1983) *Nietzsche*, London: Routledge.

Schilpp, Paul Arthur (ed.) (1942) *The Philosophy of G.E. Moore*, Evanston, IL: Northwestern University Press.

Schilpp, Paul Arthur (ed.) (1944) *The Philosophy of Bertrand Russell*, Evanston, IL: Northwestern University Press.

Schneewind, J. B. (1977) *Sidgwick's Ethics and Victorian Moral Philosophy*, Oxford: Oxford University Press.

Sellars, Wilfrid and Hospers, John (eds) (1970) *Readings in Ethical Theory*, 2nd edn, Englewood Cliffs, NJ: Prentice Hall.

Sidgwick, Henry (1874) *The Methods of Ethics*, 1st edn, London: Macmillan.

Sidgwick, Henry (1907) *The Methods of Ethics*, 7th edn, London: Macmillan.

Singer, Peter (ed.) (1991) *A Companion to Ethics*, Oxford: Blackwell.

Slater, John G. (1994) *Bertrand Russell*, Bristol: Thoemmes Press.

Spinoza, B. (1951) *Ethics*, Elwes, R. H. M. (trans.), New York: Dover.

Sprigge, T. L. S. (1993) *James and Bradley: American Truth and British Reality*, Chicago and La Salle, IL: Open Court.

Stevenson, C. L. (1944) *Ethics and Language*, New Haven, CT: Yale University Press.

Stevenson, C. L. (1963) *Facts and Values*, New Haven, CT: Yale University Press.

Stirner, Max (1995) *The Ego and Its Own*, Byington, S. T. (trans.), Leopold, D. (ed.), Cambridge: Cambridge University Press.

Tait, Katherine (1975) *My Father Bertrand Russell*, New York and London: Harcourt Brace Jovanovich.

Tawney, R. H. (1929) *Religion and the Rise of Capitalism: A Historical Study*, London: Murray

Trevelyan, R. C. (1941) *Translations from Leopardi*, Cambridge: Cambridge University Press.

Trotsky, L. (1973) *Their Morals and Ours*, 5th edn, New York: Pathfinder.

Waley, Arthur (1958) *x*, New York: Grove Press.

Wiggins, D. (1987) *Needs, Values, Truth*, Oxford: Blackwell.

Wilson, D. S. and Sober, E. (1998) *Unto Others: The Evolution of Altruism*, Cambridge, MA: Harvard University Press.

Wong, D. (1984) *Moral Relativity*, Berkeley and Los Angeles: University of California Press.

Wood, Allen (1991) 'Marx against morality', in Singer, P. (ed.) *A Companion to Ethics*, Oxford: Blackwell, 511–24.

Wright, C. (1996) 'Truth in ethics', in Hooker, B. (ed.) *Truth in Ethics*, Oxford: Blackwell, 1–18.

Wright, Robert (1994) *The Moral Animal*, New York: Random House.

INDEX